October 10–12, 2013
Orlando, Florida, USA

I0050947

Association for Computing Machinery

Advancing Computing as a Science & Profession

CARIBE ROYALE
SUITES · CONVENTION CENTER · VILLAS
ORLANDO

RIIT'13

Proceedings of the 2nd Annual Conference on
Research in Information Technology

Sponsored by:
ACM SIGITE

Supported by:
EMC Academic Alliance, NetApp, Oracle Academy, ABET, & University of South Florida

**Association for
Computing Machinery**

Advancing Computing as a Science & Profession

The Association for Computing Machinery
2 Penn Plaza, Suite 701
New York, New York 10121-0701

Notice to Past Authors of ACM-Published Articles
ACM intends to create a complete electronic archive of all articles and/or other material previously published by ACM. If you have written a work that has been previously published by ACM in any journal or conference proceedings prior to 1978, or any SIG Newsletter at any time, and you do NOT want this work to appear in the ACM Digital Library, please inform permissions@acm.org, stating the title of the work, the author(s), and where and when published.

ISBN: 978-1-4503-2494-6 (Digital)

ISBN: 978-1-4503-2677-3 (Print)

Additional copies may be ordered prepaid from:

ACM Order Department
PO Box 30777
New York, NY 10087-0777, USA

Phone: 1-800-342-6626 (USA and Canada)
+1-212-626-0500 (Global)
Fax: +1-212-944-1318
E-mail: acmhelp@acm.org
Hours of Operation: 8:30 am – 4:30 pm ET

Printed in the USA

SIGITE/RIIT 2013 Chair's Message

Welcome to Orlando!

We are happy to welcome you to the 13th Annual Conference on Information Technology Education and the 2nd Annual Research in IT Conference, hosted by the University of South Florida. This year continues our IT Research conference, which was introduced last year to significant interest and participation.

Those of you who attended last year's conference in Calgary may remember a questionnaire you were asked to complete about the 2013 conference. Well, we listened. The most noticeable change from last year is the addition of a third parallel session track, providing more flexibility and, in future years, an increased number of papers at the conferences. For this year, its chief effect has been an increase in the time allotted to each paper presentation. Many of you said you might bring the family, which certainly affected our choice of conference city as well as our selection of an all-suite conference hotel that provides free shuttle service to Disney theme parks.

This year's SIGITE theme is making lemonade from the lemon grove that is our collective, resource-constrained education enterprise – in short, doing more with less. As higher education is increasingly challenged financially – a trend that shows no signs of abating – we need to open the door to economies of scale and collaborative ventures. Entrepreneurism is no longer simply something to be taught, but must be an approach to maximizing our resources and squeezing every drop of lemonade out of each lemon. And (I can't resist asking) where better to talk about lemons and lemonade than central Florida, the heart of the citrus industry?

SIGITE/RIIT 2013 kicks off with a provocative keynote by Sam Esfahani, CIO of PSCU, the leading service organization in the credit union industry. Sam is a turnaround specialist who blends innovative thinking with an uncommon ability to build high performing teams, and has been instrumental in leading PSCU's transformation as a technology leader in the credit union industry. Titled "Digit Shift: Leverage or Get Leveled," Sam's talk focuses on industry/academia collaboration, why it is so essential for the future health for both, and ways it can be cost-effectively implemented.

SIGITE/RIIT 2013 is a true team effort, and we would like to acknowledge and thank the people who have made this year's conferences possible. Rob Friedman and Ken Baker served as Program Co-Chairs, and successfully dealt with the many challenges that program chairs must. Rob, of course, also serves as SIG Chair, so had to handle twice as many questions!

Conferences are expensive events, and registration fees do not cover everything. The critically important job of garnering external support for our conferences was accomplished in great form by Sponsorship Co-Chairs Amber Settle and Terry Steinbach. To the sponsors that Amber and Terry signed up go our thanks for their generous support. Essential support has also been provided by the host for the conference, the University of South Florida, including financial support for program printing provided by the College of Engineering and audio-visual and computing support provided by Information Technology.

Behind the scenes are many others whose efforts are essential for a successful event. These people deserve special thanks, and include Abdel Ejnioui as Treasurer, Phil DuMas as Registration Chair, Colin Arnold as Local Sponsorship Chair, April Mosqus at ACM for assistance with overall planning, Lisa Tolles at Sheridan Communications for organizing the proceedings, Steven Houston for putting up all authors and presentations on our conference website, and Janet Gillis and Ryan Wakefield for designing and producing our printed conference program. Randy Connolly, last year's conference chair and the SIG's Information Director, also assisted with website matters at critical points.

Over the years, we have found our conference to be both a wellspring of ideas to address current issues and a much-needed opportunity to network and bond with fellow IT educators. We hope you find this year's conference as beneficial and rewarding as the many we have attended in the past.

Dave Armitage
Conference Chair, SIGITE/RIIT 2013

SIGITE/RIIT 2013 Program Chairs' Message

There's been a lot of change for SIGITE over the years – growth in membership, increased cooperation with other SIGs, sponsorship of affiliated conferences, and new IT programs from around the world contributing to a steadily enhanced stature for IT as a computing subarea, just to name a few. Last year's inauguration of the Research in Information Technology (RIIT) conference as a co-located event with the annual SIGITE conference is one change that has proved warranted, given the number and quality of the submissions we received this year and last. The RIIT thread complements the more widely known and more heavily subscribed SIGITE conference, given the increased interest industry continues to show in partnering with academia to address collaboratively applied research advances in areas related to our five curricular pillars. As Dave Armitage and Jeff Brewer wrote in last year's Program Chairs' message, "With a hands-on flavor and stronger connections with industry, [research in IT] is clearly differentiating itself from research in more traditional computing disciplines, and is deserving of its own conference venue."

As authors and reviewers no doubt noticed, we changed conference management systems this year. Several years ago, Grinnell University's Henry Walker was kind enough to mirror his databases and web forms used to organize SIGCSE to accommodate SIGITE, and we appreciate his consistent support. This year, however, we opted for change in this area, too. Colleagues in SIGKDD developed and manage the Microsoft CMT application we selected to use. Although there were a few bumps in the transition, most of our contributors and volunteers found it to be an easy-to-use system. 12 RIIT reviewers made recommendations on 24 submissions to RIIT, and 64 peer reviewers scored and commented on 70 submissions to SIGITE.

The number and substance of these submissions, in relation to the venue of this year's conferences, provided yet other opportunities for change in the conferences. These include providing more panel discussions, more workshops and more time allotted for individual paper presentations. As interest grows in SIGITE/RIIT, we're able to be more selective and more inclusive at the same time. 28 technical papers will be presented at SIGITE, which will significantly reduce our acceptance rate from a 6-year average of 54% to 40% this year, while RIIT's acceptance rate came in at 50%. We are able to provide inclusivity by offering 24 authors – a four-fold increase over last year – the opportunity to present their work as poster papers that are included in the ACM Digital Library. We would like to thank a highly responsive group of 76 peer reviewers, several of whom got tagged late in the process to review more papers than they bargained for.

Perhaps the most significant change to the proceedings is that they are available for download to conference registrants for two weeks preceding and two weeks following the conference dates, thus providing more opportunity for conversation among authors and attendees. From a community building perspective, this is a tremendous opportunity for advancement provided by the ACM Publications Board.

As you look through the schedule of events, you'll notice that we have doubled the panel session time from 30 to 60 minutes, and these panels will run concurrently and not opposite any technical papers, so you can participate and contribute to the topic that is most important to you. We have also moved the workshops to Saturday morning in an attempt to make the best use of a time block that in the past has not been well attended. We know that Orlando attractions beckon, but please consider taking advantage of the workshops.

All of us on the organizing committees would like to hear from you about these changes so that we can continue to innovate and provide SIGITE/RIIT attendees with the best experience possible.

We welcome you to SIGITE 2013 and RIIT 2013. Engage the panels and the paper and poster authors, meet new colleagues and reengage with old friends. Thanks for attending!

Ken Baker and Rob Friedman
SIGITE/RIIT Program Co-Chairs

Table of Contents

Paper Session G3: UML & UI

Session Chair: Tom Gibbons *(College of St. Scholastica)*

Paper Session H3: Browser and Network Analytics

Session Chair: Tsunenori Mine *(Kyushu University)*

Author Index

SIGITE/RIIT 2013 Conference Organization

General Chair: William D. Armitage, *University of South Florida, USA*

Program Co-Chairs: Rob Friedman, *University of Washington Tacoma, USA*
Ken Baker, *CH Mack, USA*

Sponsorship Co-Chairs: Amber Settle, *DePaul University, USA*
Terry Steinbach, *DePaul University, USA*

Treasurer: Abdel Ejnioui, *University of South Florida, USA*

Registration Chair: Phil DuMas, *University of South Florida, USA*

Local Arrangements Committee: Colin Arnold, *University of South Florida, USA*
Phil DuMas, *University of South Florida, USA*
Abdel Ejnioui, *University of South Florida, USA*
Steven Houston, *University of South Florida, USA*

Program Design and Printing: Janet Gillis & Ryan Wakefield, *University of South Florida, USA*

Steering Committee Chair: Rob Friedman, *University of Washington Tacoma, USA*

Steering Committee: Ken Baker, *CH Mack, USA*
Randy Connolly, *Mount Royal University, Canada*
Richard Helps, *Brigham Young University, USA*
Rick Lee Homkes, *Purdue University, USA*
Jim Leone, *Rochester Institute of Technology, USA*
Barry Lunt, *Brigham Young University, USA*
Mihaela Sabin, *University of New Hampshire, USA*
Mark Stockman, *University of Cincinnati, USA*

Reviewers:

Sohaib Ahmed, *Massey University*
Hend Al-Khalifa, *KSU*
Peter Alston, *Edge Hill University*
Larry Booth, *CSU*
Thomas Borrelli, *Rochester Institute of Technology*
Lynn Braender, *The College of New Jersey*
Jeff Brewer, *Purdue University*
Rob Byrd, *Abilene Christian University*
Sam Chung, *University of Washington Tacoma*
Randy Connolly, *Mount Royal University*
Jean Coppola, *Pace University*
Mónica Costa, Unknown
Michele Dijkstra, *Pacific Lutheran University*
Nalaka Edirisinghe, *Temasek Polytechnic*
Abdel Ejnioui, *University of South Florida*
Joseph Ekstrom, *Brigham Young University Provo*
Alan Fedoruk, *Mount Royal University*
Alessio Gaspar, *University of South Florida*
Rick Gee, *Okanagan College*
Thomas Gibbons, *The College of St. Scholastica*
Bryan Goda, *Kyushu Institute of Information Science*
Mingwei Gong, *Mt. Royal University*
Richard Helps, *Brigham Young University, IT*
Lawrence Hill, *Rochester Institute of Technology*
Ricardo Hoar, *Mount Royal University*
Edward Holden, *Rochester Institute of Technology*
Arno Hollosi, *FH CAMPUS 02*
Rick Homkes, *Purdue University*
Janet Hughes, *University of Dundee*
Michael Jonas, *University of New Hampshire*
Jane Kochanov, *Penn State Harrisburg*

Deborah Labelle, *Nazareth College*
Séamus Lawless, *Trinity College Dublin*
Jim Leone, *Rochester Institute of Technology*
Sergio Lopes, *University of Minho*
Jitendra Lulla, *Chelsio Communications*
Barry Lunt, *Brigham Young University*
Cynthia Marcello, *SUNY Sullivan*
Kevin McReynolds, *LDS Business College*
Craig Miller, *DePaul University*
Selvarajah Mohanarajah, *Edward Waters College*
Yousif Mustafa, *SimplexSystems, Inc.*
Besim Mustafa, *Edge Hill University*
Yin Pan, *Rochester Institute of Technology*
Junfeng Qu, *Clayton State University*
Hugo Rehesaar, *Griffith University*
Janet Renwick, *Univ of Arkansas - Fort Smith*
Rebecca Rutherfoord, *Southern Polytechnic State University*
Etienne Schneider, *Independent*
Amber Settle, *DePaul University*
Zaffar Shaikh, *IBA Karachi*
Edward Sobiesk, *USMA*
Mark Stockman, *University of Cincinnati*
Andrew Suhy, *Ferris State University*
Kevin Tew, *Brigham Young University*
Xinli Wang, *Michigan Tech University*
Elissa Weeden, *Rochester Institute of Technology*
James Woolen, *Ferris State University*
Nima Zahadat, *George Washington University*
Chi Zhang, *Southern Polytechnic State University*

SIGITE/RIIT 2013 Sponsor & Supporters

Sponsor:

Supporters:

Termediator: Early Studies in Terminological Mediation Between Disciplines

Jessica Richards
Brigham Young University
jessicamsrichards@gmail.com

Owen Riley
Brigham Young University
owen.g.riley@gmail.com

Joseph J. Ekstrom
Brigham Young University
jekstrom@byu.edu

Kevin Tew
Brigham Young University
kevin_tew@byu.edu

ABSTRACT

A glossary is a terminological document that binds terms to concepts to illuminate the meaning of the term within in a specific domain. Many of the same terms are bound to different concepts within different domains, which often leads to miscommunications in interdisciplinary projects. How can terminology management tools facilitate communication between domains? Would an application that performs similarity measures between terms in glossaries from different domains provide useful insights? This paper provides a status report on the "Termediator" application that begins this effort in terminology management. Termediator uses a web interface to list the terms, concepts, and similarity measures for thousands of terms compiled from 198 different glossaries. Termediator's results include obvious synonym matches and accurate relevance rankings between non-synonym terms. These results leave us optimistic about the future of terminology management tools that augment interdisciplinary communication through natural language processing.

Categories and Subject Descriptors

H.4.3 [**Communications Applications**]

Keywords

Communication, terminology, glossary, XML, processes

1. INTRODUCTION

Miscommunication between related fields often occurs in the different meanings that each field assigns to the same term. For example, a software engineer and a business process analyst both use the word "process" quite frequently, but they mean different things in the engineering and business worlds. If the engineer and the analyst need to have a conversation, they may talk in circles about "processes" without realizing that the root of their miscommunication lays in a difference of concept. They both are familiar with the word in question, and they both know what the word means within their own professional context, but translation fails when they must reconcile their definition with their colleague in another discipline.

Mediating communication between fields thus requires us to delve into terminology management to heighten awareness of meaning. When we say "terminology," many will assume we mean that all IT professionals should grab a dictionary before a company meeting. We are actually referring to the discipline of terminology, which uses glossaries, not dictionaries. Dictionaries are mainly descriptive and do not suit the ambiguity of this research. A dictionary groups homonyms together because they sound the same—even if their meanings are completely different—because a dictionary concerns itself with lexicographical representation, not the terminological concept. However, a glossary ignores homonyms and instead groups synonyms together—determining that the concept behind the words is the most important factor. Consider when a systems engineer and a software engineer have an argument, where does the miscommunication stem from? Not how the words sound—both would pronounce "system" the same way—but what the words mean. As a result our research uses the glossary's terminological approach to attack the core problem of interdisciplinary miscommunication.

The essence of our research, however, is not pure terminology management as typically defined [1]. Our approach centers on the augmentation of terminology management through additional tools. One may question: why aren't simple glossaries enough? Consider how many meanings a single term can have, such as the word "system". A general dictionary lists five major definitions for "system", and the *sevocab* (a collection of concepts from IEEE and ISO standards in Systems and Software Engineering) adds eight more. Thirteen closely related concepts are enough to confuse anyone, especially industry professionals who rely on precise terminology to successfully complete work assignments. An electronic engineer uses system to mean "an interdependent group of people, objects, and procedures constituted to achieve defined objectives or some operational role by performing specified function," while the information technologist defines the same term as "something of interest as a whole or as comprised of parts." Though similar, the engineer believes that a system must achieve a defined objective, while the IT analyst believes a system is anything made up of component parts. Communication between these two professionals could easily lead to confusion and frustration. Clearly tools that resolve these terminological collisions would be useful to people in computing fields that constantly interact with each other, yet come to the table with different meanings for the same term.

In 2012, we set out to create an integrated glossary tool [2] that would identify vocabulary collisions. A collision is when the same concept is bound to multiple terms, or when different concepts are bound to the same term. Such collisions frequently occur between fields that developed similar ideas in parallel, and therefore use different terminology to express similar ideas. The first step of this work was to acquire terminology data from existing resources. The core source was the *sevocab* [3] which is an aggregation of glossaries [4] in systems engineering and software engineering. The *sevocab* exists because systems and software engineers needed a common base for terminological information. To acquire and normalize the data from these resources, we created custom parsers and created an online GUI to grant web access to our integrated glossary. In the end, this system allowed us to see all the concepts (from multiple sources) bound to a term and which terms had the most concepts (and therefore were the most likely candidates for miscommunication).

Overall, significant progress was made in 2012, but room was left to improve and extend the glossary application. To continue and expand that application, we created the "Termediator" as the next-generation integrated glossary tool. Our first steps were to fulfill the expectations we delimited at the end of 2012: a standardized XML format with more detailed attributes, a merging script with a validation mechanism, full source citations, and a larger source data set. In addition, we attempted to further augment terminological awareness through concept similarity measurements and visualization features. We used Salton's vector space model [5] to create relevant rankings that identified which terms have the most commonalities and are most likely to collide. For visualization, we created a new web application (http://termediator.byu.edu) that provides a master list of terms as well as search capability. Users can click on a term to see its aggregated concepts as well its ranked relevance to other similar terms.

Through the Termediator's terminology aggregation, vector similarity measurements, and associative visualization, we have noticed certain statistical trends. These trends leave us optimistic that future IT tools can enhance interdisciplinary communication.

2. CONTEXT
In this section we discuss the significance of terminology management, how we standardized our source material using an XSD, and why we retain domain information for each glossary concept.

2.1 Terminology Management
The lay individual may assume that a glossary and a dictionary are essentially the same thing. However, subtle distinctions exist that are relevant to our research. Lexicography creates dictionary relationships that begin with the term and analyze it to produce a hierarchy of definitions that are ranked from the "most appropriate" or "most recognized" definition to the "least appropriate" or "least recognized" definition. Consider just a small sample of dictionary definitions of the word "set":

1. To put (something or someone) in a particular place: *to set a vase on a table.*
2. to place in a particular position or posture: *set the baby on his feet.*
3. to place in some relation to something or someone: *we set a supervisor over the new workers.*

4. to put into some condition: *to set a house on fire.*
5. to put or apply: *to set a fire to a house.*
6. to pass below the horizon; sink: *the sun sets early in winter.*
7. to decline; wane.

According to lexicography, there may be multiple definitions but the first one is preferred over the others. If we took that same list of definitions and placed it in a glossary, a terminologist would say that the "right" definition depends entirely on the context of its use. Conversely, a glossary starts with the concept and associates it with an appropriate term. Determining which term's concept to use depends on the context of the use. A term may have multiple concepts that are of equal importance, just as one would not say that a software engineer or a systems engineer was more important than the other–they simply fulfill different roles. Terms may also encompass multiple words, which further increases ambiguity. Take "task", for example—how many short phrases have the word system in them? Background task, noncritical task, task behavior specification, sprint task, apportioned task; although each term uses "task", their concepts are not necessarily strongly related.

In this light, a glossary is better suited to our needs as it seeks to facilitate understanding between simultaneous concepts while a dictionary seeks to subordinate definitions in a ranked order. However, a glossary's looser associative structure comes with a challenge: there is no "right" definition, and one term can be bound to multiple different concepts by multiple terminologists in multiple domains. Any terminological structure we devise must be flexible enough to handle such ambiguity.

2.2 Integrated Glossary XSD Structure
An XSD is a schema that defines the structure of an XML document. We chose to create an XSD in order to standardize the individual XML glossaries so that we can seamlessly merge them into an integrated glossary compendium.

Our XSD conforms to the XML Schema standard version 1.0. This is the most widely accepted version of the language at the time of this writing. A short example of a glossary's tag structure is as follows:

Table 1. Glossary's XML tag structure.

```
<Glossary>
<Entry>
    <Term>Term Text</Term>
    <Concept>Concept 1 Text</Concept>
    <Concept>Concept 2 Text</Concept>
</Entry>
</Glossary>
```

As you can see from the example, each glossary contains a root `<Glossary>` that contains `<Entry>` tags. Each `<Entry>` has one term and one or more linked `<Concept>` tags.

Additionally, `<Glossary>` tags have three attributes: OriginName, OriginAuthor, and OriginURL. Terms can optionally contain child `<TermAnnotation>` elements of four types: Note, SeeAlso, Synonym, or Reference. *Appendix A* contains an example of a XML glossary populated with attributes and content.

2.3 Domains
The 2012 project [2] primarily used the *sevocab* [3] in order to identify and resolve collisions in the space where Software Engineering and Systems Engineering intersect. As we developed the Termediator, we realized that IT professionals must interact with almost every field, since IT has become the universal toolkit for document creation and management. To analyze a broader set

of terminological collisions, we added terminology from the Enterprise Architecture, Business Process Management, and Workflow domains. We will continue to add domains and their terminology as the research continues.

To store the domain information, we added the OriginDomain attribute to the `<Glossary>` XML tag. You may ask, what is a Domain and why did we store it? As our source list grew, we realized it would be useful to permanently store not only the glossary from which a Concept originated, but also the field, or "domain", it came from. This information is valuable because glossaries come from standards and organizations that naturally clump into domain supersets. Domains are a crucial attribute that helps us understand where and why terminology collisions occur. For example, it is worthwhile to note that conflicts between Information Technology and Business Process Management terminology frequently occur when "agents" and "processes" are involved, but conflicts between Business Process Management and Workflow cluster around "activity" and "case."

3. IMPLEMENTATION

The first challenge in creating Termediator was to collect the source material, transform it into a standardized XML format, and then merge all terms and concepts into an integrated glossary. The second challenge was creating a useful user interface that illustrated relationships between the terms and concepts. The current interface presents a hierarchical tree that generates each term at the root of its relationship to other terms and associated concepts.

3.1 PDF Parsing

Many of the relevant glossaries were only available in PDF format. For these glossaries Adobe Acrobat's "Transform to XML 1.0" function was used to create each glossary's source XML file.

A custom Python parser was created for each individual glossary. The parser takes a source file, extracts the term and concepts, and builds glossary entries from that information. The entry XML format conform to our XSD.

At first the source XML and content was transformed into a navigable XML tree through Python's built-in ElementTree library [6]. It soon became apparent that the built-in implementation of ElementTree was incapable of handling many of our source documents. The transformation from PDF to XML often produced sloppy or malformed XML. ElementTree's search capabilities were also somewhat limited, which posed a problem because many of our source XML documents only had formatting information, such as paragraph tags or line breaks, to delineate content. Without meaningful content tags, it was necessary to define and search for the formatting tags that should translate into glossary entries. ElementTree's built-in implementation could not handle these more complex search cases. We switched our main parsing functions over to the lxml ElementTree library [7] that expands the base ElementTree functionality with better handling for malformed XML and more advanced searching capabilities.

3.2 Web Scraping

Many other glossaries were available on the web, and so we created web scrapers to extract and normalize this online content. Simple one-page online glossaries were typically saved as a local HTML document and parsed into XML. We then constructed a custom Python parser, similar to the ones used for PDF source documents, to extract content and build glossary entries from that content. Parsers for web files were built around the BeautifulSoup library [8], which creates navigable trees from HTML code.

When online glossaries contained more than one webpage, we used the Python urllib library to scrape all relevant pages directly from the website. We then brought the retrieved pages into BeautifulSoup to create a navigable HTML tree. Relevant HTML tags were then identified and their content copied to XML tags in our standardized structure.

The HTML code we pulled frequently had very sloppy syntax. As the syntax errors varied with each glossary, correctly parsing the HTML required frequent debugging cycles. To shorten the time between each cycle, we added caches to the web scrapers that enabled us to debug the parser without fetching the same data over and over from the web.

HTML documents also contained a lot of whitespace, which was translated by BeautifulSoup as literal HTML entities (carriage returns, line breaks, no break spaces, and so on). There were also many entities in our source material that were incompatible with the final glossary's UTF-8 encoding. Part of the parsing process was stripping unnecessary entities or converting incompatible ones. The following function was used in some parsers to convert incompatible characters, such as curly quotes, to compatible characters, such as straight quotes.

Table 2. Function that strips unnecessary entities and converts incompatible characters into compliant ones.

```
def clean_input(text):
    replace_dict = {u'\u2014':'-', u'\u2013':'-',
                    u'\uf0b7':'', u'\u201c':'"',
                    u'\u201d':'"', u'\u2019':"'",
                    u'\u2026':'...', u'\u2192':'',
                    u'\u03a9':'omega',
                    chr(195)+chr(188):'u',
                    chr(195)+chr(168):'e',
                    chr(195)+chr(167):'c',
                    chr(195)+chr(171):'e'}
    for i, j in replace_dict.iteritems():
        text = text.replace(i, j)
    return text
```

In addition, some glossaries chose to illustrate concepts primarily through diagrams or other images, which made it necessary to include these essential images in Termediator's XML documents. Since online references to images may result in broken links over time, we chose to download the images and provide local references in the XML. Images are referenced via ImageData tags that are nested as child tags of Concepts, for example:

```
<Concept>BPMN 2.0 diagrams combine swimlanes and
conditional statements, as illustrated below:
    <ImageData src="images/bpmn_diagram.jpg">
</Concept>
```

3.3 Merged Output

Once we had individual glossary content parsed into a standardized XML document, we merged all of the documents into a glossary compendium. An example of merged output is provided in *Appendix B*.

The merger is a python program that accepts a list of XML documents. The core merger function integrates two glossaries at a time. First, it parses both XML glossary documents into navigable trees using the lxml ElementTree library. After the trees are parsed, every concept tag in each tree is assigned a child ConceptAnnotation tag that marks the concept's source. Concepts in both trees are then sorted alphabetically by term. The merger then goes through each tree, term by term, and makes a comparison version with downcased characters. The comparison version of the term is used to sort and merge the two trees into one alphabetical tree. When two identical terms are encountered, the entries are merged so that the term in the merged compendium has concepts from both trees.

To merge every glossary in our data set, first a complete merge is performed on the first and second glossaries in the list, so that Glossary A + Glossary B = merged Compendium. The next glossary on the list, Glossary C, is combined with the compendium, which gives us Glossary C + Compendium = new Compendium. This process is repeated until the list is empty.

3.4 Visualization

Visualization was preliminarily attempted in the 2010 project through an alphabetical list of terms and built-in browser search that assumed the full glossary text was part of the visualization. In the Termediator we add direct search capability that lets users search for any term they desire. When users click on a term, Termediator pulls up the aggregated concepts as well as its ranked relevant to other similar terms.

4. Concept Similarity

Our current similarity measure uses vector space model to perform relevance rankings that identify which terms have the most commonalities and are therefore most likely to be misunderstood and misused.

We used Gerard Salton's vector space model [5] for information retrieval as Termediator's similarity measure. In the Salton model, documents and queries are represented as vectors of term counts. When a concept is converted to a vector, associated angles are created. Those angles can be used in a similarity measure comparison by comparing the angle deviation between two vectors (which represent two terms in the glossary compendium). The most convenient way to perform this measurement is to calculate the cosine of the angle between the two vectors.

Each concept's vector has N dimensions corresponding to the total number of distinct terms. For example, consider the following two phrases P1 and P2:

P1 = The red cat
P2 = The angry red dog

First, we take each distinct term and create vectors such that the vectors of P1 and P2 become:

Table 3. Basic vector creation.

	The	Red	Cat	Angry	Dog
P1	1	1	1	0	0
P2	1	1	0	1	1

Thus, P1 can be represented as the vector (1,1,1,0,0) and P2 can be represented as (1,1,0,1,1). Once concepts are converted to vectors, we use the cosine similarity measurement to determine how close the two angles made by the vectors are which results with a value between zero and one. A value of zero means there is no similarity (there are no shared dimensions between the vectors) and a value of one means there is perfect similarity (the vectors are the same). Specifically, the cosine similarity used for this project is currently:

$$Sim(a,b) = \frac{\sum_{i=1..t} a_i \times b_i}{\sqrt{\sum_{i=1..t} a_i^2 \times \sum_{i=1..t} b_i^2}}$$

Where t is the total number of distinct terms between a and b. Or in simplest terms, it is the dot product of the two vectors divided by the product of their norms. Calculating this for "the red cat / the angry red dog" example gives us a similarity measurement of approximately 0.577.

Salton's model was chosen primarily out of convenience. While it provided a foundation as we forayed into concept similarity measurements, this model resulted in an undesirably high number of false positives in our results. Future implementations of Termediator will experiment with other similarity measures.

4.1 Stop Word Removal

Using the similarity measure above as a foundation, Termediator is able to compute the "distance" between concepts in the space of terms, however, all terms are not created equal. The first optimization performed was stopword removal. In many of the concepts, there are words that do little to contribute to the semantic meaning of the others. Some simple examples of such words are "it", "there", and "a". Removing these words "increases retrieval efficiency and generally improves retrieval effectiveness" [9]. In our application, stop word removal takes place when a concept is converted into a vector. The list of stop words used for this function is included in an online appendix at http://termediator.byu.edu/stopwords.

4.2 Stemming

In addition to removing the stop words in each concept, another technique called stemming is applied. Stemming is the process of "[capturing] the relationships between different variations of a word" [9]. This is critical for comparing concepts because without it, words such as "computer" and "computing" would be considered completely different dimensions in the concept vector. With stemming, words are broken down to a root word so that these and other similar words can be compared together.

To perform the stemming, this application uses a common algorithmic stemmer called the Porter stemmer. It follows a series of steps to transform an input word into a common stem and "has been shown to be effective in a number of… evaluations and search applications" [9]. The current stemmer script currently being used is a Python version obtained from the "official home page for distribution of the Porter Stemming Algorithm, written and maintained by its author, Martin Porter" [10]

4.3 User Interface

Termediator was built as a web application using the Django web framework, although the glossary functionality is nearly independent of the chosen web platform [11]. Django is a Python based framework meaning that the majority of the pages are rendered from a collection of different python scripts. In addition to python scripts, the project also utilizes the jQuery JavaScript library to enhance the user experience. The user, when brought to the initial conceptual clustering page, will see the entire list of terms in alphabetical order from the compendium. At the very top is a search filter that uses a jQuery plugin called Fast Live Filter [12]. This filter will adjust the list of terms displayed based on what is entered in real time. It uses a simple regular expression to find any terms that contain all of the entered text, so entering the word "data" will show a list containing both the term "data" and the term "database".

When a term is selected by clicking on it, a request is made to the server that returns every concept associated with that term from the compendium.

Figure 1. The "system" term and child concepts as presented in the Termediator UI.

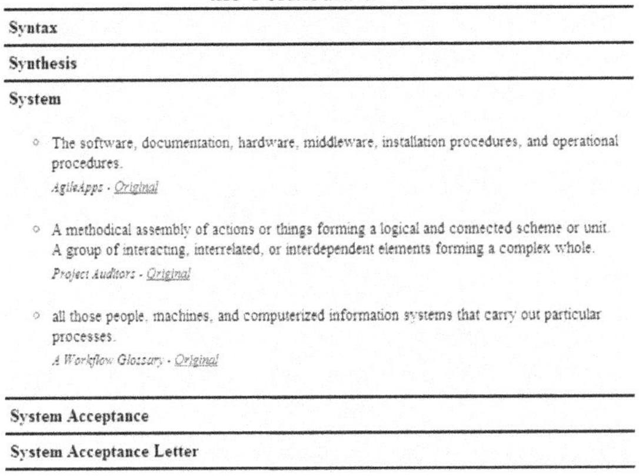

These concepts are retrieved using simple xQuery statements made against the compendium XML file. In addition to displaying the concept text, the source from which the concept was retrieved is also displayed with an external link to the original. When a concept is selected by clicking on it, the application loads the matrix that contains the similarity values, creates the complete row of similarities as described in the previous section, and then sorts it. Currently the system will return the top three values, with ties being sorted alphabetically. These top three terms will be displayed below the selected concept and work the same as the terms in the original list, the only difference being a similarity value being displayed after the term (See *Figure 2*).

Figure 2. The "system" term, child concepts, and similarity ranking of matched concepts.

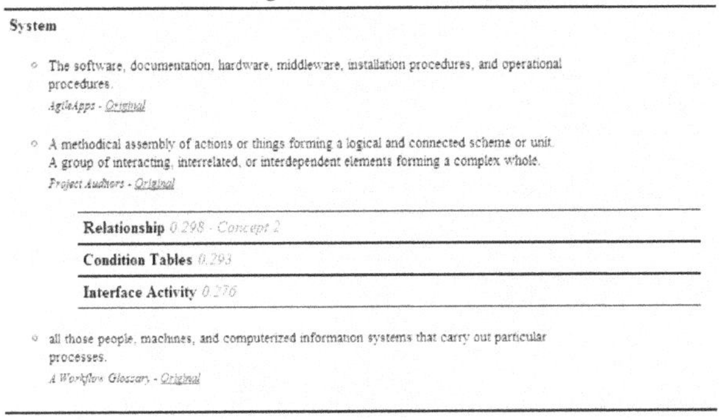

4.4 Analysis Functionality

To aid the user in identifying the connections between concepts, an initial analysis tool has been implemented into the application and can be used by clicking on the "Show Analysis" button below a concept at least one level deep. This will recreate and display the vectors that were used to compute the distance between the parent concept with the selected concept and display it in a human readable form. Terms that were found in both documents are highlighted to help aid in the analysis. Figure 3 shows the analysis tool being used on concepts from the terms "System" and "Operations and Maintenance Manual".

Figure 3. The term "system" and its analysis chart.

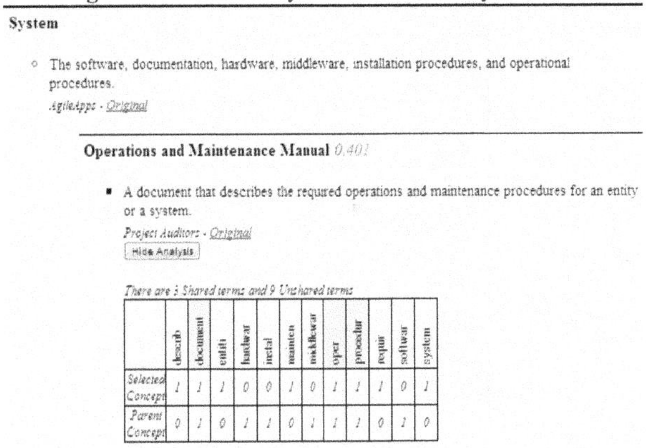

5. RESULTS

This section presents a breakdown of sources and terms in the glossary compendium, and provides an analysis of similarity values and their overall effectiveness. Main data points were collected using Python scripts, which can be re-used in the future to create the same analytic structure; this allows us to compare future iterations using a standard set of metrics. Statistical information is also provided on the Termediator web interface.

5.1 Compendium

The compendium contains 294 different glossaries; 131 included in the sevocab and 163 from other sources. When merged, these glossaries contain 31980 terms and 50621 concepts. A complete breakdown of terms by number of concepts is found in *Table 4*.

Table 4. Terms by number of concepts.

Concept Count	Term Count
1	9707
2	1241
3	448
4	199
5	90
6	46
7	26
8	14
9	12
11	11
13	7

The data shows that roughly 89% of the terms represent a single concept. About 3% of the terms have three or more concepts, and the max number of concepts under a single term is 13. The top 14 terms with the most concepts are displayed in *Table 5*, which are all terms with eight or more concepts each.

Table 5. Top fourteen terms with the most child concepts.

Term	Concept Count
Process	22
Activity	18
Task	17
Baseline	15
Constraint	14
Stakeholder	14
Risk	13
C(A)	12
Gantt chart	12
Software	12
Milestone	8
Project	8
Six Sigma	8
Task	8

5.2 Similarity Values

In addition to analyzing the compendium, we also analyzed Termediator's stored similarity values. A total of 28,506,368 similarity values are stored. These values range from one to zero and represent how similar one concept is to another. *Figure 4* is a histogram illustrating the distribution of the similarity values. It uses a logarithmic scale to show frequency and only stores non-zero similarity values.

Figure 4. Histogram of similarity value distribution.

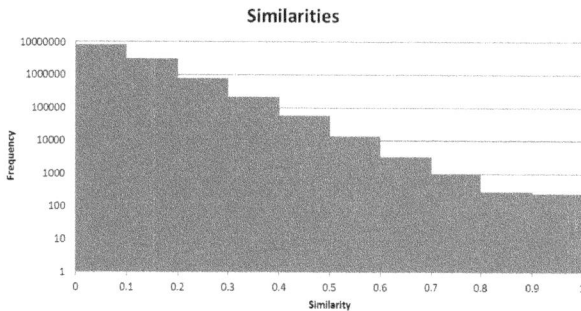

Our current concept similarity measurement implementation shows that the vast majority—or approximately 67%—of stored values are extremely low between 0 and 0.1. These low similarity values do not give relevant results and are of little use to the Termediator. This finding shows that more than half of the storage is not needed, and indicates changes to be made to scale the Termediator vector implementation more efficiently in the future.

5.3 Similarity Effectiveness

Termediator's overall effectiveness in its current implementation is dependent on a number of factors. One factor is concept length and is shown in *Figure 2*. This figure shows two different concepts under the term "process" along with the three most similar terms for each concept.

This figure shows two different concepts under the term "process" along with the three most similar terms for each. The first concept on the left is composed of a handful of short sentences whereas the concept on the right has a paragraph of text. Looking at the similar terms, we can see that the short concept had lower similarity scores returned which is evident by looking at the similar terms. The longer concept had much higher similarity scores that results in terms that have a noticeable similarity with the term "process".

Based on these results it would appear that the vector space model using only term frequencies has many limitations. Lack of concept normalization tends to give longer concepts higher value than their shorter counterparts as evidenced in the previous figure. The compendium, with all 8,986 concepts, has less than a tenth of a percent of the stored similarity values over 0.5; this shows that improved similarity measures need to be implemented. With the web platform established and analysis tools available, the Termediator is ideal for applying different similarity measures in the future and performing side by side analysis to compare overall effectiveness.

6. CONCLUSION

Termediator's results include obvious synonym term matches, accurate term matches, and false positives.

Obvious synonym mathes are most often found in "See Also" terms. A "See Also" term's entire concept references another term, such as the term "AI" which has the concept "See Artificial Intelligence." The Termediator succeeds by listing "Artificial Intelligence" as the most relevant match for "AI". These synonym matches show that the Termediator may work on a fundamental level.

The Termediator also makes some accurate matches between non-synonym terms. Some examples of these results exist in the terms: Abstraction, Agile Development, Help Desk Management, Information Processing, Source Code, Terminal, Trojan, Twisted Pair Cable, URL, User Interface.

Figure 6.1. "Abstraction"

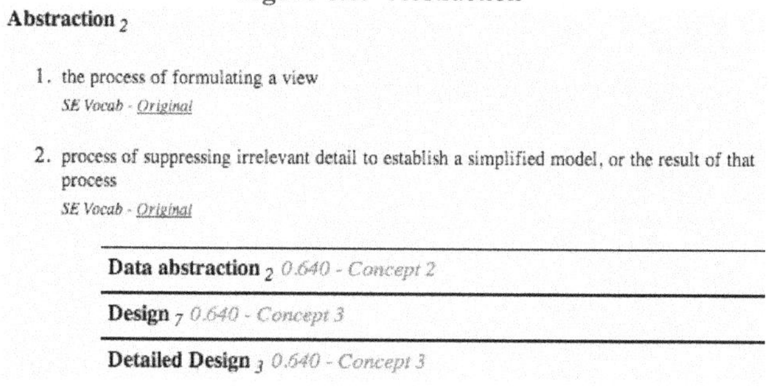

Figure 6.2. "Acceptance Criteria"

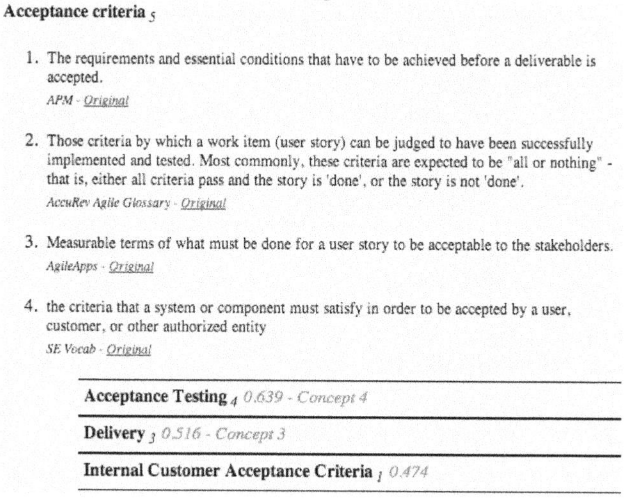

Figure 6.3. "Agile Development"

Agile Development *₂*

1. Agile development is a way of thinking about software development as expressed in the Agile Manifesto, and acts as an "umbrella" for a group of methodologies. The methodologies are based on process-centric and iterative development, where requirements and solutions evolve through collaboration between self-organizing, cross-functional teams. Agile development is a conceptual framework that promotes evolutionary change throughout the entire life cycle of the project and represents a new, more flexible approach to development than the traditional methods that have previously been the norm for software development.
AccuRev Agile Glossary - Original

2. software development approach based on iterative development, frequent inspection and adaptation, and incremental deliveries, in which requirements and solutions evolve through collaboration in cross-functional teams and through continuous stakeholder feedback
SE Vocab - Original

Agile Methodology *₂ 0.545*	
Agile Software Development *₃ 0.541*	
Agile Processes *₁ 0.473*	

Figure 6.4. "Help Desk Management"

Help Desk Management *₁*

1. Help desk management services provide centralized information and support management service to handle a company's internal or external queries and operational problems about IT-related processes, policies, systems and usage. Services include product support capabilities, including elements of hardware and software support, logging of problems, and results analysis (results analysis means analyzing the results of calls taken to resolution of those calls for entry into self-help database, problem trends to suggest permanent fixes and so forth); dispatch of service technicians or parts; training coordination; and other IT-related issues.
Gartner - Original

Hardware And Software Maintenance Services *₁ 0.472*	
Product Support Services *₁ 0.448*	
Technical Lead / Technical Point of Contact *₁ 0.447*	

Figure 6.5. "Information Processing"

Information Processing *₂*

1. The handling of information by computers in accordance with strictly defined systems of procedure.
Iowa State IT Glossary - Original

2. the systematic performance of operations upon information, which includes data processing and may include operations such as data communication and office automation.
SE Vocab - Original

Data processing (DP) *₁ 0.688*	
Process *₂₂ 0.662 - Concept 18*	
Abstract data type *₁ 0.574*	

Figure 6.6. "Source Code"

Source Code *₄*

○ A sequence of instructions, including comments describing those instructions, for a computer system. Also known as program code, program source code, or simply as code.
AgileApps - Original

Program instruction *₁ 0.585*	
Computer Programming *₁ 0.571*	
Computer Technology *₁ 0.571*	

Figure 6.7. "Terminal"

Terminal *₉*

○ Computer-like device that includes a screen and a keyboard for both display and input. It connects to the server. It is called "dumb" because it can do very little on its own. It is not a computer by itself. The programs it "runs" are located on the server. Also called a dumb terminal.
AAO IT Glossary - Original

Servers *₁ 0.401*	
Workstation *₃ 0.400*	
Telnet *₂ 0.369 - Concept 2*	

Figure 6.8. "Trojan"

Trojan *₁*

○ A harmful application (or routine) that hides it malicious activities by masquerading as a more useful, harmless and desirable application. In many respects a Trojan is like a virus, except that it does not provide a means to copy itself. A Trojan instead relies upon the fact that it masquerades as something useful that people will recommend or copy-on the application. Trojan's are often found in software that is freeware, although it must be stressed that most freeware is free of viruses and Trojans. Anti-virus applications will typically scan for many known Trojans. Anti-virus writers tend to classify a Trojan as one of the following depending on what the Trojan does: Trojan Downloader - downloads and installs new software on the computer. Trojan Dropper - installs new software on the computer. Trojan Proxy - turns the computer into a proxy server providing anonymous access to the internet for the Trojan writer. Trojan PSW - password stealer, hunts the computer for stored usernames and passwords and forwards these to the Trojan writer. Trojan Spy - any form of spyware application, such as keyloggers, password stealers etc. Trojans get their name from the classical Greek story of the Trojan horse, used in the Trojan war. The Trojan horse was a large wooden horse left as a gift from the Greeks to the Trojans, the Greeks then sailed away (apparently admitting defeat). The Trojans moved the horse inside their city walls and then celebrated their apparent victory. Unfortunately for the Trojans the Trojan Horse contains a number of Greek soldiers who then killed the guards and let the remainder of the Greek army into the city who then sacked Troy. A Trojan is also known as a Trojan horse. For more information see: www.cryer.co.uk/resources/antivirus.htm - List of anti virus products that are free for personal use. www.historyforkids.org/learn/greeks/religion/myths/trojanhorse.htm - Summary of the Trojan Horse story (for children) http://everything.explained.at/Trojan_horse_(computing) - Trojan horse explained.
Brian Cryer's IT Glossary - Original

Trojan horse *₄ 0.040 - Concept 2*	
RAT *₁ 0.446*	
Malware *₂ 0.297*	

Figure 6.9. "Twisted pair cable"

Twisted pair cable *₁*

○ The type of cable used for most telephone wiring. It has pairs of copper wires twisted together to minimize electrical noise. There are shielded twisted pair (STP) and unshielded twisted pair (UTP) cables. In shielded twisted pair cables, each pair has a metal sheath around it for better protection against interference.
AAO IT Glossary - Original

STP *₄ 0.734*	
UTP *₁ 0.699*	
Shielded Pair *₁ 0.514*	

Figure 6.10. "URL"

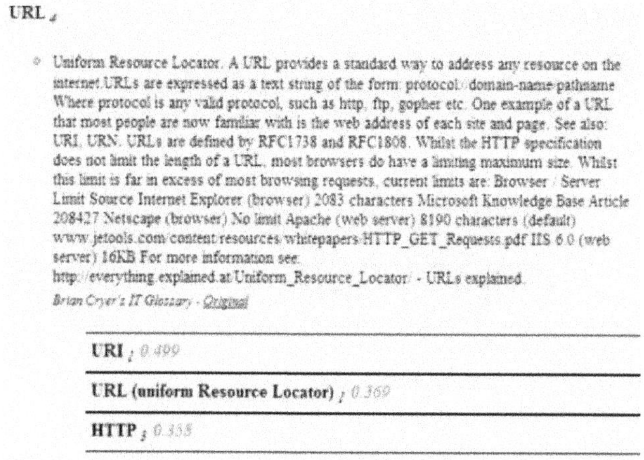

URL [4]

○ Uniform Resource Locator. A URL provides a standard way to address any resource on the internet. URLs are expressed as a text string of the form: protocol://domain-name/pathname Where protocol is any valid protocol, such as http, ftp, gopher etc. One example of a URL that most people are now familiar with is the web address of each site and page. See also: URI, URN. URLs are defined by RFC1738 and RFC1808. Whilst the HTTP specification does not limit the length of a URL, most browsers do have a limiting maximum size. Whilst this limit is far in excess of most browsing requests, current limits are: Browser / Server Limit Source Internet Explorer (browser) 2083 characters Microsoft Knowledge Base Article 208427 Netscape (browser) No limit Apache (web server) 8190 characters (default) www.jetools.com/content/resources/whitepapers/HTTP_GET_Requests.pdf IIS 6.0 (web server) 16KB For more information see: http://everything.explained.at/Uniform_Resource_Locator/ - URLs explained.

Brian Cryer's IT Glossary - Original

URI [1] *0.499*	
URL (uniform Resource Locator) [1] *0.369*	
HTTP [3] *0.355*	

Figure 6.11. "User Interface"

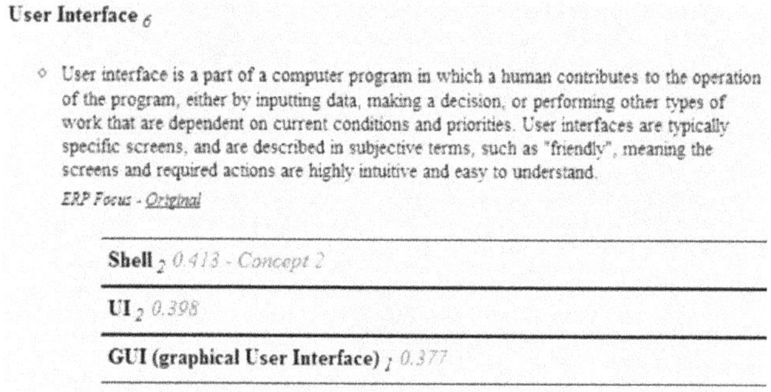

User Interface [6]

○ User interface is a part of a computer program in which a human contributes to the operation of the program, either by inputting data, making a decision, or performing other types of work that are dependent on current conditions and priorities. User interfaces are typically specific screens, and are described in subjective terms, such as "friendly", meaning the screens and required actions are highly intuitive and easy to understand.

ERP Focus - Original

Shell [2] *0.413 - Concept 2*	
UI [2] *0.398*	
GUI (graphical User Interface) [1] *0.377*	

False positives exist in the Termediator due to a number of factors. The short length of glossary concepts makes it difficult to perform precise natural language processing. Termediator's term comparison also relies heavily on direct word matching, which often links concepts that share similar words without sharing context.

Our usage of a vector space model also could be improved: the basic idea is sound, but we need to explore more sophisticated techniques and further specialize our vector implementation to achieve more useful results. Term context is not fully utilized: we are comparing concepts to concepts in our analysis, without using the context of the term itself. In many technical glossaries, a large portion of a term's meaning is located in the term itself. In the future, superior results may be obtained by comparing concepts in context with their attached terms.

Lastly, it should be noted that any technical glossary expects the user to have a knowledge set in place before reading the glossary. Most of the concepts we compiled do not contain enough information to describe a technical term to the layperson, which gives us less detail to work with overall.

The current status of the Termediator leaves us optimistic that enhanced terminology management tools will be able to augment interdisciplinary communication through natural language processing.

7. REFERENCES

1 Cabre, M. Teresa. *Terminology: Theory, methods, and applications.* John Benjamins North America, Philadelphia, 1999.

2 Ekstrom, Joseph J. Experience with a Cross-Disciplinary Aggregated Glossary of Technical Terms. *SIGITE* (2012).

3 IEEE. SEVOCAB. *IEEE Computer Society* (Dec. 2010).

4 ISO. ISO/IEC/IEEE 24765:2010. *Systems and software engineering -- Vocabulary* (Dec. 15, 2010).

5 Salton, Gerard, Wong, A., and Yang, C.S. A Vector Space Model for Automatic Indexing. *Information Retrieval and Language Processing* (1975).

6 PYTHON API. *ElementTree.* 2013. http://docs.python.org/2/library/xml.etree.elementtree.html.

7 LXML API. *lxml: XML and HTML with Python.* 2013. http://lxml.de/.

8 BEAUTIFULSOUP API. *BeautifulSoup.* 2013. http://www.crummy.com/software/BeautifulSoup/.

9 Croft, W. B., Metzler, D., & Strohman, T. *Search engines: Information retrieval in practice.* 2010.

10 Porter, M. *The Porter Stemming Algorithm.* 2001. http://tartarus.org/martin/PorterStemmer/index-old.html.

11 DJANGO PROJECT. *Django.* 2013. http://www.djangoproject.com.

12 Bush, Anthony. *Fast Live Filter.* 2013. http://anthonybush.com/projects/jquery_fast_live_filter/.

Appendix A

This segment of code illustrates a Glossary with one Entry. The Entry contains one Term. The Term contains two TermAnnotations and one Concept. This sample conforms to our XSD.

```
<Glossary OriginName="AccuRev Agile Glossary" OriginURL="http://www.accurev.com/agile-
glossary" OriginAuthor="AccuRev" OriginDomain="Workflow">
    <Entry>
        <Term>Acceptance Criteria</Term>
            <TermAnnotation type="SeeAlso">Acceptance Testing</TermAnnotation>
            <TermAnnotation type="SeeAlso">Acceptance Testing Driven Development
(ATDD)</TermAnnotation>
            <Concept>Those criteria by which a work item (user story) can be judged to have been
successfully implemented and tested. Most commonly, these criteria are expected to be "all or
nothing"—that is, either all criteria pass and the story is "done", or the story is not
"done". </Concept>
    </Entry>
</Glossary>
```

Appendix B

This segment of code is the sample of a glossary merger. The APM, AccuRev Agile, and Agile Apps glossaries all contained the term "acceptance criteria". When these glossaries were added to the compendium, their concepts linked to "acceptance criteria" were merged into one entry and a `<ConceptAnnotation>` tag was added to each `<Concept>` to indicate where the concept originated. This sample conforms to our XSD.

```
<Entry>
  <Term>Acceptance criteria</Term>
    <Concept>The requirements and essential conditions that have to be achieved before a
deliverable is accepted.
        <ConceptAnnotation>APM</ConceptAnnotation>
    </Concept>
    <Concept>Those criteria by which a work item (user story) can be judged to have been
successfully implemented and tested. Most commonly, these criteria are expected to be "all or
nothing" - that is, either all criteria pass and the story is 'done', or the story is not
'done'.
        <ConceptAnnotation>AccuRevAgileGlossary</ConceptAnnotation>
    </Concept>
    <Concept>Measurable terms of what must be done for a user story to be acceptable to the
stakeholders.
        <ConceptAnnotation>AgileApps</ConceptAnnotation>
    </Concept>
</Entry>
```

Advancing the IT Research Agenda

William W. Agresti
Johns Hopkins University
Carey Business School
100 International Drive
Baltimore, MD 21202
(001) 410-234-9403
agresti@jhu.edu

ABSTRACT

The potential benefits of pursuing an intentional community-wide development of a research agenda for IT are discussed. Motivation to undertake this task arises from the continuing evolution of IT as a distinct discipline. There is an opportunity to mark progress by developing an IT research agenda that has broad involvement from the community. Alternative formats for an agenda are discussed and potential research topic areas are proposed, drawing upon prior contributions. To help inform the discussion, 24 other research agendas are profiled, providing useful examples of agenda-development processes and alternative formats for the recommended IT research agenda.

Categories and Subject Descriptors

K.3.2 Computer and Information Science Education; K.7.0 Computing Profession - General

General Terms

Management, Measurement, Documentation, Standardization

Keywords

Research, discipline, profession, agenda

1. INTRODUCTION

This paper makes a case for the potential benefits of pursuing an intentional community-based development of a research agenda for IT. Having a recognizable and visible research agenda will represent progress in the coalescence of IT as a distinct discipline. "The standing of a field may be measured by its capacity to set its own agenda." [16, p.9]

In advocating for an IT research agenda, we will discuss the motivation for doing so, the potential benefits of having one, what form such an IT research agenda might take, what might be the IT research content areas, how to proceed to develop it, and what evaluation criteria we would use to determine if we had a useful one. To inform the discussion and provide examples for IT, 24 other research agendas are examined and profiled.

2. MOTIVATION

A principal reason for a research community to develop its own research agenda is to signal the growing maturity of a discipline. We are echoing the contention by Reichgelt that "… to the extent

RIIT'13, October 10–12, 2013, Orlando, FL, USA
Copyright 2013 ACM 978-1-4503-2494-6/13/10…$15.00.
http://dx.doi.org/10.1145/2512209.2512210

that it is desirable for IT to establish itself as a respected academic discipline, the field must communicate its distinctive nature through the formulation of a research agenda." [23, p. 248]

There is an evolutionary process as disciplines emerge; developing a research agenda is a natural stage in this maturation process. As indicators of its maturing, IT now has research conferences, journals, doctoral programs, and academic units at the department and school level. IT is recognized as a discipline by curricular and accreditation bodies (e.g., [15, 1] respectively). Nevertheless, when the attention turns to a distinct research legacy, IT is not as prominent as its related disciplines in the computing space, such as computer science and information systems, as discussed in [2], which also discussed jurisdictional issues for theory-driven IT research. The prior decade has witnessed the evolution of IT as a discipline that is distinct from these nearest neighbors, while still related to them, as they are to each other. So, we look to shore up the research foundations of IT.

Characterizing it as "community-based," means that we recommend pursuing an IT research agenda as an intentional activity by a research community. Doing so will gain the benefits of diverse opinions. The process of developing this agenda in an open fashion will serve to further define the IT research community, simply by researchers self-selecting to participate in the exercise. A community-based agenda will convey more stature than one put forward by any single entity. Research agendas in other fields (e.g., [18, 24]) prominently cite their origins from a diverse collaborative base as if to imply that greater authority should accrue to agendas from a broadly engaged community.

Being able to refer to an IT research agenda may be more than (to use colloquial requirements analysis terminology) a "nice to have" and may be a "must have." As Ekstrom observes, "The likelihood of IT surviving as an academically sound discipline is greatly enhanced if it can establish a distinct research agenda." [8, p. 19]

In addition to a motivation based on contributing to the evolution of IT as a discipline, further motivation comes from the potential benefits of having an IT research agenda.

3. POTENTIAL BENEFITS

Why is there this call to pursue a research agenda for IT? Why not let it simply define itself as a consequence of research being performed? One clear potential benefit is to serve as a reference for those undertaking IT research. Researchers will know when they are tackling research questions that the community has

declared to be critical to further advancement of the field. Aggregating over the totality of research investigations, it means that there may be a better use of scarce resources -- the talents of IT researchers who may now see an opportunity to have greater impact on the field by addressing challenges that have been identified as being roadblocks to progress. A defined IT research agenda can assist PhD advisors and students by serving as a repository of critical research topics. Similarly, it can be valuable input to non-profit and industry R&D centers to see potential roles for their contributions.

A visible and community-endorsed research agenda for IT can facilitate research coordination. Having a reference architecture of research questions can help to arrange for articulated academia-industry projects. An IT research agenda may help to define the most effective roles for the large and diverse IT practitioner community, such as engaging business and industry as platforms for empirical work, to test out theories, and to build prototypes. There can be greater potential for longitudinal studies and "hand-offs" of more theoretical research to organizations whose mission involves prototyping or first application of new ideas, such as industrial research laboratories or university and government incubators. The Infosec Research Council [13] provides an example in which U.S. Government funding agencies maintain awareness of each other's information security research initiatives, so the results coming from an applied research project funded by one agency can be moved along for testing by a demonstration project funded by another agency – thereby accelerating the transition from ideas into actual use.

An IT research agenda would be timely in light of the trend in funding agencies to target larger and more complex challenges, frequently requiring collaboration among teams of researchers and multiple performing organizations --- often including universities, non-profits, and industry. A resulting recommendation may be for organizations to collaborate and pursue funding for sharable IT research platforms, benchmark datasets to facilitate experimentation, and research centers such as those funded by the U.S. National Science Foundation (NSF).

As an example, consider the potential benefit if there were a reference architecture of anonymized co-located data and service requests from multiple organizations in a well-defined and representative cloud-computing environment that could be used to test alternative policies and practices for provisioning, security, and privacy.

The process of developing an IT research agenda may result in breakthrough ideas or call attention to neglected areas, as was pointed out in [11, 12, and 22] for information systems research.

A community-derived research agenda can serve a cohesive role for future research. Researchers will be able to associate their research as it contributes to the larger community agenda, which may facilitate integration of their results with those of other researchers. The research questions or goals could be adopted by journals and conferences as index terms to facilitate summarizing the relevant research to mark progress in addressing each question or goal.

4. DEVELOPING A RESEARCH AGENDA

This section explores what an IT research agenda might look like, in terms of its format and contents, and the process of developing it, along with consideration of how we may know if we are successful.

4.1 Possible Formats

It seems reasonable to focus on the end product: what would an IT research agenda look like? Historically, the most famous research agenda is likely to have been the address given by David Hilbert, the preeminent mathematician of his time, at the International Congress of Mathematicians in Paris in 1900. To mark the start

of a new century, he described 23 problems upon whose solution "… an advancement of science may be expected." [27, p. 395] So, one form of a research agenda is a list of critical problems that are seen as key obstacles to advancement of the field and whose solution would mark significant progress.

As a way to investigate additional possible formats and organizing constructs for research agendas, we examined 24 examples from various domains and disciplines. The agendas were chosen because they were in subject areas that were computing-related, or, like IT, also featured a large community of practice in addition to active research. The entities producing the research agenda were groups of individual researchers, committees, and task forces that were associated with professional societies, scientific societies, workshops, or national organizations.

We selected the 24 agendas to provide equal coverage to IT topics, applications of IT, and non-IT subjects, so there are eight agendas in each category. The appendix shows features of the 24 agendas: title; sponsoring activity or entity; notes about the process, format, or end product; and a reference. The research agendas are for the following subjects:

Group 1. Information technologies
1-1   Information security
1-2   High assurance computing
1-3   Data mining
1-4   Software engineering
1-5   Networked systems of embedded computers
1-6   Cloud computing
1-7   Knowledge management
1-8   Heterogeneous and distributed environments

Group 2. Applications of IT and computing
2-1   Computing at the margins (digital divide)
2-2   Information literacy
2-3   IT and governance
2-4   IT for manufacturing
2-5   Computing and the social sciences
2-6   IT and healthcare
2-7   Computer-based assessment
2-8   IT and technology commercialization

Group 3. Non-IT research agendas
3-1   American Dental Association
3-2   U.S. National Institute of Justice
3-3   Innovative Medicines Initiative
3-4   Influenza
3-5   Science Policy
3-6   Primary Care
3-7   Arts, Lifelong Learning, and Individual Well-Being
3-8   Agricultural Education

As noted in the appendix, the formats of the examined agendas exhibited some variation. Some were reminiscent of Hilbert in articulating key problems whose solution would most advance the field. The most widely used format showed agendas that were constructed as a list of critical research areas or topics that were defined and discussed. Some formats consisted of several goals, each of which was further broken down into more specific, and ideally measurable, objectives.

Distinctive features of certain agendas were notable as they might be useful for an IT research agenda. The research agenda for agricultural education [3] was organized as six research priorities, with each one described by its background, challenges, and "opportunities to respond." Each priority also cited one or more key expected outcomes, which begins to address potential success criteria.

Related to this notion of documenting expected outcomes, the hard problems list of the IRC [13] includes metrics for each problem: What are measurable success criteria? How will you know if you are making progress in solving the hard problem? How do you know when the problem is solved?

In a technological subject like IT, it would be natural for its research agenda to feature technical topics. However, other agendas may offer a suggestion for the IT community. The research agenda on IT for manufacturing [19] features both a technology part and a non-technology part, recognizing that there were significant research questions that needed to be addressed so that the IT would actually get applied appropriately in the manufacturing environments. Research was needed to understand non-technical influences such as social and organizational dynamics, training, and globalization.

Analogously, the research agenda for networked systems of embedded computers provides for three broad areas: "(1) research that is needed to build robust and scalable [networked systems of embedded computers], (2) research on social, ethical, and policy issues that result from the deployment of [networked systems of embedded computers]; and (3) research on component technologies that is unlikely to be addressed by the general IT research community." [20, p. 175]

In addition to organizing agendas as problem lists, goals/objectives, research questions, and research areas/topics, there were other dimensions noted in the appendix:

- Research Timeline: Objectives were identified as being near-term, mid-term, or long-term

- Structural Relationships: Some agendas did more than list problems or goals/objectives and included the inter-relationships among them, for example, as a taxonomy or architecture.

- Audience: To differing degrees, the examined agendas made it clear about the intended audience for the agenda, for example in [5], policy-makers, researchers, practitioners, educators, funding sources. It also seems reasonable that additional audiences, such as new members of the IT research community, would find a IT research agenda as providing very useful guidance.

In addition to these dimensions, we offer additional ones that we believe may be beneficial, based on our experiences:

- Contextual Paradigm: This dimension highlights the research as being associated with what is known and predictable versus more "out of the box", innovative, or, as referred to in [14], "game-changing" or "think-big" ideas. There are related notional contrasts in this dimension: Incrementalism/Wild Card; Known Unknowns/Unknown Unknowns; Evolutionary/Revolutionary; Linear/Nonlinear.

- Research Market Economy: A research agenda can also reflect the push and pull of the supply and demand for research. The research community would analyze the supply-side: what is being produced now under the rubric of IT research? The demand-side of the agenda would articulate the consumers of IT research: What do individuals, communities, and organizations want and need? Are there scenarios of various "ideal" states on future uses of IT products and services by individuals and organizations?

What do people expect from IT, for example, in terms of security, privacy, reliability, mobile access, context-awareness, and automated support for tasks and decisions and actions? The demand and supply can be the basis for a gap analysis to identify IT research themes.

- Disciplinary Architecture: A research agenda may also reflect what may be understood from analyzing the place of IT in the context of related computing disciplines, as explored in [2]. So, a possible driver of the IT research agenda is expectations: how important is it to the IT research community that the broader research establishment and society in general will be able to say, "Those research areas are effectively being addressed by the IT research community"?

4.2 Content of an IT Research Agenda

If the IT community developed a research agenda, it would not need to start from scratch. There have been many thoughtful analyses and observations on the research themes in IT. Orlikowski and Iacono [22] stressed the importance of developing conceptualizations and theories of IT artifacts: how they are composed, how they are used in various contexts, and how they change.

Investigating IT artifacts was also a recommended research thrust in [2], along with enterprise architectural infrastructure, interaction models, system performance, and domain induction. Variations of these thrust areas appear also in other proposals, such as Reichgelt also proposing research on generalizing from domains [9]. On a topic related to the thrust in enterprise architectural infrastructure, Ekstrom highlighted the need to address complexity arising in IT practice from aggregating services from various systems into systems of systems [9].

In two proposed IT research agendas, one follows a "top-down" approach and the other is "bottom-up." Reichgelt (top-down) proposed research questions organized around three themes [23]:

- Can we establish a theory about how to provide value to users at an acceptable cost?

- In providing value, what are the trade-offs associated with an IT application, its components, and the wider context in which it is used?

- How can we better understand the complex interactions involving an IT application, its users, and the environment in which it is introduced and used?

In exploring an IT research agenda, Ekstrom et al. used a bottom-up approach of examining the subject areas of 70 IT master's theses [8]. The theses fell into five categories: development projects and case studies; education (concept learning and applying IT in an educational setting); information assurance; project management; and technology (including evaluation and testing).

The appendix provides examples of what is possible when diverse elements of a community come together to develop a research agenda. The discussion of the cloud computing research agenda [7] offers an iconic example when theoretical principles meet practical considerations in the process of deciding on research priorities. Implementers of large and prominent cloud computing environments pointed out the ramifications of enforcing tight synchronization, which is a prominent academic research topic. The interactions among the researchers and implementers led to the realization that it is more critical to maintain stability: research is needed to further understand decoupling behavior and loose synchronization.

4.3 Process of Agenda Development

The recommendation here is for an IT research agenda to be the product of a broad-based community activity, which will have beneficial side effects of serving as another opportunity for the community to self-organize. Given the nature of IT, participation should include industry and IT practitioners in addition to academia.

If we look to other disciplines and domains and the processes they have used to develop research agendas, there are several examples that may be useful practices for consideration by the IT community. Developers of the research agenda to combat influenza intentionally paid attention to less well-addressed areas during their process and facilitated discussions among researchers and professionals [26]. The science-policy agenda development similarly engaged policy makers, practitioners, and researchers to identify key research questions [24]. Developers of the U.S. National Institute for Justice agenda used dedicated listening sessions with practitioners [18].

Awareness of the target format of the research agenda can influence the solicitation to potential contributors. In developing the science-policy research agenda, the solicitation was for key research questions, "which, if addressed through focused research and enquiry, might not only help resolve important theoretical challenges but might also improve the mutual understanding and effectiveness of those who work at the interface of science and policy. " [24]

Developers of the agricultural education agenda used a single question to start its process: "What are the primary/major/fundamental problems and issues in the broad agricultural education discipline (including education, communication, leadership, and extension) that should be addressed through research in the next five years?" [3]

With any solicitation about IT, given its broad scope, it may easily prompt return questions about what is meant by IT in the context of developing a research agenda. We would recommend that if anchoring the concept of IT is needed, use the definition in [15, p. 8] that IT "... is concerned with issues related to advocating for users and meeting their needs within an organizational and societal context through the selection, creation, application, integration and administration of computing technologies."

If we were to pursue as a target an agenda organized around research questions and were to propose a single query to solicit contributions, we recommend a question oriented to Reichgelt's "central research drive in IT": What are key research questions, whose solution will contribute to establishing a "theory about how to provide value to users at an acceptable cost through the selection, creation, application, integration and administration of computing technologies." [23, p. 253]

To support agenda development, it has been possible in the past to submit proposals to agencies and professional societies for funds to cover the costs of meetings and other logistical needs. NSF sponsored some of the workshops referenced in the appendix and is currently funding a two-day workshop entitled "Articulating the Computing Research Agenda in Social Computing Research." [21]

4.4 Evaluation Criteria

If the research community does come together to plan and develop an IT research agenda, it should first give thought to the same basic elements that are part of any such exercise:

- Why are we doing this?
- Who is the audience?
- How will we evaluate our work product?

Regarding evaluation or success criteria, when Hilbert pondered how to judge the "value of a problem", it was " ... the gain which science obtains from the problem." [27, p. 390] In this spirit, indicators of the gain from a successful and useful IT research agenda could include several factors:

- How often is the agenda cited in journal articles and research proposals?
- Has the agenda been the stimulus or rationale for funding?
- Has the emphasis of research shifted to topics from the agenda, based on analysis of publications before and after the release of the agenda?
- What was the impact of papers that addressed topics from the agenda? Were the papers highly cited? Did the papers win awards?
- Did research advocated in the agenda lead to new IT products and services that helped people and organizations?
- In the review and update of the agenda, were the research questions solved? Was measurable progress made toward solutions?

5. RECOMMENDATIONS

We recommend that the IT research community come together to undertake the creation of an IT research agenda. We believe that the benefits discussed here provide motivation that such an agenda can be a potentially valuable reference document for the community itself and other audiences in academia, industry, and government.

There is support for the claim that research agendas can be useful to a research community. Papers reporting on the research agendas in ecology and global agriculture were the most downloaded from their respective journals [24].

Any such IT effort would not need to start from scratch, as noted earlier in citing existing proposals for IT research topics. The overlaps among research topics in these proposals are encouraging that the community may be successful in reaching some broader consensus about major subject areas of IT research. A dedicated community-wide effort may even succeed in moving beyond research subjects and topics to more specific research questions/goals/objectives/outcomes that can serve as a valuable reference point for IT researchers. If we need further inspiration, Hilbert's list of problems has been "an organizing force in mathematics" for more than a century. [27, p. 3]

6. REFERENCES

[1] ABET. 2010. Criteria for Accrediting Computing Programs, Accreditation Board for Engineering and Technology, Baltimore, MD.

[2] Agresti, W. 2011. Toward an IT agenda. *Communications of the Association for Information Systems*, *28*, 1, 255-276.

[3] American Association for Agricultural Education. 2011. National research agenda. Retrieved May 15, 2013 from http://aaaeonline.org/nationalresearchagenda.php#

[4] American Dental Association. 2012. Research of importance to the practicing dentist. Retrieved May 15, 2013 from http://www.ada.org/sections/about/pdfs/doc_research_agenda.pdf

[5] American Library Association. 2011. Research agenda for library instruction and information literacy. Retrieved May 15, 2013 from http://www.ala.org/acrl/aboutacrl/ directoryofleadership/sections/is/iswebsite/projpubs/researchagen dalibrary

[6] Anderson R. 1997. A research agenda for computing and the social sciences. *Social Science Computer Review* 15, 2, 123-134.

[7] Birman, K., Chockler, G., and van Renesse, R. 2009. Toward a cloud computing research agenda. ACM *SIGACT News* 40, 2, 68-80.

[8] Ekstrom, J., Dark, M., Lunt, B., and Reichgelt H. 2006. A research agenda for information technology: Does a research literature already exist? In *Proceedings of the Sixth Conference on Information Technology Education* (SIGITE '06). (Minneapolis, MN, October 19-21, 2006). ACM, New York, NY, 19-24.

[9] Friedman, R., Stockman, M., Reichgelt, H., Agresti, W., and Ekstrom, J. 2012. Defining IT Research, In *Proceedings Research in IT Conference* (Calgary, Alberta, Canada, October 11-13, 2012). ACM, New York, NY, 49-50.

[10] Geisler E., and Kassicieh, K. 1997. Information technologies and technology commercialization-the research agenda, *IEEE Transactions on Engineering Management* 44, 4, 339-346.

[11] Gill, G., and Bhattacherjee, A. 2009. Whom are we informing? Issues and recommendations for MIS research from an informing science perspective. *MIS Quarterly* 33, 2, 217-235.

[12] Hardaway, D., Mathieu, R., and Will, R. 2008. A new mission for the information systems discipline. *IEEE Computer* 41, 5, 81-83.

[13] Infosec Research Council. 2005. Hard problems list. Retrieved May 15, 2013 from http://www.infosec-research.org/docs_public/20051130-IRC-HPL-FINAL.pdf

[14] Innovative Medicines Initiative. 2010. Scientific research agenda. Retrieved May 15, 2013 from http://www.imi.europa.eu/content/research-agenda

[15] Lunt, B., Ekstrom, J., Gorka, S., Hislop, G., Kamali, R., Lawson, E., LeBlanc, R., Miller, J., and Reichgelt H. 2008. Information technology 2008: Curriculum guidelines for undergraduate degree programs in information technology. November 2008, ACM, New York, NY,

[16] Mahoney, M. 2004. Finding a history for software engineering. *IEEE Annals of the History of Computing* 26,1, 8-19.

[17] March, S., Hevner, A., and Ram, S. 2000. Research commentary: An agenda for information technology research in heterogeneous and distributed environments. *Information Systems Research* 11, 4, 327-341.

[18] National Institute of Justice. 2013. Research agenda and goals. Retrieved May 15, 2013 from http://www.nij.gov/about/research-agenda.htm

[19] National Research Council. 1995. *Information technology for manufacturing: A research agenda.* Committee to Study Information Technology and Manufacturing. Computer Science and Telecommunications Board. National Academies Press, Washington.

[20] National Research Council. 2001. *Embedded Everywhere: A Research Agenda for Networked Systems of Embedded Computers.* Committee on Networked Systems of Embedded Computers, Computer Science and Telecommunications Board. National Academies Press, Washington.

[21] National Science Foundation. 2013. Articulating the computing research agenda in social computing research. Retrieved May 15, 2013 from http://www.nsf.gov/awardsearch/ showAward?AWD_ID=1249835

[22] Orlikowski, W., and Iacono, C. 2001. Research commentary: Desperately seeking the 'IT' in IT research – a call to theorizing the IT artifact. *Information Systems Research* 12, 2, 121-134.

[23] Reichgelt, H. 2004. Towards a research agenda for information technology. In *Proceedings of the Fourth Conference on Information Technology Education* (SIGITE '04) (Salt Lake City, UT, October 28-30, 2004). ACM, New York, NY, 248-254.

[24] Sutherland W., Bellingan L., Bellingham J., Blackstock J., Bloomfield R., et al. 2012. A collaboratively-derived science-policy research agenda. PLoSONE 7, 3 e31824. DOI=10.1371/ journal.pone.0031824

[25] Truch, E., Ezingeard, J-N., and Birchall, D. 2000. Developing a relevant research agenda in knowledge management - bridging the gap between knowing and doing. *Journal of Systems and Information Technology* 4, 2, 1-11.

[26] World Health Organization. 2009. *Public Health Research Agenda for Influenza.* Retrieved May 15, 2013 from http://www.who.int/influenza/resources/research/2010_11_report_ of_the_first_global_consultation_november_2009.pdf

[27] Yandell, B. 2002. *The Honors Class.* A.K. Peters, Natick, MA.

[28] Yang Q. and Wu, X. 2006. Ten challenging problems in data mining research. *International Journal of Information Technology and Decision Making*, 5, 4, 597-604.

APPENDIX

The appendix shows characteristics of the 24 research agendas: title; sponsoring activity or entity; date; notes about the process, format, or end product; and a reference:

- Group 1. Information Technologies
- Group 2. Applications of IT and Computing
- Group 3. Non-IT Research Agendas

Group 1. Information Technologies

1-1, Infosec Research Council (IRC) Hard Problems List, 2005; Identified eight hard problems, each one described by definition, threat, motivation, challenges, approaches, metrics; IRC consists of U.S. Government agencies that sponsor research in information security. [13]

1-2, High Assurance Computer Systems: A Research Agenda, 1995; Workshop on challenging problems; defined four pillars of a research agenda; more meta-level on research program directions, http://www.nrl.navy.mil/chacs/pubs/5-1221 2344.pdf

1-3, Ten challenging problems in data mining research, 2006; Conducted a survey, leading to ten problems. [28]

1-4, Scaling Up: A Research Agenda for Software Engineering, 1989; Workshop; Recommendations made regarding perspective, engineering practices, and modes of research; organized by short-term (1-5 years) and long-term (5 -10 years), http://www.nap.edu/openbook.php?record_id=1467&page=1

1-5, Embedded Everywhere: A Research Agenda for Networked Systems of Embedded Computers, 2001; Identified eight critical research areas; more details on issues in each area. [20]

1-6, Toward a Cloud Computing Research Agenda, 2009; Defined five research themes, with discussion of issues and questions under each theme. [7]

1-7, Developing a relevant research agenda in knowledge management, 2000; Used a survey and refinement of the responses to identify three research themes of user perspectives; organizational turbulence and flexibility; and the balance between people, process, and technology. [25]

1-8, Research Commentary: An Agenda for Information Technology Research in Heterogeneous and Distributed Environments, 2000; Identified three research areas (mobile computing, intelligent agents, and net-centric computing) and six prevailing themes for research such as performance, scalability, and pervasive heterogeneity. [17]

Group 2. Applications of IT and Computing

2-1, Creating a Research Agenda in Computing at the Margins, 2010; Workshop, Research is needed to bridge the digital divide; identified three broad research areas of access, empowerment and innovation, with research topics under each area, http://computing-margins.org/workshop.pdf

2-2, Research Agenda for Library Instruction and Information Literacy, 2011; Organized into four main topical sections, then defined research questions within each section. [5]

2-3, Information, Technology, and Governance: A Grand Challenges Research Agenda, 2011; Workshop; Used group facilitation and multi-voting to identify top five challenges, for defined research and practice questions, gaps, intended audiences for research agenda, http://www.ctg.albany.edu/ publications/reports/ITG_workshop/ITG_workshop.pdf

2-4, Information Technology for Manufacturing: A Research Agenda, 1995; Recognized both a technology agenda, with research questions in four areas, and a non-technology agenda: on IT being used appropriately in manufacturing. [19]

2-5, A Research Agenda for Computing and the Social Sciences, 1997; Conference; two major themes: research on social aspects of Internet and social science applications of advanced I. [6]

2-6, IT Research Challenges for Healthcare: From Discovery to Delivery, 2010; Summarizes workshop into four research areas and research enablers and inhibitors, such as the roles of the workforce, open platforms, and test beds,

http://www.cra.org/ccc/files/docs/init/Information_Technology_R esearch_Challenges_for_Healthcare.pdf

2-7, Towards a Research Agenda for Computer-Based Assessment, 2007; Eight research questions under three perspectives: assessment methodologies, assessment tools, and implementations/delivery, http://bookshop.europa.eu/en/ towards-a-research-agenda-on-computer-based-assessment-pbKJ8108495/

2-8, Information technologies and technology commercialization-the research agenda, 1997; Develops six research questions based on exploring two aspects of the IT-commercialization intertwining: IT as a major contributor to innovations that are commercialized and IT as a facilitator for commercialization. [10]

Group 3. Non-IT Research Agendas

3-1, Research of Importance to the Practicing Dentist, 2012-13; Defined four goals, each with 2-3 objectives that are reviewed biennially. [4]

3-2, U.S. National Institute of Justice (NIJ) Research Agenda and Goals, 2013; Based on five strategic goals of NIJ, identified ten goals for research agenda, with objectives under each goal. [18]

3-3, Innovative Medicines Initiative (IMI), Scientific Research Agenda, 2010; Defined four inter-related research areas and a multiannual plan with eight research priorities, with annual implementation plans. [14]

3-4, World Health Organization Public Health Research Agenda for Influenza, 2009; Defined a framework of five research streams that are variously described in terms of areas of focus, critical factors, questions, road maps, priorities, etc. [26]

3-5, A Collaboratively-Defined Science-Policy Research Agenda, 2012; Participants submitted questions which were organized and refined, leading to the identification of six research themes with a total of 40 questions. [24]

3-6, Research Agenda for Primary Care, 2002; Identified five major research areas and seven current areas of research, with list of relevant research topics in each area, http://www.ahrq.gov/research/findings/factsheets/primary/pcagen da/index.html

3-7, Framing a National Research Agenda for the Arts, Lifelong Learning, and Individual Well-Being, 2011; Identifies three key challenges and three research recommendations; some are meta-level on how to conduct and manage the research, with issues and questions in each area, http://www.nea.gov/ research/taskforce/Arts-and-Human-Development.pdf

3-8, National Research Agenda, American Association for Agricultural Education, 2011, Defined six key research priority areas for 2011-15, with key outcomes for each area. [3]

Using Agent Technologies to Correlate and Compare Anti-Malware Software

Kellie Kercher	Dale C. Rowe	Haley Dennis
Brigham Young University	Brigham Young University	Brigham Young University
265 CTB	265 CTB	265 CTB
Provo, UT, 84602	Provo, UT, 84602	Provo, UT, 84602
(801) 422 6051	(801) 422 6051	(801) 422 6051
kkercher@somethingk.com	dale_rowe@byu.edu	haleylyndennis@gmail.com

ABSTRACT

Malware is a fast growing threat that consists software used to disrupt, or impact the confidentiality, availability or integrity of a user's computer experience. Antivirus software can help protect a user against these threats. There are numerous vendors users can choose from for their antivirus protection, each with their own set of virus definitions and various resources that are capable of recognizing new threats. However, there is no established system or process to measure and display data on the performance of antivirus vendors to new malware over an ongoing time period in real time. Such a mechanism would better inform end users of their security options in addition to informing organizations of prevalent threats occurring in networks. In this paper, we propose a cloud sourced malware reporting system that uses distributed agents to assess the performance of antivirus software based on malware signatures.

Categories and Subject Descriptors D.4.6

[OPERATING SYSTEMS]: Security and Protection - *Invasive software (e.g., viruses, worms, Trojan horses)*

Keywords

Agent Technology, Malware, Peer Reporting

1. INTRODUCTION

Malware is a fast growing threat facing all end user devices. In 2011, the antivirus, Symantec, detected and blocked more than 5.5 billion types of malware. This was an increase of 81% from the previous year's detection [9]. In addition, businesses are typically slow to detect malware breach activity with the average time for detection being 210 days in 2012 [1]. Intrusion Detection Systems (IDS), firewalls and antivirus software can be used to combat these types of attacks and secure devices against intrusions. While an IDS and firewall typically protect a *network* against intrusion, end devices commonly employ antivirus software to protect the individual device. There are numerous

antivirus vendors, (ie: Microsoft Security Essentials, McAfee, AVG, and Avast) that vary in resources and capabilities at recognizing new pieces of malware. Each vendor releases their own virus updates they have discovered for protecting a device against the latest threats. However with the increasing number of these threats, vendors compete to be first responders to a piece of malware in order to win over the majority of the market share.

Currently, there is not a system available that measures the performance of antivirus software in responding to new strands of malware over an ongoing period of time. Research shows that current evaluations have been for a fixed time point. These reports do not show the ongoing trends in detection response time. Without this data, it is difficult to perform ongoing analysis into detection efficiency and thus inform end users of their security options. This data will benefit the research community in that it will provide comparison information between different antivirus vendors and contain information on active regional threats to better inform clients.

This report discusses a novel approach that employs distributed agents in a malware quarantine analysis and update data collection framework. This information will be delivered to a centralized server in order to present real time antivirus activity. An agent is a primitive form of artificial intelligence. It is aware of its environment and will make necessary actions to maintain the state of an environment [18].

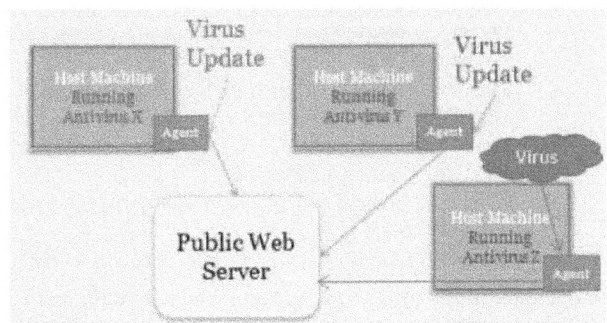

Figure 1: Proposed Distributed Agent Collection Design

This technology will be used to detect new malware quarantines and updates sent by the antivirus vendors to a client. Following detection, the agent will dissect the data and deliver items of interest to a web server database, where the data will be publically available. It is the intent of the project that the reported information will be used to compare the performance of different antivirus vendors in responding to active threats. The project will also be used to universally describe malware across multiple versions of antivirus software. This research will

RIIT'13, October 10–12, 2013, Orlando, Florida, USA.
Copyright © 2013 ACM 978-1-4503-2494-6/13/10...$15.00.
http://dx.doi.org/10.1145/2512209.2512212

ideally encourage further study in antivirus technologies along with providing information that will help users in their antivirus software decisions.

We hypothesize that there is not a single best antivirus vendor. One vendor may be a first responder to a specific piece of malware while another vendor may discover and respond to a different malicious threat more rapidly. Each vendor has different capabilities and resources that enable it to respond and release new virus updates. These virus updates contain useful information that will be used to identify malware across different vendors.

The proposed framework is projected to be able to capture antivirus data overtime to support the idea that a host device may benefit from multiple vendor software installations. Different vendors will vary in their response times and capabilities in identifying malware and updating client devices. A single installation of an antivirus alone is not enough to prevent a system against all new strands of malware. A combination of antivirus vendors will decrease the time a device is vulnerable to a threat and improve the device's defenses.

2. BACKGROUND
2.1 Malware

Malware is a malicious script or piece of software that is used to prevent, publicize or interrupt computer operations. A piece of malware can be classified into multiple categories. Some of these categories include [3, 19]:

- Adware – A piece of software that automatically delivers advertisements to the client.
- Backdoor - A method that bypasses expected authentication procedures. It can be used to secure entry into a system.
- Bot – An automated process that interacts with other network services. Through bots, a third party can indirectly interact with a system over a network.
- Logic Bomb – A threat that consists of two parts, a payload and trigger. The payload is a specific action to perform and the trigger is a condition that controls the execution of the payload.
- Rootkit – A program designed to take control of a system. It attempts to seize administrative or root system privileges without authorization.
- Spyware – A piece of software that discretely reports user activity to a third party.
- Trojan horse - A malicious script or piece of software disguised as a safe application.
- Virus - A malicious application that self-propagates across devices.
- Worm - A script that self-propagates across a network.

A single piece of malware may perform numerous tasks and be classified in multiple categories. Users can contract malware by downloading the immediate strand of malware or by downloading a piece of software packaged with the malware. Malware can be hidden in media files, advertisements, email attachments or peer-to-peer shared file.

2.2 Antivirus Variations

According to Maggi et al. antivirus vendors are inconsistent with their naming convention for malware specimens [11]. The proposed project, along with analyzing the performance of different antivirus vendors will provide the ability to view correlation data based on agent-generated hashes to identify naming variations for the same piece of malware. This information will be provided by the collection server's web interface. This visual will help reduce confusion and aid further research in analyzing malware across vendors.

An important feature of the proposed project is the ability to read virus updates from different anti-viruses. Sanok examines the techniques of signature detection, heuristics and general decryption that different anti-virus applications use to detect and quarantine viruses [16]. This information is beneficial in understanding how anti-viruses treat signatures and where they are stored in order to allow an agent to discover and disclose a signature.

2.3 Antivirus Protection

A study by Rob Lee measured the protection level that antivirus software provides. He designed a lab environment running where systems that had the popular anti-virus McAfee installed. With a team of college students, he attempted to exploit the system with a combination of well-known malware. Form this experiment; it was found that anti-virus software is only effective in protecting systems against low-level malicious activity [10]. Lee's findings stress the importance of a new security model to fortify end-users against popular threats in today's networks. His research supports the claim that a single antivirus on its own is not enough to prevent malware attacks on a host machine. We believe this project will further validate this claim.

2.4 Existing Antivirus Comparisons

Sukwong et al. analyzed six popular antivirus products in responding to 1,115 distinct malware samples over a 5 month period of time [17]. The antivirus software analyzed by this study includes:

- Avast 4.8 Professional v.4.8.1335
- Kaspersky Internet Security 2009
- McAfee Total Protection with Security Center v.9.15
- Norton Internet Security 2009 v.16.5.0.135
- Symantec AntiVirus v.10.1.7.7000
- Trend Micro Internet Security Pro v.17.1.1250

This study evaluated the time it took an antivirus to detect an unknown piece of malware with daily virus updates scheduled. The results of the study showed that all the antivirus software were close to equal in their response to new threats. Tools varied in being first responders to a specific threat.

There are companies that regularly perform antivirus comparisons. AV-Comparatives performs regular evaluations of the antivirus software performance. Some of the antivirus vendors include:

- Avast
- AVG
- AVIRA
- Bitdefender
- BullGuard
- eScan
- Fortinet
- F-Secure
- Kaspersky
- McAfee
- Microsoft Security Essentials
- Panda
- Sophos

The company analyzes the performance and releases its finding at a later time [5]. The evaluation is not in real-time but rather an accumulation of finding results.

AV-Test ranks the protection, usability and capabilities to remove malware from an infected device on a six-point scale [2]. Despite this system consistently running a comparison on the different antiviruses, it does not provide detailed information on the exact response times to a specific piece of malware.

There are numerous other organizations that regularly compare antivirus performance. Despite these organizations and their reports, users are not provided real time information on active threats and the antivirus response. A system is needed that catches in real time and releases comparative data on antivirus software capabilities in combating new threats.

2.5 Multiple Antivirus Installations

Despite the improvements in antivirus technology, malware is still in existence and greatly spreading [17]. To analyze anti-virus software, a comparison study was performed on 32 different antivirus programs against 1,599 samples of malware. This study analyzed the effects of diversity on the detection capability as well as the time it takes an antivirus to evolve and update virus definitions. It was found that each type of anti-virus software has different capabilities of catching and updating systems against a threat [7]. The study performed identified trends display varying antivirus first responders to a specific malware threat.

It is believed that there is not a single antivirus product that is consistently the fastest at responding to a new threat or most effective in identifying the varying types of malware [20]. It is unpredictable which antivirus vendor will be the first to release a virus definition for a new strand of malware. It is advised that a user includes multiple installations of an antivirus to reduce the time a system is vulnerable to a threat [20]. This is why it is products such as Microsoft's Forefront Security includes licenses for numerous scanning engines from third-party vendors. Using more than one antivirus can greatly improve the chances of detecting and removing new strands of malware [15].

3. METHODOLOGY

3.1 Project Approach

The purpose of this research is to develop a cloud sourced malware reporting system that uses distributed agents to assess the performance of antivirus software based on malware signatures. A prototype proof of concept will be built in order to examine the effectiveness of such a system. The prototype will include the client side agent and a public facing web server to visually display antivirus updates, response times, naming conventions and further antivirus details.

3.2 Development Environment

The development environment will consist of a Windows 7 Professional operating system. The reason for programming in this environment is due to the easily accessible antivirus software supported by this platform. The following antivirus vendors are proposed to be analyzed by the prototype:

- AVG
- Kaspersky
- Microsoft Security Essentials
- McAfee
- Sophos
- Symantec

3.3 System Prototype

The agent will be programed in Python 2.7. Python is a high-level programming language that simplifies development by requiring fewer lines of code to perform functions. Python also includes a large community of developers who are actively creating and maintaining libraries that may be useful in the prototype development. The proof of concept will be programmed to look for antivirus malware quarantines and updates. Once it detects a change in the environment the agent will notify the web server and communicate data about the change.

A correlation server will be built to receive data and host antivirus statistics from the distributed agents. This server will consist of a Linux machine with the Apache HTTPS server along with a MySQL database to store data. The agent will be installed on a host machine and tested for its capabilities to communicate with the web server. Once compatibility is confirmed, the agents will be installed across multiple devices and tested on the ability to track antivirus data received.

3.4 Testing

When antivirus software detects a piece of malware on the host, the agent will look for the following variables to deliver to the centralized cloud server:

- Hash of alert
- Malware Name
- Antivirus version
- Platform
- Time and date of alert

The prototype will locate and note the following pieces of data from an antivirus update.

- Time and date of update
- Hash of update
- Name of update
- Vendor
- Platform
- Host IP

These variables are of interest to the research pertaining to the proposed hypothesis. The agent is not directly reading an antivirus update. This is due to potentially breaching the vendor licensing agreements.

Furthermore, it has been found that different antivirus vendors use different malware naming conventions to describe the same piece of malware. To test the correlation between vendors and malware names, the prototype will retrieve virus names from a host antivirus update or malware quarantine and compare it against other vendors in order to locate corresponding malware names. This data will be delivered to the web server. The names will be formatted and displayed in a table on the server for easy comparison. If there is a correlation between vendors and antivirus naming the table will display the similarities. However, if the malware names are unrecognizable between vendors, the table will be able to provide a universal connections database for virus definitions across vendors.

As previously stated, a singular installation of an antivirus alone is believed to not be sufficient to protect a system against malware. The reason being is that different antiviruses will distribute virus definition updates to endpoint host machines at different unpredictable times. We believe that a combination of antivirus vendors within the same network will decrease the time devices are vulnerable to a threat. Instead of a host relying on a single antivirus to update, networks with multiple installations will have multiple supporting vendors. The system will only have to wait for the first responding antivirus for protection.

To test this hypothesis, the prototype agents will retrieve timestamps from the retrieved antivirus updates. This data will be delivered to the web server to be displayed in a graph format. Confirming results will show antiviruses with varying response times. No single antivirus will be the first responder to all new pieces of malware over an extended period of time. In opposition to the hypothesis, if the different antiviruses repeatedly place the same in response time, there may an overall best antivirus. This would prove there is not a need to use multiple antivirus software installations.

4. EXPECTED RESULTS

It is expected that the agents will be able to analyze antivirus data in real time. This information will then be seen on a public server. From the data, it is believed the information will reveal known threats in a region along with average antivirus response times to handling a new threat. This information will aid users in their antivirus commitments along with providing awareness to active threats.

In addition, it is expected that the response times will greatly vary between antivirus vendors. With this knowledge the results are hypothesized to support the case for multiple antivirus installations. One vendor may be the first responder to one piece of malware while another vendor may address another piece of malware first.

5. CONCERNS

The proposed project is not without potential issues. There are some key concerns along with potential solutions or approaches that aim to minimize the risk of this research.

5.1 Vendor Standardization

There is not a standard mechanism for delivering updates, or recording anti-virus in the logs. For some products, this information is stored outside the standard Windows event logs in internal audit-logs. We propose to write the connectors to the 6 initially identified vendors as 'plug-in' style modules that retrieve log data in an appropriate manner.

5.2 Intellectual Property

In initial research planning the decision was made to actively avoid scenarios that would require any reverse-engineering of anti-virus applications. Although understanding the software's internal operations and in particular, the structure and content of updates would be of huge benefit, it is believed that the key objectives can be obtained without this information. This avoids any potential conflict over intellectual property, or breaches of end user license agreements (EULAs).

5.3 Agent and Correlation Server Security

With an open-system, there is the potential for abuse by miss-reporting data, manipulation of agent-to-server traffic or other such attacks on data-in-transit. For this reason all communications between the agents and server will be encrypted using industry standard protocols and libraries. Regular penetration tests will be carried out against the system along with input-fuzzing of communications inputs, and agent data collection inputs. While it may be unfeasible to protect against all potential attacks we aim to quantify the risk

associated with various elements of the project and provide this information openly at the conclusion of the project prototype.

6. CONCLUSION

In conclusion, malware presents a serious threat to endpoint user devices. In order to protect against malware, antivirus software can be installed on a device to help defend against known malware strands. To help users in their malware decisions, a distributed cloud based reporting system will be created using distributed agents. The agents will be located on end point devices in order to catch antivirus quarantines and alerts in real time. Information from these alerts will be delivered to a web server that will format and present the data to interested parties. In addition, the project will be used to universally describe malware across vendors. We hope that this research will encourage further study in antivirus technologies along with aiding users in their antivirus software decisions.

7. REFERENCES

[1] "2013 Trustwave Global Security Report." Accessed April 13, 2013. https://www2.trustwave.com/2013GSR-TY.html?aliId=1417176.

[2] "AV-TEST - The Independent IT-Security Institute: Test Procedures." Accessed April 13, 2013. http://www.av-test.org/en/test-procedures/.

[3] Aycock, John. Computer Viruses and Malware. Springer, 2006.

[4] Cambridge, Rodney D. "Method and System for Bi-directional Updating of Antivirus Database," July 18, 2006. http://www.google.com/patents?id=OaB6AAAAEBAJ.

[5] "Comparatives‖tests - Reviews - Reports." Accessed April 13, 2013. http://av-comparatives.org/comparativesreviews.

[6] Garuba, M., Chunmei Liu, and N. Washington. "A Comparative Analysis of Anti-Malware Software, Patch Management, and Host-Based Firewalls in Preventing Malware Infections on Client Computers." In *Fifth International Conference on Information Technology: New Generations, 2008. ITNG 2008*, 628–632, 2008. doi:10.1109/ITNG.2008.233.

[7] Gashi, I., V. Stankovic, C. Leita, and O. Thonnard. "An Experimental Study of Diversity with Off-the-Shelf AntiVirus Engines." In *Eighth IEEE International Symposium on Network Computing and Applications, 2009. NCA 2009*, 4–11, 2009. doi:10.1109/NCA.2009.14.

[8] Hodges, Vernon, and Shawn O'Donnell. "Method and System for Providing Automated Updating and Upgrading of ...," March 7, 2000. http://www.google.com/patents?id=TGEDAAAAEBAJ.

[9] "Internet Security Threat Report." Accessed April 13, 2013. http://www.symantec.com/content/en/us/enterprise/other_resources/b-istr_main_report_2011_21239364.en-us.pdf.

[10] Lee, Rob. "Is Anti-Virus Really Dead? A Real-World Simulation Created for Forensic Data Yields Surprising Results" Computer Forensics and Incident Response. *Blog*, April 9, 2012. http://computer-forensics.sans.org/blog/2012/04/09/is-anti-virus-really-dead-a-real-world-simulation-created-for-forensic-data-yields-surprising-results.

[11] Maggi, Federico, Andrea Bellini, Guido Salvaneschi, and Stefano Zanero. "Finding Non-trivial Malware Naming Inconsistencies." In *Information Systems Security*, 144–159. Springer, 2011. http://link.springer.com/chapter/10.1007/978-3-642-25560-1_10.

[12] Mamaghani, Farrokh. "Evaluation and Selection of an Antivirus and Content Filtering Software." *Information Management & Computer Security* 10, no. 1 (March 1, 2002): 28–32. doi:10.1108/09685220210417481.

[13] Oberheide, J., E. Cooke, and F. Jahanian. "Rethinking Antivirus: Executable Analysis in the Network Cloud." In *2nd USENIX Workshop on Hot Topics in Security (HotSec 2007)*, 2007. http://www.usenix.org/event/hotsec07/tech/full_papers/oberheide/oberheide_html/.

[14] Pikoulas, J., W. Buchanan, M. Mannion, and K. Triantafyllopoulos. "An Intelligent Agent Security Intrusion System." In *Engineering of Computer-Based Systems, 2002. Proceedings. Ninth Annual IEEE International Conference and Workshop on The*, 94–99, 2002. doi:10.1109/ECBS.2002.999827.

[15] Posey, Brien. "Microsoft Exchange Server Security Dos and Don'ts" TechTarget. *SearchExchange*. Accessed March 18, 2013.

http://searchexchange.techtarget.com/feature/Microsoft-Exchange-Server-security-dos-and-donts.

[16] Sanok,Jr, Daniel J. "An Analysis of How Antivirus Methodologies Are Utilized in Protecting Computers from Malicious Code." In *Proceedings of the 2nd Annual Conference on Information Security Curriculum Development*, 142–144. InfoSecCD '05. New York, NY, USA: ACM, 2005. doi:10.1145/1107622.1107655.

[17] Sukwong, Orathai, Hyong S. Kim, and James C. Hoe. "Despite the Widespread Use of Antivirus Software, Malware Remains Pervasive. A New Study Compares the Effectiveness of Six Commercial AV Products." Accessed April 13, 2013. http://theone.ece.cmu.edu/papers/94.commercial.2011.compmag.pdf.

[18] Sycara, K., A. Pannu, M. Willamson, Dajun Zeng, and K. Decker. "Distributed Intelligent Agents." *IEEE Expert* 11, no. 6 (December 1996): 36–46. doi:10.1109/64.546581.

[19] Tian, Ronghua. *An Integrated Malware Detection and Classification System*. Deakin University. (2011). Accessed April 24, 2013. http://dro.deakin.edu.au/view/DU:30043244.

[20] "Why one virus engine is not enough." Accessed April 13, 2013. http://www.gfi.com/whitepapers/why-one-virus-engine-is-not-enough.pdf.

MP3 Files as a Steganography Medium

Mikhail Zaturenskiy

Supervisors: Dr. William Lidinsky, Dr. Robert Carlson
Department of Information Technology and Management, Illinois Institute of Technology
201 East Loop Road, Wheaton IL 60189, +1 (630) 682-6000
mikzat@gmail.com

ABSTRACT
There is a lot of work done on hiding information inside picture files in formats such as JPEG, however not much has been done to date on hiding information inside MP3 audio files. This paper looks at ways to hide information inside MP3 files and proposes four largely unexplored techniques: unused header bit stuffing, unused side information bit stuffing, empty frame stuffing, and ancillary bit stuffing.

Categories and Subject Descriptors
E.3 [DATA ENCRYPTION], H.5.5 [Sound and Music Computing]

Keywords
Steganography

1. BACKGROUND ON STEGANOGRAPHY
Steganography is similar to Cryptography in that they are both forms of a broader topic of Secret Writing. While they both prevent unwanted entities from reading a message, they take different approaches to achieving this. Steganography relies on the fact that the presence of the message is unknown. The message is hidden in some clever way to avoid drawing suspicion. As a general rule, the shorter the message being hidden, the easier it is to keep it from being discovered. Cryptography works by running the message through a cryptographic function which scrambles it and returns it in a form that can only be read back using a key to reverse the process. The hidden message is available for all to see, but nobody can read it without the key. Ideally, a Steganographic message should also be encrypted using some Cryptographic algorithm to keep it protected even in case of discovery.

Steganography is "the art or practice of concealing a message, image, or file within another message, image, or file" [1]. The idea is that nobody except the intended recipient of the message knows that the hidden message exists. Steganographic techniques have been used for many centuries dating back to ancient Greece and China. Some techniques include invisible ink, microdots, and tattooing messages on somebody's head and letting hair grow back to conceal the message. Today, Steganography is usually associated with hiding data in digital images using computers.

Like digital images, MP3 audio files are very popular and are used all over the world. However, unlike with digital images, little work has been done applying Steganographic techniques to MP3 audio files. Because files in this format have been around for over a decade, people are comfortable with them and are not likely to suspect hidden data inside.

2. DESCRIPTION OF MP3 FILE FORMAT
The audio files we all know as MP3 files are digitally encoded using MPEG-1 Audio Layer 3 format and more recently using MPEG-2 and MPEG-2.5. Similar Steganographic principles can be applied to MPEG-1, MPEG-2 and MPEG-2.5 encoded MP3 files, but discussion of MPEG-2 and MPEG-2.5 is excluded for simplicity. The focus of this paper will be on MPEG-1 Audio Layer 3.

MP3 files are composed of a series of frames. While the data can be encoded with a variety of parameters such as different bit rates and sample frequencies, every frame contains approximately 26 milliseconds of audio data [2] [3]. This means that the number of frames is directly proportional to the duration of the audio recording.

Each frame is made up of a 4-byte header, an optional 2-byte CRC (Cyclic Redundancy Check), a 32-byte side information segment (17-byte if the MP3 file is mono), and a main data segment (length varies). Optionally, the file may begin with an ID3v2 information tag and end with an ID3v1 tag. Other less-common tags exist, but they will not be mentioned in this paper. See below for a simplified graphical representation of the structure of an MP3 file.

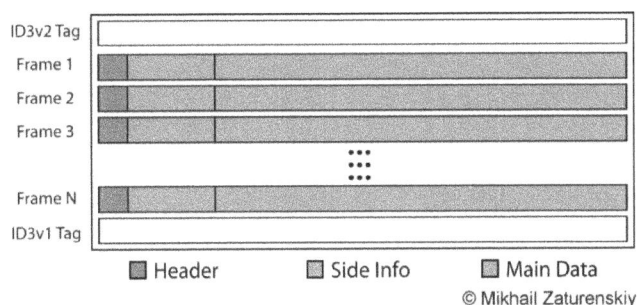

© Mikhail Zaturenskiy

Figure 1. MP3 File Basic Structure

The following is an illustration of a frame header and its components.

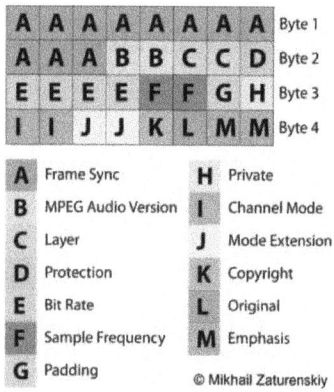

Figure 2. Frame Header

Legend:
- **A** Frame Sync
- **B** MPEG Audio Version
- **C** Layer
- **D** Protection
- **E** Bit Rate
- **F** Sample Frequency
- **G** Padding
- **H** Private
- **I** Channel Mode
- **J** Mode Extension
- **K** Copyright
- **L** Original
- **M** Emphasis

© Mikhail Zaturenskiy

If the frames are protected by a CRC (indicated by the "CRC/Protection" flag of the frame header), then the header is immediately followed by a 2-byte CRC and the side information begins after the CRC. The CRC is computed on the last two bytes of the frame header and the whole side information section.

In the following illustration of what the side information segments may look like in stereo and mono MP3 files, we can see that the granule side information in a mono MP3 file describes only one channel, compared to the two channels in the stereo MP3 file.

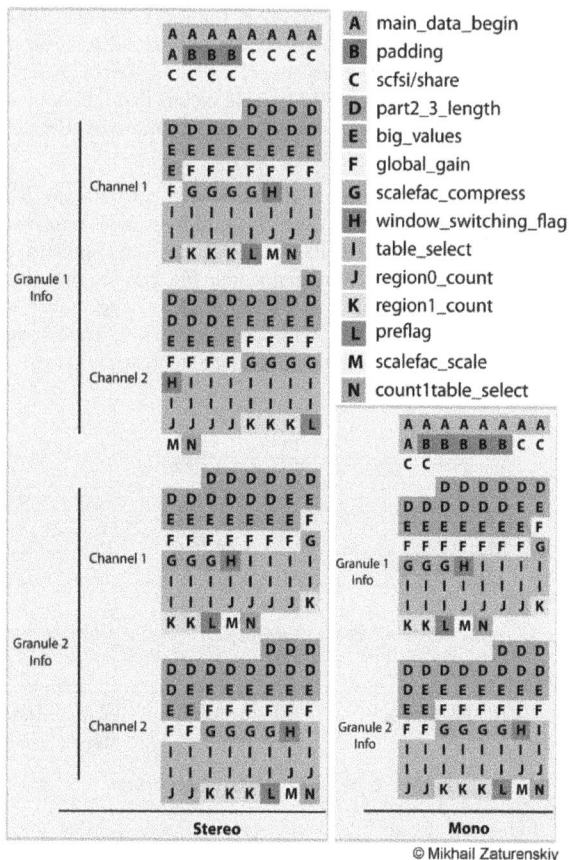

Legend:
- **A** main_data_begin
- **B** padding
- **C** scfsi/share
- **D** part2_3_length
- **E** big_values
- **F** global_gain
- **G** scalefac_compress
- **H** window_switching_flag
- **I** table_select
- **J** region0_count
- **K** region1_count
- **L** preflag
- **M** scalefac_scale
- **N** count1table_select

© Mikhail Zaturenskiy

Figure 3. Side Information for Mono and Stereo files

The contents of the side information for a granule may differ if the "window_switching_flag" is set, as shown below.

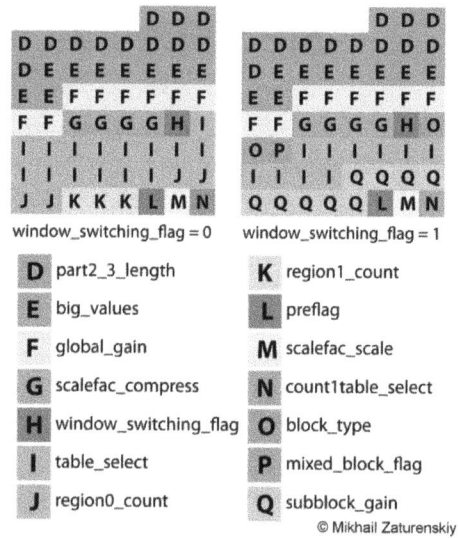

window_switching_flag = 0   window_switching_flag = 1

Legend:
- **D** part2_3_length
- **E** big_values
- **F** global_gain
- **G** scalefac_compress
- **H** window_switching_flag
- **I** table_select
- **J** region0_count
- **K** region1_count
- **L** preflag
- **M** scalefac_scale
- **N** count1table_select
- **O** block_type
- **P** mixed_block_flag
- **Q** subblock_gain

© Mikhail Zaturenskiy

Figure 4. Granule Side Information variation

Below is a simplified illustration of the main data section of a frame, the part that contains the actual audio data, from a stereo MP3 file. This looks the same in a mono MP3 file, except that each granule does not split off into two channels.

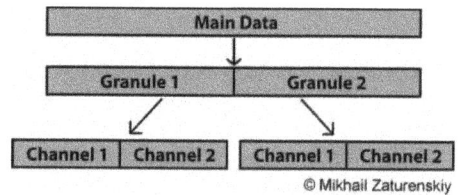

© Mikhail Zaturenskiy

Figure 5. Stereo MP3 File's Main Data

Due to the nature of the MP3 format, the main data segment for a particular frame may actually begin before that frame and may not use up all of the space available in the frame. The side information has a main_data_begin field that indicates how far back this frame's main data section starts. This is because each frame requires a different amount of space to store its audio information, so some frames can "donate" their unused space to the frames after them. This space taken from previous frames is usually referred to as the "bit reservoir". See Fig. 6 below for a visual.

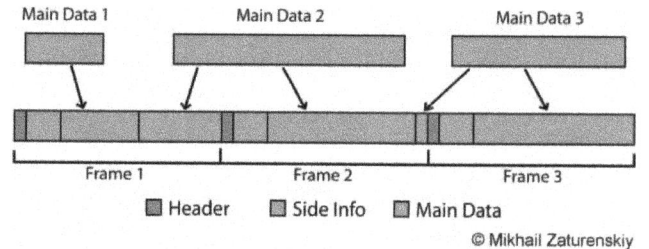

© Mikhail Zaturenskiy

Figure 6. How MP3 Bit Reservoir Works

For a particular frame, the main data section is made up of two pieces called "granules". Each granule contains data for either one or two channels depending on whether the MP3 file is mono or stereo, respectively. After the two granules it is possible that there may be some space left until the beginning of the next frame's main data section. This space is called "ancillary data" and does not contain any important information. See below for a visual representation of ancillary data.

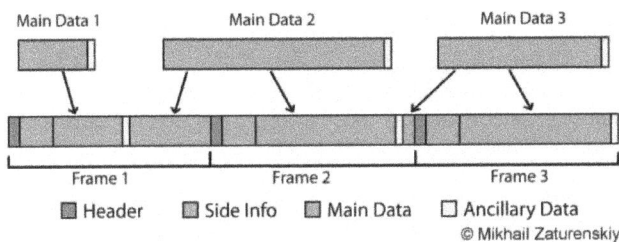

Figure 7 - Ancillary Data

3. CURRENT WORK ON MP3 STEGANOGRAPHY

The first and probably the most well-known program for performing MP3 Steganography is called "*MP3stego*", developed by Dr. Fabien Petitcolas [4]. His algorithm injects data into the audio during the encoding process before the audio is optimized and attempts to reduce the amount of audible distortion introduced to the output file, though my testing has shown that the process does cause minor audio anomalies to be present in the resulting MP3 file. "*MP3stego*" requires access to the source WAV file and has strict limitations on the properties of that source: it must be 44100Hz 16-bit mono and the covert data can be no more than a few hundred bytes after compression and encryption. This is very limiting and is not practical for general Steganographic use, but it is understandable as this program was developed as merely a proof-of-concept.

An example of a post-encoding Steganography application is another project also called "*mp3stego*" developed by Lukasz Grzegorz Maciak, Micheal Alexis Ponniah, and Renu Sharma [5]. Their goal was to use an approach they referred to as "padding byte stuffing" to embed lyrics into MP3 files. According to their results, they had trouble with the method causing significant audio data corruption and my investigation revealed a flaw in their approach, which will be discussed in the "Potential Hiding Methods" section.

Another popular program developed by Achmad Zaenuri is called "*mp3stegz*" [6]. This uses a post-encoding approach, referred to here as "empty frame stuffing". His algorithm searches for frames with homogenous bytes and then injects covert data into those frames, making the assumption that those frames do not contain audio data. A challenge with this technique is remembering where you put the data so you could retrieve it later. "*mp3stegz*" tackles this issue by injecting the string "XXXX" before inserting data in a frame. Retrieval works by searching for the "XXXX" string. While this approach is not quite stealthy and loses four bytes per frame, it does work without affecting audio quality or file size. The downsides to this program are that it is very slow, requires that the file you want to hide has a 3-character file extension, and the method does not guarantee that any space will be available in a given MP3 file.

Other software exists for hiding data in MP3 files, but the three programs mentioned above are among the more popular and, for the purpose of this discussion, offered a good sample of ways to hide data in MP3s.

4. POTENTIAL HIDING METHODS
4.1. Encoding-Time Methods

There are ways of hiding data into an MP3 file as the file is being encoded from raw WAV format into the compressed MP3 format. An IBM research group has discussed several approaches to doing this. Some of those approaches are "low-bit coding", "phase

coding", "spread spectrum", and "echo data hiding" [7]. However, these methods all require access to the source audio file from which the MP3 is created. This is an issue because it is rare for an end-user to have access to the source audio. Another downside is the complexity of efficiently implementing such techniques and the necessity to build custom encoders/decoders. Also, the generated MP3 files with injected data may potentially be audibly different from the original, leading to suspicion which we are attempting to avoid. Fear of causing audible anomalies severely limits the amount of data that can be injected with these methods. While the injection methods are viable, they will not be discussed here in more detail due to these limitations.

4.2. Post-Encoding Methods
4.2.1. Padding Byte Stuffing

Some MP3 files encoded with Constant Bit Rate (CBR) contain frames that have a padding byte. The presence of this extra byte in a frame is determined by checking the value of the "Padding" bit in the frame header. If the assumption is made that these bytes are not filled with useful data and are located at the end of a frame, using them for storing covert information has the benefits of not affecting MP3 file size or the audio quality while allowing a potentially significant amount of data to be injected. This assumption, however, is incorrect. To understand why, let's first see how padding bytes work.

The purpose of padding bytes is to keep the average Bit Rate of the MP3 file constant by increasing the length of some frames by one byte. Frame length is calculated as follows [3, 5]:

$$\text{Frame Length} = 144 * \left(\frac{BitRate}{SampleRate}\right) + Padding$$

"Padding" is equal to either 0 or 1. If we assume a Bit Rate of 160kbps and a Sample Rate of 44.1khz, then we have:

$$\text{Frame Length} = 144 * \left(\frac{160000}{44100}\right) + 0 = 522.448 \rightarrow 522$$

$$\text{Frame Length} = 144 * \left(\frac{160000}{44100}\right) + 1 = 523.448 \rightarrow 523$$

These values result in the Frame Length not being a whole number. This is not possible because Frame Length must be an integer, so it is automatically rounded down to 522 bytes, which is a little less than it should be and throws off the average Bit Rate over time. To compensate, some frames are lengthened by one byte to make their Frame Length 523 bytes. This allows the average Bit Rate to remain constant. Fig 8 shows a simple visual representation of the result.

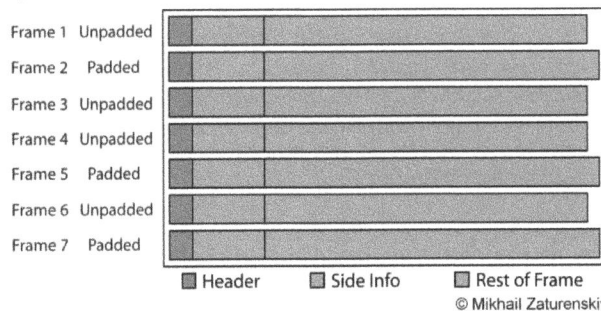

Figure 8 - Frame Padding

We can see that the padding byte is not just filled with some unimportant data that can be overwritten. The padding byte is just a 1-byte extension of the MP3 frame length, allowing a little more audio information to be stored. This explains why attempting to overwrite these bytes with custom data results in audio damage.

4.2.2. Custom Frame Injection

This technique has not yet been explored much; it involves inserting extra frames which may contain hidden data. The header of such tailored frames should be invalid to force the MP3 Player to skip them during playback, or have the side information tailored to say that the frame contains no audio data. These frames are best placed in the beginning (after the ID3v2 tag, before the first real frame) and end (before the ID3v1 tag, after the last real frame) of the MP3 file, to avoid interfering with actual audio data. Injecting in the middle of the file may cause a pause or interfere with the MP3 bit reservoir. The benefit of this technique is that it allows potentially limitless storage at the cost of increasing file size. The theories regarding this technique are yet to be tested.

4.2.3. Empty Frame Stuffing

Often MP3 files have frames with no valid audio data, usually at the beginning or the end. Properly injecting data into such audio data parts may allow a significant amount of storage without affecting audio quality or MP3 file size. Depending on the frame's length, it may be possible to gain hundreds of bytes for storage of covert data from a single empty frame. The difficulty with this technique is detecting the empty frames and reliably injecting data in a manner that would allow it to be easily retrieved when needed. Other downsides are that the search for such frames may be time consuming and the storage capacity is unpredictable.

4.2.4. Partially Empty Frame Stuffing

Some frames may be partially empty. All channels of both granules are not necessarily used in a particular frame. Theoretically, if in a stereo MP3 file there is a frame that uses only one channel of one granule for audio data, then the space in the whole second granule as well as the second channel in the first granule may be usable for storage. This has yet to be tested.

4.2.5. Unused Header Bit Stuffing

Every MP3 frame header contains several bits that are rarely used. If we assume that nothing is going to look at those bits, we can overwrite them with our own data without causing any actual damage. This technique does not cause changes in file size and allows a predictable amount of data storage since we can usually determine the total number of frames in the file without much difficulty. The issue with "unused header bit stuffing" is that the space we have is very limited (just a few bits per frame), so maximum data storage is directly bound by the length of the audio data. Also, there is potential for unpredictable behavior if any program actually attempted to use the bits we have overwritten.

4.2.6. Side Information Bit Stuffing

Exactly as with "unused header bit stuffing", every side information section of an MP3 frame contains several bits that are rarely or never used and can be used for storing our data. The benefits and downsides of this method are identical to that of "unused header bit stuffing".

4.2.7. Ancillary Bit Stuffing

The "ancillary data" can be used to store information. Properly detecting the location of these spaces allows us to insert our own data into them. Ancillary data rounds the end of the main data piece up to the beginning of the next frame's main data, which means it might not exist at all for a particular frame if rounding is not required. However, each ancillary data space is usually several bits long, which adds up over the length of the MP3 file.

5. SELECTED METHODS

The Steganographic methods evaluated here are "unused header bit stuffing", "unused side information bit stuffing", "empty frame stuffing", and "ancillary bit stuffing". For all of these post-encoding methods, there are benefits of being independent of parameters such as Bit Rate, Sampling Rate, and Variable/Constant Bit Rate encoding, as well as providing a significant amount of space for storage without affecting audio data and without changing the original file size. To evaluate the feasibility and efficiency of the four methods, as well as their Steganographic security, an application was developed that can reliably embed any file (within size limits) into any MP3 file (or a set of mp3 files).

6. METHOD DETAILS
6.1. Unused Header Bit Stuffing

One challenge of "unused header bit stuffing" is deciding which header bits are "unused". One bit we know we can use with confidence is the "Private" bit (see Fig. 2). This should not be used by anything for any reason (except by us). The "Copyright" bit can also be overwritten as it does not affect audio playback, same with the "Original" bit. This, so far, gives us 3 bits per frame for injection. There are also two "Mode Extension" bits that are theoretically only used when the "Channel Mode" bits are set to the "Joint Stereo" mode value, so for all other modes these two bits may also be usable for storage, however this has not yet been verified. The two "Emphasis" bits are also candidates for being "unused", but my experimentation has shown that this is not completely true.

It was found that after overwriting "Emphasis" bits, popular audio programs such as *Winamp*, *iTunes*, and *Windows Media Player* still play the file fine, but it does result in significant audible distortion when played back on other less-popular audio software and some portable MP3 players including the *Creative Zen Stone*. Overwriting only the most significant bit of the "Emphasis" field fixed the distortion on portable MP3 players, but some media players still had the distortion issue: *Media Player Classic* which is part of the "K-Like Codec Pack", as well as Linux-based players like *Totem*. Based on this analysis we can comfortably overwrite 3 of the header bits ("Private", "Copyright", and "Original"), and potentially the "Emphasis" bits, depending on how much we are willing to risk detection.

It is a good idea to leave the headers of the first few frames unmodified. This is because media players display some information about the MP3 file by reading headers from the first frame or two, the rest of the frames are probably assumed to have equivalent information and therefore are not read. If we were to change the first frame's "copyright" or "original" bits, then the value seen by the media player would be different from the original, but if we skip a few frames and then change everything afterward, the changes would be invisible to the media player. It is possible that some programs check more than one frame just to verify the values they read in frame one. Skipping one frame seems sufficient for Windows Media Player 11, but not for Winamp 5, so there is some uncertainty about how many frames should really be skipped. My tests have shown that skipping two frames was sufficient, but there may be instances that require more.

The locations of unused header bits are easy to determine. First, it is necessary to find the first frame in the MP3 file. After this, every next frame can be found by calculating the current frame's length using the equation shown in Section 4.2.1. Within a frame, the header always has the same format, so the proper bits can be quickly located by their standard offsets.

When changing any of the bits in the header, it is important to consider whether or not the frame is protected by a CRC. If this is the case, changing the bits will render the affected frames unplayable due to a mismatched CRC. In order to ensure that the MP3 file remains audibly identical to the original, a new CRC must be calculated for each affected frame after all changes are made.

6.2. Side Information Bit Stuffing

In "side information bit stuffing", there are multiple "padding" bits, all of which may be used for storage. These bits immediately follow the main_data_begin field. In a stereo MP3 file there are 3 padding bits, while in a mono MP3 file there are 5. Because these bits are only used to round the side information section up to an integer number of bytes, their value has no purpose and they are always skipped. This means we can safely insert data into them without interference with standard media player functionality. There may be other places in the side information that can serve as storage for our data, but this needs to be further researched.

Locating the side information padding bits is a little trickier than finding the unused header bits. It is possible that a 2-byte CRC field immediately follows the header of a frame. This can be determined by reading the "CRC" bit in the header. If the bit is not set, then the side information immediately follows the header, but if it is set, then 2 bytes must be added to skip the CRC. From there, the padding bits always have the same offset.

As with "unused header bit stuffing", when changing the side information bits in CRC-protected MP3 files, a new CRC must be calculated for each modified frame.

6.3. Empty Frame Stuffing

For "empty frame stuffing", one challenge is efficiently determining which frames are actually "empty", that is, they do not contain any audio data. The most straightforward way of doing this is by scanning the main data section of each frame and checking its uniformity (all 1's or all 0's). This is a brute-force approach and would take a very long time to compute. Aside from the time-inefficiency, this also introduces a problem with recovering your data. Once you write your data in, that frame is no longer empty, so you cannot use the same method for recovery. It is necessary to leave some sort of identifier that could be searched for when attempting to retrieve.

As an example, Achmad Zaenuri's "mp3stegz" utility mentioned earlier, which implements a similar injection method, marks used frames by filling the first 4 bytes of the empty space with "XXXX" - 4 ASCII "X" characters [8]. There is a risk of having an incorrect frame accidentally match this pattern during retrieval, but it is highly unlikely. To increase the efficiency of this method we can use the observation that almost all such frames occur in the beginning of the MP3 file and at the end. By searching from the beginning until the first non-empty frame and from the end until the last non-empty frame, a lot of time can be saved at the expense of potentially missing a few empty frames.

The speed of "empty frame stuffing" can be greatly improved using more sophisticated detection methods. One such method is the analysis of the side information for clues about whether or not the frame contains audio data. By analyzing the side information in a number of MP3 files containing empty frames, it became apparent that the big_values and table_select fields of the side information in empty frames always equal zero, while in non-

empty frames they always contain non-zero values. By adding the big_values and table_select fields for both granules and all channels of a frame (2 pairs in mono MP3s, 4 pairs in stereo MP3s), we can quickly tell whether or not the frame contains audio data without scanning the whole main data section. This also opens up the door to using partially empty frames as previously mentioned in "partially empty frame stuffing". Using the side information to determine the "empty" status of a frame also allows for easy retrieval: since the side information fields used for this calculation are not modified we can use the same method to find the frames our data is stored in.

An important thing to keep in mind when using advanced detection methods for "empty frame stuffing" (such as analysis of the side information section) is the location of the beginning of the empty space. In the brute-force method used by "mp3stegz", the empty section starts from the byte following the side information and ends with the byte before the next frame's header. When detected via side information fields, however, the beginning of the "empty" section may not occur immediately after the side information, instead it is at the beginning of the main data section for that frame. This may be before the current frame's header, as determined by the main_data_begin field of the side information. This also means that the ending of the empty section needs to be determined, which can be done by locating the beginning of the next main data section.

It is a good idea to leave the main data of the first few frames unmodified because these are often used to store special tags which may contain important information, especially so in Variable Bit Rate (VBR) MP3 files.

6.4. Ancillary Bit Stuffing

In "ancillary bit stuffing" covert data is stored in tiny spaces in-between main data sections of frames. To find the ancillary data spaces we first need to find the beginning of the current frame's main data section using the main_data_begin field of the side information. Next, we need to look at the previous frame's main_data_begin and determine what portion of its main data is filled with audio information. To calculate the length of the audio data, we can add all the part2_3_length fields in the side information of that frame. There are two such fields in a mono file - one per granule, and four such fields in a stereo file - one per channel per granule. Using this information, we can determine where exactly the previous frame's audio information ends. Once we figure this out, the ancillary data is made up of the bits between the end of the last frame's audio information and the beginning of the current frame's main data. This is usually between 0 and 7 bits as this data is mostly used to round the previous frame's main data section up to a full byte, but it could be larger if the previous frame's audio ended early.

As with "empty frame stuffing", it is a good idea to leave the main data of the first few frames unmodified to avoid damaging any tags which may be present.

7. METHODS AND DETECTION STRATEGIES

While all of the four methods used will cause no audible damage and no change to the properties of MP3 files, they do vary in the amount of difficulty a Steganalyst would have attempting to do blind detection on the utilized MP3 file, that is, trying to determine the presence of any covert data without initially knowing whether something extraneous is stored in the MP3 file and without having access to the original "clean" MP3 file. "Unused header bit stuffing" and "unused side information bit stuffing" are the methods easiest to detect, while "empty frame stuffing" and "ancillary bit stuffing" provide more of a challenge. Note that even if the presence of covert data is detected, all the methods prove to be about equally as challenging for an attempt to retrieve that data if any unused space is filled in with random bits. The biggest challenges involve determining the size of the stored data, determining what options were used for injection, and figuring out if this file is part of a set of MP3s that the covert data is stored in. Also, because the four methods are independent of one another, it is possible to inject four different covert files into the same MP3, or set of MP3s, creating the possibility of having several decoys. If the stored covert data is encrypted, it further increases the difficulty of retrieval.

7.1.   Unused Header Bit Stuffing

In a standard clean MP3 file, all the headers are practically identical for one another, with the exception of several bits such as the "Bit Rate" and "Padding". Using this knowledge, it is not difficult to scan through all the frame headers of an MP3 file and measure the degree of variation between the headers. This is a simple scan and is significantly more effective if only looking at the uncommonly used bits (the ones available for data injection). If there is significant variation between these bits, then it is very likely that covert data is stored in them.

7.2.   Unused Side Information Bit Stuffing

The padding bits of the side information are always 0. This means that it is very easy to detect injected data by checking if any of these padding bits are equal to 1.

7.3.   Empty Frame Stuffing

This is where we start to run into some difficulties. We do not know what the main data section looks like in a clean file - it is not necessarily uniform. Even if we use the side information fields to locate the potentially empty frames, there is no good way to tell if this frame contains covert data or just something meaningless. While not a guarantee, often these frames do seem to contain patterns (sometimes they even are composed of all 1s or 0s). Using this information, statistical methods can be developed to determine with some level of significance whether there is covert data or not. This would involve analyzing MP3 files we know for sure are clean.

7.4.   Ancillary Bit Stuffing

The challenges here are identical to that of "empty frame stuffing". Even if we were to locate all the ancillary bits and put them together, we have no knowledge of what their initial values should be so it may be difficult to determine the presence of covert data. Once again, some level of confidence may be obtained by performing statistical analysis on the values of ancillary bits in clean MP3 files to obtain a statistical model.

8. CONCLUSION

Keeping in mind that our interest is in Steganography, not Cryptography, we are trying to make sure nobody knows that the covert data is present. The four methods evaluated here, "unused header bit stuffing", "unused side information bit stuffing", "empty frame stuffing", and "ancillary bit stuffing", all do a sufficient job in preventing accidental detection by allowing data to be injected into/retrieved from MP3 files without modifying any visible or audible properties of the MP3 files. The methods of "empty frame stuffing" and "ancillary bit stuffing" also provide additional resistance to Steganalysis, making them a better choice for more sensitive covert data.

Future work on this project could involve investigating additional injection techniques such as "partially-empty frame stuffing" and "custom frame injection". Also the methods can be applied to more practical applications such as secure key distribution or making a karaoke-like music player utilizing "unused header bit stuffing" and "unused side information bit stuffing" to store lyrics and display them synchronously as the MP3 file is played.

9. REFERENCES

[1] Steganography. (2009). In Merriam-Webster Online Dictionary. Retrieved October 24, 2009, from http://www.merriam-webster.com/dictionary/steganography

[2] Hacker, Scot, "MP3, The Definitive Guide", 1st Edition, March 2000, O'Reilly Publishing.

[3] M. Ruckert, Understanding MP3, Vieweg, 2005, ISBN 3-528-05905-2.

[4] Petitcolas Fabien A. P., "MP3stego", 1997–2005, http://www.petitcolas.net/fabien/steganography/mp3stego/

[5] Maciak, L. G., Ponniah, M. A., & Sharma, R., "MP3 STEGONOGRAPHY: Applying Stenography to Music Captioning", 2005.

[6] Zaenuri, A., "Hide any file inside mp3 file -- MP3 steganography", 2008 Achmad Z's Archives, http://achmadz.blogspot.com/2008/05/hide-any-file-inside-mp3-file.html

[7] Bender, W., Gruhl, D., Morimoto, N., & Lu, A., "Techniques for data hiding", 1996 Ibm.com, http://www.research.ibm.com/journal/sj/353/sectiona/bender.txt

[8] Zaenuri, A., "Mp3stegz algorithm", 2008 Achmad Z's Archives, http://achmadz.blogspot.com/2008/06/mp3stegz-algorithm.html

The Emergence of an IT "Profession"

Joseph J. Ekstrom
Brigham Young University
Provo, Utah
jekstrom@byu.edu

William Agresti
Johns Hopkins University
Baltimore, Maryland
Agresti@jhu.edu

Gregory W. Hislop
Drexel University
Philadelphia, Pensylvania
hislop@drexel.edu

Han Reichgelt
Southern Polytechnic State University
Marrieta, Georgia
hreichge@spsu.edu

Charlene (Chuck) Walrad
Davenport Consulting, Inc
San Diego, California
cwalrad@daven.com

ABSTRACT

Whenever society comes to depend on the services of a group of skilled individuals, society demands a way to recognize if a particular individual has the skills needed to support that dependency. Doctors, lawyers, engineers, dentists, plumbers, construction contractors, and even hairdressers are certified or licensed. Information and communication practitioners have arrived at the point where society is demanding certification of their skills. More and more organizations are requiring certifications for people to fill certain roles. Once sanctioned by government, an official organization is formed to assure integrity of practice by establishing codes of ethics, standards of practice, and in relevant areas, technical standards.

The United Kingdom, Canada, Australia, New Zealand, and many others have already "chartered" organizations to govern the IT profession. In 2009 the British Computer Society rebranded itself by changing its logo and marketing materials to "BCS-the chartered organization for IT". This action is symbolic of the times. The BCS is no longer an association of people interested in computing; rather, it is the body officially recognized by the British government to police the IT profession. The Australian Computer Society(ACS) and the Canadian Information Processing Society (CIPS) have similar status in their respective countries.

Categories and Subject Descriptors:

K.7.0 [The Computing Profession]: General

Keywords

Information Technology Profession

1. Moderator: Joseph Ekstrom

This panel was proposed with the goal of initiating a conversation in SIGITE relative to the role of academic IT in the wider evolution that is taking place in the world. We would hope that we could begin to understand the following:

- What is a profession?
- What is the current status of the Profession of IT in the United States?

RIIT'13, October 10–12, 2013, Orlando, Florida, USA.
ACM 978-1-4503-2494-6/13/10.
http://dx.doi.org/10.1145/2512209.2512231

- Why is IT recognized as profession in other parts of the world?
- What role should certifications play in the profession of IT?
- Are there areas of IT practice that are already emerging as professions?
- What role should SIGITE play in the process?

2. Position: William Agresti

Can we draw upon aspects of professionalism, such as having individuals with certain licenses or certifications related to IT, to provide value to organizations and society? Efforts to advance professionalism in IT should be guided by a "pull" from demonstrated needs or potential benefits. We should engage people outside of IT who would be on the receiving end of professional services to learn more about their needs.

If we speculate on a possible outcome of such outreach, we may find that the most useful contribution we can make is to focus on high impact areas in the interface of IT with the public, such as safety or privacy properties of IT applications and systems. Of course, any such efforts depend on our having established parameters for the use of particular models and practices as being effective in providing the desired properties. This notion of defining useful "subsets" of broad areas of practice is found elsewhere, such as CPAs who are certified in business valuation or financial forensics. Perhaps in IT we should consider a "bottom-up" approach starting with focused IT-related practices where there is the most value to society.

3. Position: Gregory Hislop

In considering the profession of IT, it may be useful to examine the Software Engineering (SE) experience as a relevant example.

Academic Programs – Both SE and IT have relatively small but growing numbers of undergraduate and professional master's degree programs. Neither discipline has significant PhD program activity, although there are a few PhD programs for SE. Both disciplines have ACM/IEEE-CS curriculum models, with the first versions created in 2004 and 2008 respectively, and revisions currently underway.

Accreditation and Licensing - In the U.S., both IT and SE are accredited by ABET, but with SE is in the Engineering Accreditation Commission of ABET, while IT is in the Computing Accreditation Commission. It is possible to be licensed in the U.S. as a Professional Engineer in Software

Engineering, but currently only in Texas. Licensing via engineering has been problematic, since much of the Fundamentals of Engineering exam is not addressed by a typical SE degree program. In the U.S., licensing (and to some extent accreditation) of SE has been a divisive issue, with many in the Computer Science community having significant reservations about these efforts. This tension within the computing disciplines has not occurred in other countries.

In summary, when considering a profession IT in light of the SE experience some of the interesting questions are: How does a profession of IT relate to Computer Science, which is clearly the dominant computing discipline? Is engineering the right professional model for IT? Should there be licensing of IT professionals and what would the intent of that license be? How do you draw the boundaries within the computing disciplines? Do the issues of professionalism apply differently to different aspects of IT?

4. Position: Han Reichgelt

One of the hallmarks of established professions is the existence of licensures and/or other qualifications that are recognized by the profession and achievement of which is typically required to be able to practice that profession. Clearly, IT (and computing in general) does not have anything that resembles the bar exam required for lawyers or the Uniform Certified Public Account Examination that candidates have to pass in order to be able to

practice as CPAs. However, IT has seen the emergence of a large number of professional certifications. While some of them tool specific (e.g, CCNA, CCNP, and the various Microsoft certifications), others, such as the various ITIL and ISACA certifications, are more general. Such certifications have a certain value in the market place. However, the IT education community has consistently struggled with the question whether, and if so, how, to integrate these certifications in its various educational programs. One of the questions the community may wish to ponder as it strives for a broader recognition of IT as a profession, is whether it is possible to integrate such certifications in its degree programs, and if so, what the best way to achieve this is, especially when set against the criteria that our accreditation agencies wish us to meet.

5. Position: Chuck Walrad

In order to be recognized as a professional, it's necessary to know what the world expects of a "profession." About 15 years ago, as part of its work to define and encourage the profession of software engineering, the IEEE Computer Society launched a study of the literature concerning the key elements that make up recognized professions. The result of that effort is captured in a Model of a Profession that is now being used to foster the development of key elements of an IT profession. This session presents that model and some efforts now underway to establish those key elements.

ChronoZoom: Travel Through Time for Education, Exploration, and Information Technology Research

Robert L. Walter
University of Washington
Center for Web and Data Science
bobw1@uw.edu,
bob@bobwalter.net

Sergey Berezin
Lomonosov Moscow State University
sergey@mstlab.org

Ankur Teredesai
University of Washington,
Center for Web and Data Science
ankurt@uw.edu

ABSTRACT

In this paper, we describe the architecture, infrastructure requirements, and technical evolution of ChronoZoom, a unique infinite-zoom, temporal-data-visualization open-source platform. With ChronoZoom, it is possible to browse through time and history and fill the browser with events that span from 13.8 billion years to a single day. ChronoZoom, originally a tool to teach Big History, offers significant information technology challenges for integrating IT best practices in HCI (browser based zoomable interfaces), Cloud Computing (client-server architectures) and Big data (storage and retrieval) infrastructure technologies. This paper offers an overview of the ChronoZoom platform, outlines the technical issues we encountered, and the corresponding design decisions that enable scaling the server to support rendering millions of timelines for thousands of concurrent, interactive users. This paper is also a testament to how a distributed team of IT developers across two continents successfully collaborated to ship an open-source, online, educational tool that is set to have tremendous impact on how we view and interact with history.

In addition to providing a tool to visualize history, ChronoZoom offers a unique data visualization tool that offers an intuitive, graphic interface for temporal display. While this paper focuses on the use of ChronoZoom to display historical information, it is equally well suited to show scientific, personal, or statistical data with its unique ability to permit temporal zoom.

Categories and Subject Descriptors

K.3.1 [**Computer Uses in Education**]: Computer Assisted Instruction, Collaborative Learning D.2.6 [**Programming Environments**]: Interactive environments, Graphical Environments, Cloud Computing

Keywords

Temporal Zoom, Cloud Computing, Big History, Zoomable User Interfaces, Timelines, ChronoZoom

1. INTRODUCTION

ChronoZoom (www.chronozoom.com) is an open source data visualization tool that permits *zooming through time* to explore timelines that extend from the Big Bang to the present. ChronoZoom can perform a zoom that goes from a 13.8 billion year view down to a single day. ChronoZoom's five trillion to one zoom ratio, and its ability to permit easy navigation through history has captured the imaginations of educators, scientists, and the general public alike. In early 2013, ChronoZoom was named the "Best Educational Resource" at the 2013 South by Southwest[1] conference.

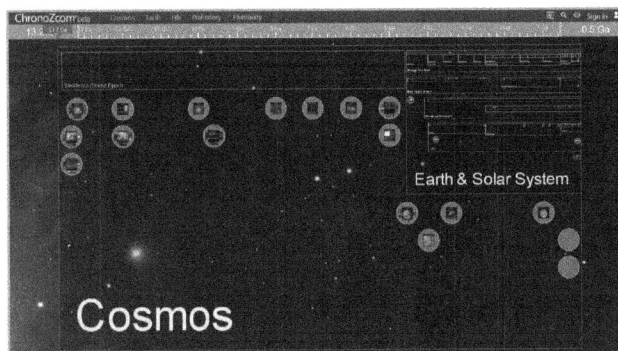

Figure 1: This is the fully zoomed-out ChronoZoom canvas. At this level of zoom, each pixel on the screen represents over 14 million years.

Almost a decade ago, Ben Bederson implemented PAD++[2], an infinite resolution, sketchpad. He envisioned this as an intuitive "stream of consciousness method of computing." Over time, this concept came to be called ZUI (Zoomable User Interface[3]). PAD++ was created as an extension of PAD, which allowed drawing within a window. This technology was extended first by Seadragon[9], which was acquired by Microsoft, and extended into the DeepZoom[4] product from Microsoft Live Labs. This evolution defined a technology that permitted merging images representing various details of an object or scene to be assembled so that a user could zoom in and out of what appears to be a single picture to reveal virtually infinite detail.

The initial idea for ChronoZoom originated as a Big History[20] class project at the University of California, Berkeley. Then student Roland Saekow noticed that timelines offered varying levels of detail, and to get a more or less detailed view of events of interest, a different timeline, often in another book, had to be accessed. He reasoned that if one could "zoom" into a timeline in a way analogous to zooming in to an image to get more detail, a viewer would be able to "browse" time; and instantly control the level of detail desired. He was aware of Microsoft's work with their DeepZoom technology and wondered if it could be used to create the zoomable timelines he envisioned. He took this idea to his advisor, Prof. Walter Alvarez, who immediately understood the importance of this observation. This led to Microsoft Live Labs and Alvarez collaborating to produce a zoomable timeline canvas as a Deep Zoom[5] image that contained timelines spanning the life of the universe down to historical timelines only a few years long.

The resulting DeepZoom image provided a novel and exciting way to quite literally, dive into history. However, there were several drawbacks. Editing and adding content required a very laborious process of recreating the many images that Deep Zoom needs to perform its magic. Silverlight[18], a proprietary Microsoft browser plugin is required for viewing. While content density was theoretically infinite, there were finite limits to the amount of data that could be displayed with this technique.

These limitations, particularly the complexity of arranging images of independent timelines so that the illusion of optical zoom is possible, made it clear that the DeepZoom paradigm would prove difficult to maintain and expand over time.

In its first attempt to simplify creating new timelines, the project centered on developing an efficient authoring tool to create deep zoom images. After several months of effort, it was deemed impractical and the process to rethink ChronoZoom from the ground up was initiated. The current version which replaces the DeepZoom image with a data driven system where timelines are rendered on-demand in the browser, is a study in how a team of information technology developers across two continents collaborated to develop a fully open-source cloud-hosted zoomable big history interface.

In this paper we first review ChronoZoom as a zoomable user interface. We describe how we define a recursive structure to represent time in Section 2.2. Then, in Section 3 we outline the technical details of the architecture of the ChronoZoom platform. In particular, we demonstrate the innovative approach for intelligently managing the client-server data interaction to enable a fast, scalable, and responsive interface that allows for near-infinite zoom.

2. CHRONOZOOM OVERVIEW

As we started the new design, we built on knowledge gained during the first attempt to create a dynamic deepzoom version of ChronoZoom. During this first effort, a one-dimensional zoom was contemplated but was far too complex to achieve with deepzoom.. These learnings informed our team during the redesign. We understood that the ChronoZoom "zoom" is not a two-dimensional, photographic zoom. It is one-dimensional. Zooming-in has the effect of displaying a shorter duration of time, not enlarging a section of an image. For example, when fully zoomed out, ChronoZoom shows the full 13.8 billion years of the universe's life (figure 1) – all of time. Zooming in has the effect of filling the screen with a much shorter interval (figure 2). However, for the visualization to work the zoom had to be two-dimensional, expanding the height of objects along with the horizontal magnification. The vertical dimension is rendered but has no significance relative to the data being displayed.

2.1 Moving From Images to Data

As shown in the original Live Labs project[5], a similar level of zoom is also supported. Our improvement was to go from a DeepZoom representation of many images, to a very simple data-driven presentation where images representing ChronoZoom primitives are artifacts rendered dynamically by the client.

This was a tremendous improvement over the previous implementation, which tried to dynamically render deepzoom image pyramids with different imagery at different zoom levels to simulate semantic zoom where the content would shift and change as the user zoomed in. What was extraordinarily difficult to accomplish with deepzoom became much easier with dynamically rendered objects on a HTML5 canvas.

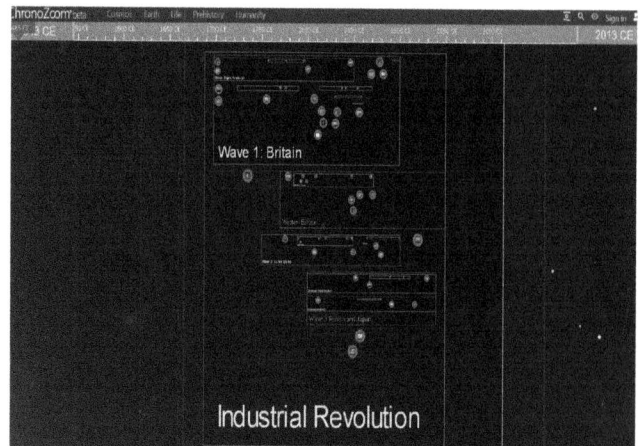

Figure 2: Zoomed in to show the Industrial Revolution, the screen is filled with the much shorter period of only 600 years. ChronoZoom is capable of a three trillion to one zoom ratio. The zoom can continue until the screen shows a single day.

Timelines are stories[7]. Each timeline displays a sequence of events that lead to a specific conclusion. Functionally, a timeline can be thought of as a container that is bounded by its start date and end date. To build the container, the only information needed is *the begin and end dates* (a,b) and *a title*. Events along the timeline (called exhibits in ChronoZoom) are simply objects with an event date, description, and references to any other content desired to be displayed.

We imagined a timeline as a room in a museum. Inside this "room" are exhibits. Each exhibit has one or more artifacts to illustrate its topic. For ChronoZoom we created a "content item" object that relates to a specific item within the exhibit.

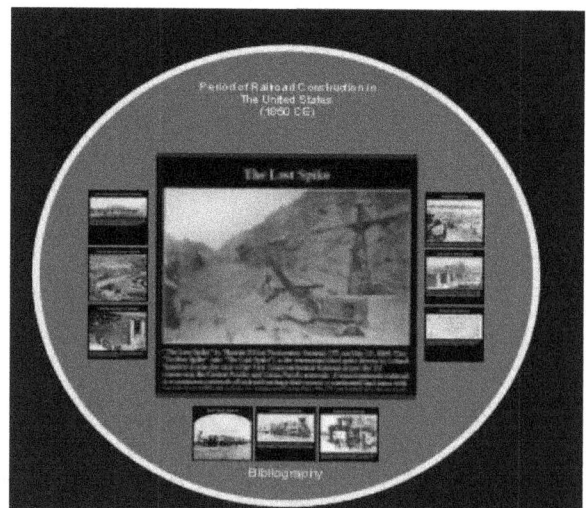

Figure 3: Exhibit inside the U.S. Industrial Revolution timeline discussing early railroads. The exhibit is a container for content items that reveal information relevant to the exhibit.

For example, in our Industrial Revolution for the United States timeline, we have an exhibit about developing the American Railroad (figure 3). In this exhibit are several content items that highlight some of the early American Railroads. We defined a simple hierarchy for ChronoZoom's data: the timeline itself, exhibits that show events relevant to the timeline, and content items that display and discuss specific content relevant to that exhibit.[8] Only content items contain images, videos or documents.

2.2 Defining the Structure of Time

Once we defined a simple data model that describes the timeline, exhibit, and content item, we are left with the most significant question: how do we build a data structure that will allow us to build out all of time and all of the timelines that can be created?

Our answer is based on the very simple concept that if one considers a timeline to be a container that can hold not only exhibits, but also other timelines, we can define a simple recursive data structure to support this: a tree.

Our ChronoZoom tree is a simple, hierarchical bidirectional graph where each node represents a timeline. Child nodes are timelines contained within the parent above it (Figure 4). Each node carries a data payload that is a list of exhibits within that node (timeline). Given that the Cosmos timeline contains all time from the Big Bang to the end of time, all other timelines must, by definition, be within this root timeline (node).

Each node has start and end date properties. Implicit is a third property: duration. For example the Cosmos timeline extends from   with a duration of   . The Industrial Revolution, on the other hand extends from 1685 CE to 1950 CE with a duration of only 265 years.

All of this data is easily stored within a relational database. Any images, videos, or documents included in content items are referenced by a URI that points to the location of that content, generally an external website. All other graphic artifacts are generated by the browser.

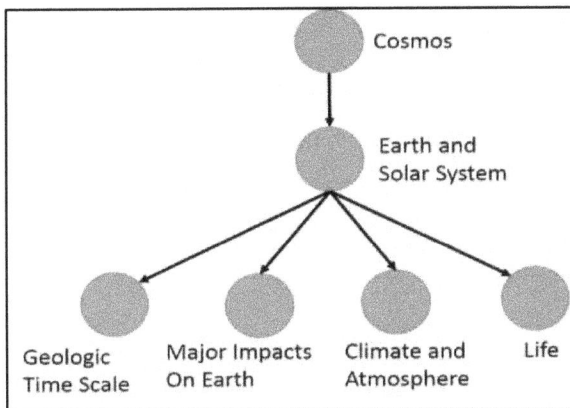

Figure 4: The top of the ChronoZoom tree. The root node is the Cosmos timeline. All other timelines are child nodes. Data can be organized such that the children of a particular node represent logical subsets of the parent's topic. For example, all of the children of "Earth and Solar System" are logical timelines that relate to earth and the solar system.

This redefinition of ChronoZoom moved it from the DeepZoom / seadragon[9] zoomable graphic to a data-driven, dynamically-drawn canvas that can be simply edited and expanded. ChronoZoom was no longer just a way to zoom through history, it became a versatile data visualization tool that could supply a graphic, zoomable, and interactive interface for any data that would benefit from this treatment.

3. TECHNICAL DETAILS

ChronoZoom presents some technical challenges to both the server and the browser client. The server must manage and deliver data payloads that represent the current area of interest to the user. The client is required to dynamically render the graphic primitives ChronoZoom displays. This is accomplished using a HTML 5 graphic canvas.

3.1 Living in the Cloud

To develop such an ambitious project, substantial server hardware is required. ChronoZoom is designed as a classic three-tier application. To avoid the cost and complexity of a data center solution, ChronoZoom is implemented with virtual servers in Microsoft's Azure cloud[10]. As described in Figure 5, the data tier is composed of an Azure SQL data base and a blob, both contained in a single Azure instance. Service calls are processed in a virtual middle tier contained in the top, Azure Websites tier.

Developing and supporting a cloud application proved to be quite different from more traditional data center infrastructures. Some of the anticipated issues like inter-tier communication and load balancing were solved by the cloud itself. Others, unanticipated by the team, like deployment and database constraints, proved challenging.

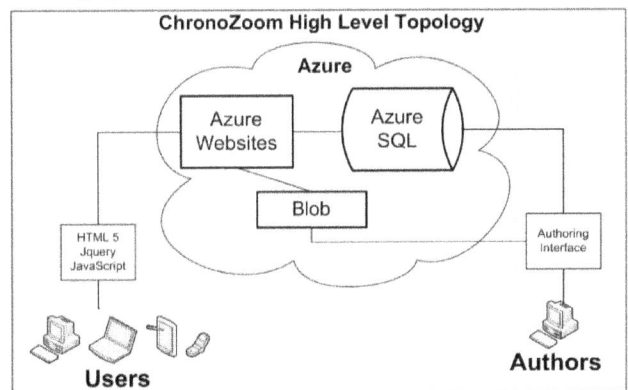

Figure 5: ChronoZoom topology. All server functionality is contained in two Microsoft Azure instances: one for the web server and service tier; the other, Azure SQL. The browser uses HTML 5 and JavaScript to convert the server payload into the ChronoZoom canvas. Authors use a graphical UI to create timelines, exhibits, and content items.

When the first beta of the data-driven ChronoZoom was developed in 2011, Azure only offered "compute" instances. These instances are essentially Windows virtual servers. Customers have no assurance that their applications will reside on any particular machine in the cloud. Azure can move and reassign instances as needed. All compute instances, therefore are read-only. Code changes can't be directly pushed to the current virtual machine (VM). Actually, they can be, but the changes will be lost when Azure takes care of its internal business and reassigns an instance to a new VM. Also, if the application is deployed to multiple instances, there is no way to identify and populate each individually. This is solved by the Azure management software. Changes are pushed to the Azure manager, which handles the actual deployment of code to the instances. This process had a long learning curve for the team. Once mastered, however, deployments took only a few minutes.

33

This has been changed somewhat over the last year or so. Now there are not only compute instances, but also web server instances. The web server instances do permit what feels like direct updating using FTP or with the Microsoft WebMatrix[11] tool. All complexity is hidden from the user. The current ChronoZoom release's web servers are sited in these new web server instances.

In order to see ChronoZoom's data visualizations, clients must support HTML 5[12]. Most modern browsers, including tablets and phones have this capability. The visualizations are all generated on a graphic canvas. This is accomplished using html 5 graphic functionality supported by JavaScript. ChronoZoom supports tablets, smart phones, and touch PC's with a multi-touch interface as well. ChronoZoom also offers an extensible navigation architecture built using Reactive Extensions[21].

3.2 Managing "Infinite" Zoom

Which timelines and exhibits are visible at any level of zoom is dependent on the length of the timeline. For example, at 13.8 ga (fully zoomed out) on a typical canvas of 950 pixels, each pixel represents about 14 million years. To be visible, a timeline would have to be at least 10 pixels wide. That means nothing with a duration less than 140 million years can be seen on the fully-zoomed-out canvas.

ChronoZoom features temporal zoom. This is very different from optical zoom. When you perform optical zoom, an object it appears closer; everything enlarges at the same rate. The zoom affects both the perceived height and width of the object. A temporal zoom, on the other hand, only changes one dimension: the x-axis. In a view of the history of the universe, the timescale (x-axis) covers 13.8 ga (giga-anum: billions of years).

3.3 The Virtual Canvas

Given the ability to expose vast amounts of information as the user zooms in and out, ChronoZoom must be able to efficiently manage very large amounts of data and display this data as required. Additionally, it must provide an engaging set of zoom animations. In the original, DeepZoom version, the user was actually performing a two-dimensional graphic zoom so the visual effects were part of the DeepZoom experience. In the data-driven ChronoZoom, artifacts are generated based on numerical data supplied by the database so any zoom effects must be generated through animations[13, 14].

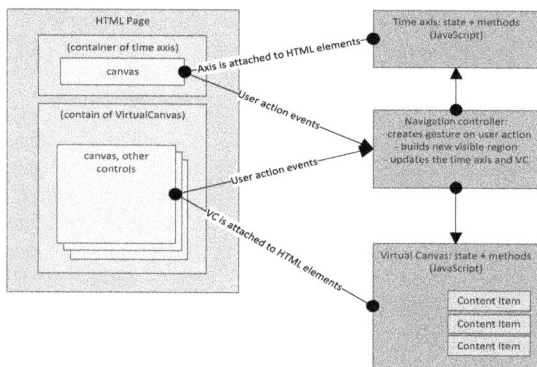

Figure 6: The HTML page contains two "canvases" that permit graphic generation of ChronoZoom objects. The time axis canvas is where the time scale at the top of the page is created. The virtual canvas is populated with timelines, exhibits, and content items.

The virtual canvas represents $\mathbb{R}^2$ space and a hierarchical set of objects placed in that space. A subset of that space, the viewport, represents the area visible to the user.

The space includes a coordinate system with units of measurements: t along x-axis, and $\hbar$ − unit along y-axis. A parameter of the virtual space is an aspect ratio $\gamma\,[\hbar/t]$, which says how much $\hbar$ units is in one t unit; in other words, a rectangle of size $1 \times \gamma$ should appear as a square in the virtual space. Aspect ratio is a constant for each virtual canvas.

We use superscript $*^v$ to say that $p^v = (x^v, y^v) \in \mathbb{R}^2$ is a point in the virtual space coordinate system. The superscript $*^p$ indicates that screen coordinates in pixels are used. Units of a value are provided in square brackets; e.g. $x[t]$ indicates that value x is measured in t.

A visible region $\mathcal{V}$, which is a rectangle within the virtual space:

$$\mathcal{V} = (c^v, w^p, h^p, \alpha),$$

where $c^v = \left(c_x^v, c_y^v\right)$ is a center point of the $\mathcal{V}$ in virtual coordinates, $w^p \times h^p$ is the size in pixels of the visible region (i.e. size of the physical canvas to draw), $\alpha\,[t/\text{pixel}]$ is a scale, which say how many t units are contained in a single screen pixel.

The screen coordinate system has its origin in the left-top corner of $\mathcal{V}$; the x-asis is directed to the right, the y-axis is directed to the bottom.

$$x\,[\hbar]$$

The next function gets the width and height of $\mathcal{V}$ in pixel coordinates:

$$w^v[\hbar] = \alpha w^p,\; h^v[t] = \gamma\alpha h^p.$$

Then, the next function transforms a point p^v into a screen coordinate system of the virtual canvas $\mathcal{V}$:

$$p_x^p(p_x^v; \mathcal{V}) = \frac{p_x^v - c_x^v}{\alpha} + \frac{w^p}{2},$$

$$p_y^p(p_y^v; \mathcal{V}) = \frac{p_y^v - c_y^v}{\gamma\alpha} + \frac{h^p}{2}.$$

And finally, virtualToScreen: $(p^v, \mathcal{V}) \rightarrow p^p$:

$$\text{virtualToScreen}\,(p^v, \mathcal{V}) = \left(p_x^p(p_x^v), p_y^p(p_y^v)\right).$$

Screen to virtual coordinates transformation can be inferred as reverse functions of the calculations above.

A virtual canvas content object $\mathcal{C}$ is an object defined in the virtual coordinates which can be rendered on a physical canvas. Its location is defined as

$$\mathcal{C} = (p_c^v, w_c^v, h_c^v),$$

where $p^v = \left(p_{cx}^v, p_{cy}^v\right)$ is the left-top corner of the content object in virtual coordinates. $w_c^v \times h_c^v$ is the size of the visual representation of the object in virtual co-ordinates.

Transformation of $\mathcal{C}$, attached to $\mathcal{V}$, from virtual space into screen coordinates of $\mathcal{V}$:

$$\mathcal{C}^p = \begin{pmatrix} \text{virtualToScreen}\,(p_c^v; \mathcal{V}), \\ w_c^p = \dfrac{w_c^v}{\alpha}, \\ h_c^p = \dfrac{h_c^v}{\gamma\alpha} \end{pmatrix}.$$

Thus, the size of $\mathcal{C}$ in pixels is $w_c^p \times h_c^p$.

The function determining visibility of an object is as follows:

1. Determine whether bounding rectangle of C intersects visible region $\mathcal{V}$. If not, it is not rendered.
2. If either w_c^p or h_c^p is less than a predefined threshold (say, 10 pixels), it is not rendered.
3. Otherwise, render the object on a canvas of the layer associated with this object. Thus the virtual canvas can be defined as a 3-tuple:

$$\mathbb{V} = (\gamma, \mathcal{V}, C),$$

where $C = \{\mathcal{C}_i^p\}_{i=0}^{n-1}$ is a set of virtual canvas objects.

The virtual canvas is implemented in JavaScript using a JQuery[15] UI widget. The virtual canvas API allows changing the visible region and defining the viewport.

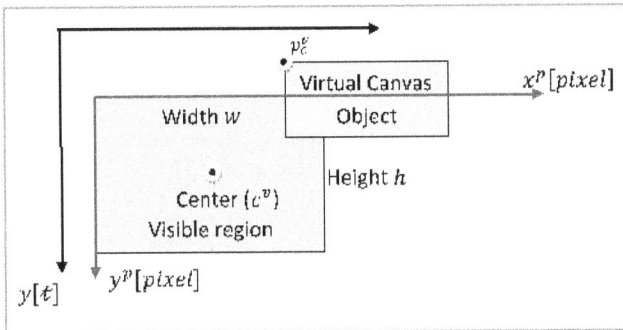

Figure 7: The virtual canvas object is used to compute the Visible region (viewport). The virtual canvas is implemented in JavaScript JQuery and an API allows creating the viewport and moving it.

```
/* find the fork node of the current interval */

CREATE PROCEDURE `fork_node`(IN `start_time`
INT(32) UNSIGNED, IN `end_time` INT(32) UNSIGNED,
OUT `node` INT(32) UNSIGNED) BEGIN
        SET `node` = ((`start_time` - 1) ^ `end_time`) >>
1;
        SET `node` = `node` | `node` >> 1;
        SET `node` = `node` | `node` >> 2;
        SET `node` = `node` | `node` >> 4;
        SET `node` = `node` | `node` >> 8;
        SET `node` = `node` | `node` >> 16;
        SET `node` = `end_time` & ~`node`;
END $$
DELIMITER ;
```

Figure 8: Calculation to determine which timelines are required for a given viewport. Note that this calculation essentially populates the entire canvas with all objects that are visible at the current level of zoom. The viewport, itself, may only show a subset of these objects. This is sufficient given a reasonable number of available objects in the current release.

3.3.1 Serving the Right Data

Since the ChronoZoom virtual canvas can contain a vast amount of information, even with the compressed nature of the data-driven application, downloading the entire virtual canvas would take too much time to be practical for a web application. In addition, a given PC may not have sufficient memory to contain all of the data in the full virtual canvas.

ChronoZoom must attempt to provide data on an as-needed basis. As the prior code (Fig 8) demonstrates, it is possible for the browser to know which timelines are required for a viewport at any given zoom level. This requirement can be expressed simply by specifying the minimum time span visible as well as the date range covered by the viewport.

To convert this information into the required payload, the server must very rapidly locate timelines, exhibits, and content items intersecting a given viewport. Standard B-Tree search on start time and end time of each timeline in a relational database does not offer reasonable performance on such intersection queries required by ChronoZoom. Instead, a static Relational Interval tree is created to handle intersections.[16] The RI tree utilizes a virtual full binary tree to index timelines. The binary tree is never fully materialized in the sense that nodes of the tree are only stored as integers representing their order of appearance in an in-order traversal, rather than as actual tree nodes with children pointers. Each timeline [a, b] (where a and b are positive integers denoting the start and end years of a timeline plus an offset of 13,700,000,001) is indexed by its fork value $f(a, b)$, where $f(a, b)$ is simply the least common ancestor of node of a and b in the aforementioned full binary tree, and f(a, b) can be computed very efficiently in a static RI tree.[17]

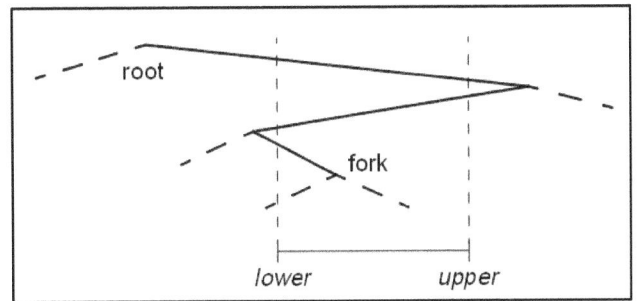

Figure 9: Fork node of an interval in the RI tree[19]

A RI tree associates a fork value with each timeline interval to enable efficient pruning of a majority of intervals not intersecting a given query range. In addition, because all timelines in ChronoZoom reside within a known fixed year range, a *static* RI tree[17] can be used so that further optimizations replacing disk accesses with fast arithmetic can be implemented.

Once the timeline intervals are known, simply searching a list of timeline ranges delivers the actual timeline information as well as the related exhibit and content item id's required. All that is left is to extract this set of data along with accompanying blob content and send it off to the browser. This method completely avoids recursion as well as expensive, multiple queries to the database.

4. CONCLUSION AND FUTURE WORK

Very few real-world platforms exist for showcasing how tools-oriented IT research can help multidisciplinary education. As outlined in this paper, a combination of IT tools comprising web development to cloud computing and big data infrastructure contributed to the development of an innovative platform to help educators teach big history.

Timelines represent stories. ChronoZoom has taken the very old idea of the timeline, which graphically represents a sequence of events that leads to a result, and provides the ability to create a rich tapestry of interactive timelines that span very large and very small periods of time. For the first time, users can start with a story that spans billions of years and then zoom in to follow a timeline (story) that spans a single week. As ChronoZoom evolved from a deep zoom image to a data-driven visualization tool, its true power as a zoomable UI tool is now unfolding.

Architecturally, the value of ChronoZoom goes far beyond teaching history. Combined with data mining and semantic search, there is an opportunity to algorithmically generate timelines and exhibits that can help researchers in various fields, as well as the general public. Since ChronoZoom is open-source software, IT educators and researchers can freely use the code to provide a platform for completely new applications.

5. ACKNOWLEDGEMENTS

Additional contributors to this paper: From the University of Washington; Joel Larson, Yitao Li, Charu Chandiram, and Ling Ding; From Microsoft Research: Javier Luraschi, Jay Beavers, Michael Zyscowki, Donald Brinkman, Rane Johnson; from Lomonosov Moscow State University: Eugene Nourminsky, Dmitry Voitsekhovsky, and Wahib Faizi.We would like to acknowledge the support of the entire team who made ChronoZoom possible and who have contributed so much to it. From the University of California, Berkeley: Walter Alvarez whose teaching, encouragement, and creativity inspired ChronoZoom. David Shimabukuro, Roland Saekow, and Chris Engberg provided the Big History content for the original (beta) release. From Microsoft Research Connections: Tony Hey, Lee Dirks, Roy Zimmermann, Rane Johnson, Daron Green, Alex Wade, Derick Campbell, Jim Pinkleman, Roman Snytsar, Alyssa Felda, and Kimberley Lane who provided the leadership, inspiration, and support that made this project possible. Thanks go to the University of Washington, Information School faculty, Joseph Tennis and Mike Crandall who developed the metadata strategy ChronoZoom. From Moscow State University: Maria Nourminskaya, Natalia Stepanova, Nikita Skoblov, Dmitry Grechka, Michael Kalygin, Alexander Zenchenko, Victor Chugunov, Yury Zhaivoronok, Giorgiy Lutidze and Ivan Samylovsky who developed, tested, and improved the application.

6. REFERENCES

[1]. "ChronoZoom Named Top Educational Resource at 2013 SXSW Interactive." Web log post. *Microsoft Research Connections Blog.* Microsoft Corporation, 13 Mar. 2013. Web. 30 May 2013. <http://blogs.msdn.com/b/msr_er-archive/2013/03/13/chronozoom-named-top-educational-resource-at-2013-sxsw-interactive.aspx>.

[2]. Bederson, Ben B. (1994). "Pad++ advances in multiscale interfaces" in Conference companion on Human factors in computing systems (0-89791-651-4, 978-0-89791-651-6), (p. 315).

[3]. Bederson, Ben B. The promise of zoomable user interfaces, Proceedings of the 3rd International Symposium on Visual Information Communication, Beijing, China, Sept. 28–29, 2010

[4]. Rodriguez, Jamie. "Jaime Rodriguez On Windows Phone, Windows Presentation Foundation, Silverlight and Windows 7." Web log post. *MSDN Blogs.* Microsoft, 31 Mar. 2008. Web. May-June 2013. <http://blogs.msdn.com/b/jaimer/archive/2008/03/31/a-DeepZoom-primer-explained-and-coded.aspx?PageIndex=2>.

[5]. The original ChronoZoom student project can be viewed at http://eps.berkeley.edu/~saekow/chronozoom/launch/index.html.

[6]. Rosenberg, Daniel, and Anthony Grafton. *Cartographies of Time: A History of the Timeline.* New York: Princeton Architectural, 2012. Print.

[7]. Johnson-Stempson, R. ChronoZoom Tutorial, Microsoft Research, http://research.microsoft.com/apps/video/-default.aspx?id=161243, March 12, 2012.

[8]. "Seadragon Software." Web log post. *Wikipedia.* Wikimedia Foundation, 31 May 2013. Web. 31 May 2013. <http://en.wikipedia.org/wiki/Seadragon_Software>.

[9]. Micorosoft Corp. N.p.: Micorosoft, n.d. *Windows Azure.* Microsoft. Web. 30 May 2013. http://www.windowsazure.com/en-us/develop/net/fundamentals/intro-to-windows-azure/>.

[10]. N.p.: n.p., n.d. *WebMatrix 3.* Microsoft. Web. 30 May 2013. <http://www.microsoft.com/web/webmatrix/>.

[11]. Bluttman, Ken. *Create Great Graphics with the HTML5 Canvas.* Tech. IBM Developer Works, 8 Feb. 2011. Web. 30 May 2013. <http://www.ibm.com/developerworks/library/wa-html5canvas/>.

[12]. Igarashi, T. and Hinckley, K.Speed-dependent automatic zooming for browsing large documents, Proceedings of the 13th Annual ACM Symposium on User Interface Software and Technology, San Diego, CA, Nov. 5–8, 2000.

[13]. Cockburn, A., Savage, J., and Wallace, A. Tuning and testing scrolling interfaces that automatically zoom, Proceedings of the SIGCHI Conference on Human Factors in Computing Systems, Portland, OR, April 2–7, 2005.

[14]. "JQuery." *Wikipedia.* Wikimedia Foundation, 31 May 2013. Web. 31 May 2013. <http://en.wikipedia.org/wiki/JQuery>.

[15]. Enderle, J., M. Hampel, and T. Seidl. "Joining Interval Data in Relational Databases | Chair of Computer Science 9." *Proc. ACM SIGMOD Int. Conf. on Management of Data (SIGMOD 2004), Paris, France* (2004): n. pag. *Joining Interval Data in Relational Databases | Chair of Computer Science 9.* ACM - New York, NY, USA. Web. 30 May 2013. <http://dme.rwth-aachen.de/en/publications/2041>.

[16]. Martin, Laurent. "A Static Relational Interval Tree." *A Static Relational Interval Tree* (2011): n. pag. *Solidq.com.* Solidq, Sept. 2011. Web. 30 May 2013. <http://www.solidq.com/sqj/Pages/2011-September-Issue/A-Static-Relational-Interval-Tree.aspx>.

[17]. Lawton, G. "New Ways to Build Rich Internet Applications." *Computer* 41.8 (2008): 10-12. *IEEE Xplore.* Aug. 2008. Web. 04 June 2013. <http://ieeexplore.ieee.org/xpls/abs_all.jsp?arnumber=4597127>.

[18]. Kriegel, H. P., Pötke, M., & Seidl, T. (2000, September). Managing intervals efficiently in object-relational databases. In *Proc. 26th Int. Conf. on Very Large Databases (VLDB)* (pp. 407-418).

[19]. Christian, D. (2004). *Maps of time: an introduction to big history* (Vol. 1). Berkeley: University of California Press.

[20]. Microsoft Reactive Extensions library <http://msdn.microsoft.com/en-us/data/gg577609.aspx>

Design Patterns as First-Class Connectors

Sargon Hasso
Technical Product Development
Wolters Kluwer Law and Business
Chicago, IL
sargon.hasso@wolterskluwer.com

Carl Carlson
Information Technology and Management
Illinois Institute of Technology
Wheaton, IL
carlson@iit.edu

ABSTRACT

We propose a technique using design patterns as an abstract modeling construct to connect software components built individually by software developers. Given a set of requirements structured as design problems, we can solve each problem individually by selecting appropriate design pattern in the intended traditional way of using it. Much of the published literature on design patterns spends much effort in describing this problem–design pattern association; however, there is no systematic and practical way that shows how to integrate those individual solutions together. Our compositional model is based on design patterns by abstracting their behavioral model using role modeling constructs. This approach describes how to transform a design pattern into a role model that can be used to assemble a software application. Our approach offers a complete practical design and implementation strategies, adapted from DCI (Data, Context, and Interaction) architecture. We demonstrate our technique by presenting a simple case study complete with design and implementation code. We also present our approach in a simple to follow software composition process that provides guidelines of what to do and how to do it.

Categories and Subject Descriptors

D.2 [**Software**]: Software Engineering

Keywords

Software Composition, Design Patterns, Role Model, Software Architecture, DCI Architecture, Connectors, Traits.

1. INTRODUCTION

In our previous work [4], we laid out the foundational theory for constructing system architecture by composing components using design patterns [3] as a solution to integration problems. In this current research, we extended it by providing an implementation strategy. The use of patterns as integration mechanisms is different from using them, as

originally conceived, as solutions to design problems. The literature abounds with techniques to help designers practice and apply design patterns in building applications; however, very little attention is paid on how to assemble applications in a systematic way from pattern-based components.

Any one who carefully studied how Lexi editor was assembled in Gamma et al. [3] book, or how the hierarchical file system (HFS) was assembled in Vlissides [16] book, both case studies introduce the reader to design with patterns, will attest that components get fused together through a shared object. In our teaching experience, we assign to our students software application problems similar to Lexi and HFS and ask them to structure the requirements as design problems. We then ask them to find a design pattern that addresses or solves each individual requirement. This exercise gives them an opportunity to learn design patterns by doing. However, since they still have to assemble and build the whole application by combining individual solutions, this is the stage when we notice they struggle greatly. Lexi and HFS don't really generalize their integration mechanisms. It is this very issue that motivated us to research this problem and come up with an approach to integrate components using design patterns themselves as an abstraction mechanism to integrate components and transform those abstractions into realization during implementation. In other words, we are viewing design patterns from two different perspectives. First, design patterns as elements of system computational capability; second, design patterns as elements of system composition. These two views are clearly distinct and elaborated further by Shaw and Garlan [14].

Here is how this paper is organized. In section 2, we briefly survey related work. In section 3, we lay out the conceptual background needed to use our approach. In section 4, we describe concepts from DCI architecture we need for our implementation strategy. We present in section 5 a simple to follow process for using our approach that provides guidelines of what to do and how to do it. To demonstrate our technique, we present a simple case study in section 6. Our conclusion and future work are discussed in section 7.

2. RELATED WORK

Decomposing an application into design problems and finding solutions based on design patterns creates an integration problem designers must deal with. This is also true even for design solutions that are not patterns-based. Currently, there are no systematic process to integrate patterns-based components. Case studies found in Gamma et al. [3] and Vlissides [16] use ad hoc approaches to do integration. They rely heavily on the experience of designers to come up with integration strategies.

An approach by Yacoub et al. [19] uses design patterns for composition and are referred to as *constructional design patterns*. Basically these are design patterns plus an interface specification. Gluing patterns together is accomplished by two types of interfaces: classes and operations. The biggest disadvantage of this approach is the fact that you must identify parts of the two patterns to be used as interfaces. If one pattern-based component requires an operation that a participating object from another pattern-based component does not have, this approach may not work.

Riehle [13] describes an approach that relies on roles relationships similar to class relationships. This is an unnecessary constraint during analysis phase. Furthermore, his composition technique constrains patterns integration to produce composite designs that are patterns themselves which limits the wide applicability of this approach.

Our approach offers a complete design and implementation strategies with a set of techniques that most software engineers are familiar with. Contrast this approach with the formal approaches we surveyed in the literature that are difficult to comprehend and implement unless proper software tools are available. For example, the method by Taibi [15] starts with the explicit design pattern model structure as a basis for composing patterns by specifying their structural and behavioral properties using first-order logic and temporal logic of actions, respectively. The resulting specifications are incomprehensible to most practitioners unfamiliar with formal methods for specifying designs.

3. CONCEPTUAL FOUNDATION

Design patterns conceived originally as techniques that offer solutions to commonly recurring problems when building software components or applications [3]. However, we have come up with a *compositional model* based on design patterns by abstracting their *behavioral model* using *role modeling constructs*. What we mean by compositional model is similar to what we do when we connect a software component from, say, two classes through typical software composition techniques like generalization, aggregation, and association. The compositional model exhibited by these techniques are *structural* because system functionality is decomposed into modules and arranged into any number of possible structures. Our compositional model, on the other hand, is *behavioral* because it is based on the *collaboration model* derived from design patterns that has specific semantics based on the design pattern we use. In order to describe this collaboration model, we have to specify the design patterns as role models. Each design pattern we choose will have a different role model. How do we obtain these role models? For each design pattern, we examine its participants' collaboration behavior, and factor out their *responsibilities*. A responsibility is collection of behaviors, or functions, or tasks, or services. We then specify the resulting role model much like a *collaboration* model in UML [9] where it states that "roles in collaborations will often be typed as interfaces and will then prescribe properties that the participating instances must exhibit, but will not determine what class will implement those behavioral properties". The resulting collaboration model will play the same function as a use case function in the DCI architecture [12] whose techniques we want to use to implement, in code, the integration.

It is very important to realize that we are not using design patterns to solve a design problem, we are using design patterns to solve an integration problem. The fact that a design pattern has a collaboration context with participants with prescribed behavior is what we are abstracting.

In role modeling, each distinct system activity or behavior, use case for example, is considered and modeled individually. We generally examine the roles of two or more interacting entities during behavior analysis. The same entities may assume different roles in yet other interaction scenarios describing a different aspect of system behavior. In general, one system functionality may span several objects belonging to different classes (this is the same as saying that several objects, in their different roles, are collaborating to execute a system function). Another system functionality may span the same or additional objects. However, this time the same objects may take on a different role. To describe a complete behavior of one specific object, the different roles are composed or synthesized. This resultant synthesized behavior is assembled and implemented as a class. It is highly likely that this role modeling is happening implicitly by software designers but the thought process can be made explicit and there are several approaches in the literature dealing with this problem.

Role diagrams that depict the role model is appropriate at this level of analysis because they involve the collaboration of two or more objects. These also provide the context to model the structure of object interactions [11]. This idea does not seem to be different from the way design patterns are defined: "...design pattern identifies the participating classes and instances, their roles and collaborations, and their distribution of responsibilities..." [3].

Role modeling in this discussion, therefore, is used in two different ways: first, as a way to expose different interfaces by the same object, depending how it interacts with other objects, and second, as a way to describe collaboration between two or more objects during an enactment of, say, one system functionality or one use case scenario. The former is what *traits* [8] were used for, something we are not interested in here; while the latter is what we will be utilizing to model system behavior.

We will utilize the concept of a role as a partial description of an object's specifications during collaboration with other objects. Henceforth, when discussing design pattern components (participants), we will refer to them as illustrated in Figure 1(b). Essentially, this means the design pattern, in this case the Decorator [3, p. 175], see Figure 1(a), has two components represented by two roles: *Decorator* and *Component*. It's these two roles that really get mapped or injected into objects when doing design integration using design patterns. As the diagram in Figure 1(b) shows, we use the UML's [9] collaboration as a dashed ellipse icon which represents the design pattern we are using as an integrator. In the collaborations model, we capture how a collection of communicating objects collectively accomplish a specific task. We achieve composition by the virtue of how participants in the chosen design pattern communicate. The parts in each collaboration composite structure represent the roles that we factored out from each design pattern as an abstraction that ultimately need to be bound to objects from the integrated components as illustrated conceptually in Figure 2. The interface realizations in the diagram are necessary for statically typed languages.

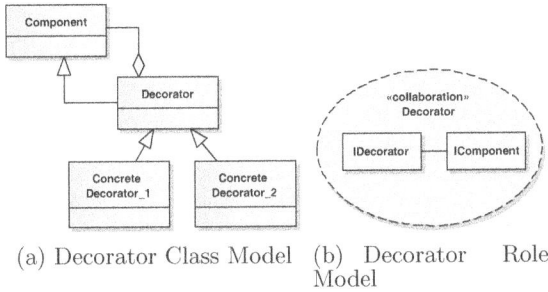

(a) Decorator Class Model   (b) Decorator Role Model

Figure 1: Illustration of the abstraction process from class model to collaboration or role model.

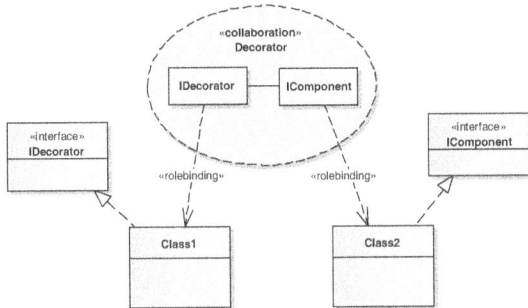

Figure 2: The Role Mapping Process to arbitrary class instances.

4. IMPLEMENTATION STRATEGY

We briefly discuss the DCI architecture and show how to use it to implement our compositional model. The DCI architecture was introduced by Reenskaug [12] and elaborated extensively by Coplien et al. [2].

In DCI, we start with the use case model as a driving force to implement an application. The architecture of an application comprises the *Data part*, this describes the makeup of the system, and the *Interaction part*, this describes system's functionality. What connects the two dynamically is a third element called *Context*. Each of these three parts has physical manifestation as components during implementation. For example, there are objects to represent the applications' domain objects; objects to represent system behavior or interactions between domain objects; and objects to represent use cases. The architecture is clean in that it makes a clear distinction between design activities corresponding to each of the artifacts, namely the *Data*, *Context*, and *Interaction*. It also makes traceability between what the user wants and where it is implemented in the code clear through the use case context construct in the architecture.

The domain objects behavioral specification are highly cohesive by making each object knows everything about its state and how to maintain it. Coplien et al. [2] refer to these domain objects as dumb objects that know nothing about other objects in the system. The interaction between domain objects, on the other hand, is a system functionality captured as system behavior and assigned to yet another type of objects conveniently named as Interaction objects. The DCI treats these objects as first class citizens. While the identification of domain object responsibilities, i.e. object behavior, is a technique known from early days of object

oriented analysis and design, check for example Wirfs-Brock et al. [17] and Coad et al. [1] who refer to this task as "Do it Myself" strategy, the interaction between objects having its own object designation is a novel concept the DCI reintroduced and made it a major activity in system architecture.

In DCI architecture, systems provide hints to system responsibilities with respect to use cases. In a typical use case scenario, system entities interact with each other through defined roles. These roles, ultimately, will be mapped onto domain objects instantiated at runtime. The DCI elaborates on this process–but all we care about at design time is identification of these object roles and what kind of behavior is expected of them. Therefore, object interactions are use case enactments at runtime. System functionality, i.e. functionality that does not belong to any one specific object type at design time, is injected onto objects at runtime. This is accomplished using a programming construct called *Traits* first introduced by Schärli et al. [8] and is defined as "a group of methods, i.e. behavior, that serves as a building block for classes and is a primitive unit of code reuse."

5. A SOFTWARE COMPOSITION PROCESS

After covering theory and practical implementation strategy, we present the following process by which we use design patterns in their role specification as new means to integrate components. The key concepts and core ideas we borrowed from DCI architecture and adapted them for our process are: role specifications, behavior injection through "traits mechanism", i.e. extending the functionality of any object, and introducing a collaboration context similar to use case context.

1. Design each component with all the required computational capability. We realize that interdependencies on services from other components are required; therefore, we assume that it may be necessary to introduce an architectural layer that provides the necessary abstraction level.

2. Determine the requirements needed for two components to interact. This step specifies the collaboration between the components.

3. Select one design pattern that satisfies this collaboration requirement.

4. Identify design pattern's participant roles.

5. Code up the roles as methodless interfaces; however, some roles may contain other roles as properties (basically, member or instance variables).

6. Identify the responsibility of each role and code it up as a Trait.

7. Select an object from each component that we need to map each role onto.

8. Map the design pattern participants' roles to these objects. The implementation is language dependent, but for statically typed languages *Interface*-like implementation is common.

9. Create a context class for the collaboration to take place identified in step 2.

6. CASE STUDY: RESORT SYSTEM

We will illustrate our approach using a case study that we intentionally made it simple to focus on key concepts presented in this paper. Due to space limitations, we will only show code fragments to illustrate the implementation using the C# language. The complete Visual Studio solution can be downloaded from GitHub [5]. This is an example of typical homework assignments we give our students structured in such a way to help them think of finding an appropriate design pattern to solve each feature requirement. This system supports these features:

1. A resort has employees, resort services, and administrative offices.

2. Resort services are either simple services (such as hotel accommodation, food, entertainment, or excursion services) or composite services/packages.

3. Service or room reservations are made by a reservation clerk at the request of a customer using a calendar of available services and rooms availability.

4. Room accommodations are identified as available, in use, waiting for cleaning or out of service pending repairs.

The application is decomposed into three distinct components depicted by class structure diagrams in Figure 3(a), 3(b), and 3(c) corresponding to our three requirements 1, 4, and 2 listed above, respectively. These three components are clearly concerned with system capabilities: resort organizational structure (Whole-part design pattern), room service availability (State design pattern), and services offered (Composite design pattern). The intent is to integrate these three components using our proposed approach based on design patterns. The integration requirement comes from requirement 3 which is a reservation task (step 1). Figure 4 illustrates how we intend to integrate the three components using the Adapter [3, p. 139] and State [3, p. 305] design patterns. We use the Adapter design pattern as an integrator because the Resort Services has an incompatible interface from the interface available in the Services part of the Resort component. By similar reasoning, we opted to use the State pattern as an integrator between the Resort Services and Room status components (steps 2 and 3). In Figure 4, we show two collaboration models corresponding to Adapter and State patterns that we will use as integrators in our case study. We will show how to code up these structures using C# language. We only describe integrating two components using the Adapter pattern; however, the process is exactly similar to integrating the other components using the State pattern (steps 4). The Adapter design pattern has two participants. In the code, these two participants have roles implemented as methodless interfaces (step 5):

```
public interface IAdapter {}
public interface IAdaptee{}
```

In the code, two objects, Services object from the Resort component and Resort Services object from the Resort Services component, will implement IAdapter and IAdaptee interfaces, i.e. roles, respectively (steps 7 and 8) and in code it looks like this:

```
public class Services : IAdapter {...}
public class Resort_Services : IAdaptee {...}
```

Of course, there is nothing to implement since these are methodless interfaces. Based on the DCI architecture strategy, they serve as identifiers for objects that will take those roles. The Adapter design pattern, basically, converts one method call into another. The ReserveResource method will be called by a Request method that we will be injecting into IAdapter type object by the Trait [8] mechanism. In C# language, it is done through extension method [7]. Extension methods enable you to "add" methods to existing types without creating a new derived type, recompiling, or otherwise modifying the original type. Extension methods are a special kind of static method, but they are called as if they were instance methods on the extended type. This is what we did in the RequestTrait class (step 6).

```
public static class RequestTrait {
    public static bool Request(this IAdapter adapter,
        IAdaptee adaptee,
        RequestType request) {...}
... }
```

The last piece of the puzzle to make all this work, is the integration. The DCI architecture creates a 'context' class for each use case; similarly in our case, we create a context that corresponds to the 'collaboration' that acts as integrator. The RequestResourceContext class is the place for this to happen (step 9).

```
public class RequestResourceContext{...}
```

As you can see, the 'integration' which is based on the 'collaboration' model is a construct that is quite traceable in the code. The integration happens when we instantiate an object of type 'RequestResourceContext' after setting up its required parts (through its constructor) and calling its 'Doit' method in the Main method of the ResortSystemCaseStudy class.

```
// demonstrate Adapter pattern integration
Services services = new Services();
Simple_Services ra = new RoomAccommodation() {...};
RequestResourceContext integration = new
    RequestResourceContext(services, ra,
    RequestType.RoomReservation);
bool rc = integration.Doit();
```

Using the State pattern adds a slight complication because the IContext requires IState property (instance variable). However, this property is of the type getter and setter whose code is automatically generated by most modern interactive development environments.

7. CONCLUSION AND FUTURE WORK

We have introduced a conceptual framework and an implementation model for software composition using design patterns. We have also created a process that should guide practitioners and students, learning how to use design patterns, in assembling individual components created by different teams. That is our contribution.

The key concepts to take away are these. First, design patterns' key principal properties are used as abstraction modeling constructs through collaboration. These, then become

(a) Resort System Component (Whole-part design pattern)

(b) Room Status Component (State design pattern)

(c) Resort Services Component (Composite design pattern)

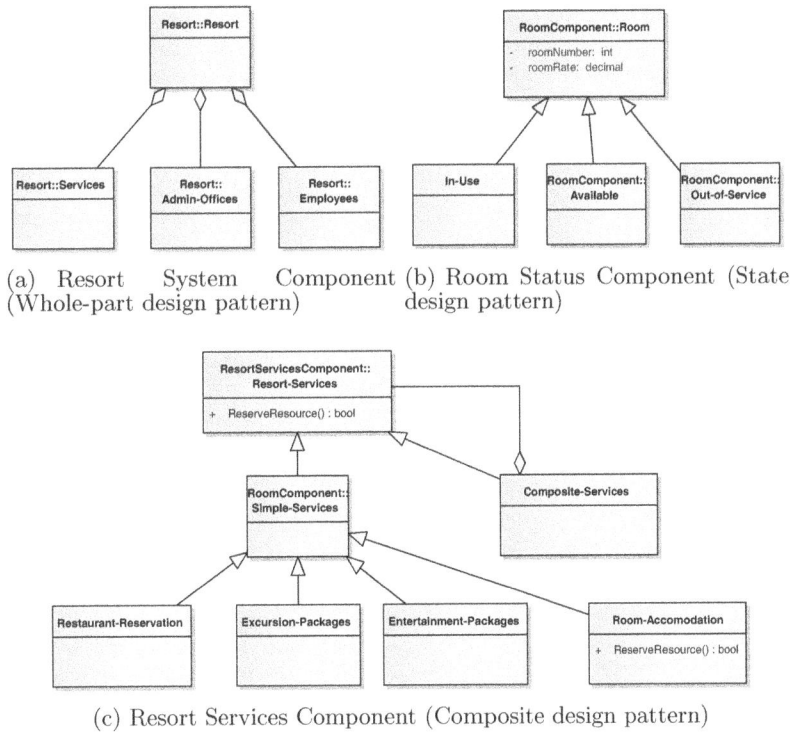

Figure 3: Model structure of the three individual components of the Resort System Sample Application.

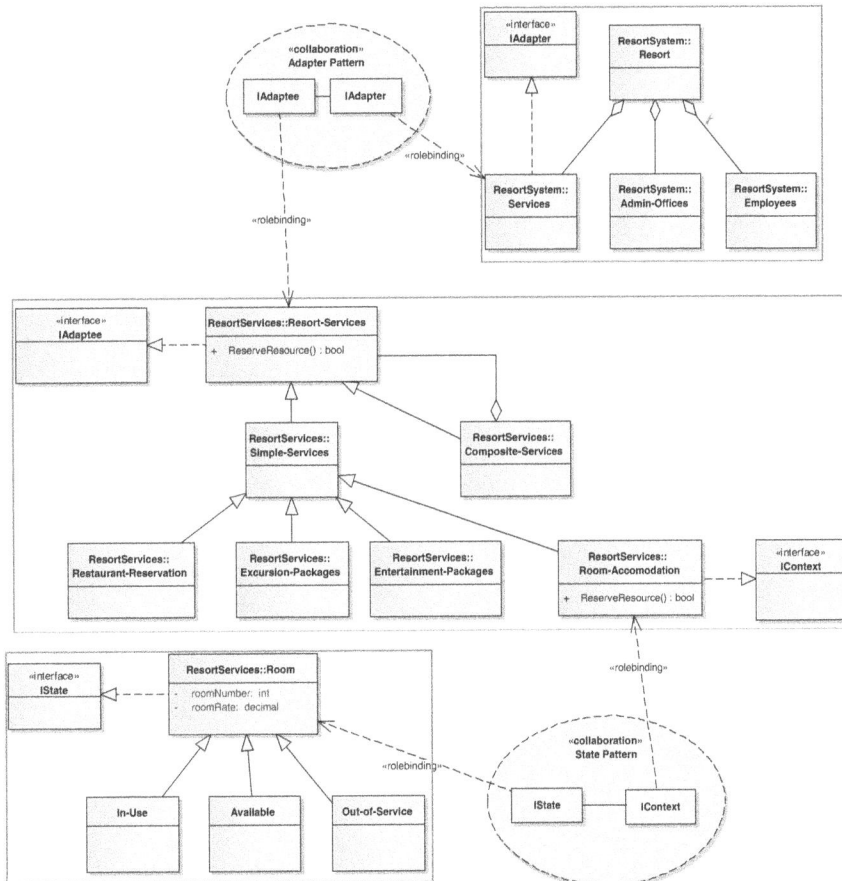

Figure 4: Resort System consisting of three components integrated using Design Patterns.

traceable artifacts through 'context' classes in the code. Second, the proposed approach allows for partial and evolutionary design. Recall, that the collaboration model captures all the integration requirements by the virtue of the role model it encapsulates. Third, role to object mapping is really binding mechanism that could be utilized effectively by this duality principle: either domain objects discovery or object roles allocation can be deferred. In other words, you can begin design with domain objects if you have settled on all of them, or you can begin design with roles required behavior and then map or bind them to objects at a later time. The latter gives you the most flexibility. Last, we provide a software composition process using design patterns anyone can learn and follow methodically.

At a minimum, two areas warrant further research. First, there is an opportunity to automate some of the implementation tasks with proper code generators, e.g. metaprogramming techniques available in some development frameworks like .NET [6]. Second, since the approach allows to defer the integration until a later stage in the development cycle, it gives an opportunity for architects or designers to identify a *variation point*, i.e. integration strategy, with *variants* [10], e.g. Adapter or Proxy.

Finally, to evaluate this proposed compositional model against other ad-hoc approaches, we intend to conduct a design experiment that is formal, rigorous, and controlled based on techniques from experiments in software engineering [18]. This effort is part of future work.

8. REFERENCES

[1] Coad, P., D. North, and M. Mayfield. *Object Models: Strategies, Patterns, and Applications*. Yourdon Press, Upper Saddle River, 1997.

[2] Coplien, J., and Gertrud Bjørnvig. *Lean Architecture: for Agile Software Development*. Wiley, West Sussex, UK, 1st edition, Aug 2010.

[3] Gamma, E., R. Helm, R. Johnson and J. Vlissides. *Design Patterns*. Addison Wesley, Reading, MA, 1995.

[4] Hasso, S. *A Uniform Approach to Software Patterns Classification and Software Composition*. Ph.D. Thesis, Illinois Institute of Technology, May 2007.

[5] Hasso, S. "Design Patterns As Connectors Source Code on GitHub". *https://github.com/shasso/cdp.git*, 2013. Accessed May 2013.

[6] Hazzard, K. and Bock, J. *Metaprogramming in .NET*. Manning Publications Co., Shelter Island, NY, 2013.

[7] Microsoft Corp. C# Programming Guide: Extension Methods. *http://msdn.microsoft.com/en-us/library/vstudio/bb383977.aspx*, 2012. Accessed Dec 2012.

[8] Nathanael Schärli, Stèphane Ducasse, Oscar Nierstrasz, and Andrew P. Black. Traits: Composable units of behaviour. In *Proceedings of European Conference on Object-Oriented Programming (ECOOP'03)*, volume 2743, pages 248Ŭ–274. LNCS, Springer Verlag, Jul 2003.

[9] OMG. *OMG Unified Modeling Language (OMG UML), Superstructure*. Object Management Group, 2.4.1 edition, Aug 2011.

[10] Phol, K., Böckle, G., and van der Linden, F. *Software Product Line Engineering: Foundations, Principles, and Techniques*. Springer, Heidelberg, Germany, 2010.

[11] Reenskaug, T. *Working with Objects: The OOram Software Engineering Method*. Manning Publications, 1996.

[12] Reenskaug, T., and James O. Coplien. The DCI Architecture: A New Vision of Object-Oriented Programming. *http://www.artima.com/articles/dci_visionP.html*, March 2009. Accessed Mar 2011.

[13] Riehle, D. "Describing and Composing Patterns Using Role Diagrams". In *Proceedings of the 1996 Ubilab Conference*, Zurich, 1996.

[14] Shaw, M. and Garlan, D. *Software Architecture: Perspective on an Emerging Discipline*. Pretice Hall, Upper Saddle River, New Jersey, 1996.

[15] T. Taibi. Formalizing Design Patterns Composition. *The IEE-Proceeding Software*, 153(3):127–136, 2006.

[16] Vlissides, J. *Pattern Hatching: Design Patterns Applied*. Software Patterns. Addison Wesley, Reading, Massachusetts, 1998.

[17] Wirfs-Brock, R., and A. McKean. *Object Design: Roles, Responsibilities, and Collaborations*. Addison-Wesley, Boston, MA, 2003.

[18] Wohlin, C., P. Runeson, M. Höst, M. C. Ohlsson, B. Regnell, and A. Wesslén. *Experimentation in Software Engineering: An Introduction*. The Kluwer International Series in Software Enginerring. Kluwer Academic Publishers, Boston, USA, 2000.

[19] Yacoub, S. M., and H. H. Ammar. "Pattern-Oriented Analysis and Design (POAD): A Structural Composition Approach to Glue Design Patterns". In *34th International Conference on Technology of Object-Oriented Languages and Systems*. *TOOLS 34*, pages 273–282. IEEE, 2000.

Improving Service Continuity:
IT Disaster Prevention and Mitigation for Data Centers

Louis Turnbull   Henry Ochieng   Chris Kadlec   Jordan Shropshire

Georgia Southern University
Dept. of Information Technology
P.O. Box 8150
Statesboro, GA 30460
(912)478-4848

louisturnbull@gmail.com   ho00027@georgiasouthern.edu   cakadlec@gmail.com   jshropshire@georgiasouthern.edu

ABSTRACT

Data centers provide highly-scalable and reliable computing for enterprise services such as web hosting, email, applications, and file storage. Because they integrate a range of different systems, data center administration is a complex process. Managing the risk of IT disaster is especially difficult. Layers of interrelated infrastructure multiply the effect of system malfunctions. Seemingly-small problems can turn into major disasters and take entire data centers offline. To cope with the myriad risks, this research develops a matrix of IT disaster prevention and mitigation techniques for data centers. The matrix is organized along two dimensions: attributes of data center infrastructure and elements of the IT disaster recovery process. It includes 134 specific techniques which were clustered into 49 cells within the matrix. An expert panel assessed the validity of the matrix and ranked the techniques within each cell. The result is a comprehensive tool for improving the resilience of data centers.

Categories and Subject Descriptors

D.4.5 [**Reliability**]: Backup procedures, Fault-tolerance, Verification.

Keywords

Data centers, IT disaster recovery, mitigation, infrastructure.

1. INTRODUCTION

Data centers are the building blocks of cloud computing systems. They incorporate commodity servers, storage arrays, and high-throughput networks into physical structures to support enterprise computing. In the aggregate, they provide a highly-scalable platform for providing information services such as email, applications, and document storage. Because they integrate a range of different systems, data centers require careful

management. Relatively small errors in configuration, minor security flaws, and isolated hardware failures have a significant effect on the stability of information services. They may even bring entire data centers offline. For instance, contractors installing a sprinkler system could accidently cut through major fiber line. Cooling systems, when facing extreme temperature swings, can overcompensate and freeze over. In such cases, they must be shut down in order to thaw. Emergency utility repairs can lead to power surges and trip power circuits or create brownouts. Unknowing employees may introduce worms and viruses into trusted zones by using infected thumb drives. Distributed denial-of-service attacks overwhelm networks and servers, blocking legitimate users from accessing services. Because relatively minor events can cause major catastrophes, IT disaster recovery planning is essential. Although it is not possible to predict every possible disaster scenario, data centers should account for a wide range of contingencies.

To assist in the planning process, a matrix of IT disaster recovery techniques was developed. It contains a comprehensive listing of disaster prevention and mitigation techniques specifically for data centers. The matrix is organized along two axes: data center infrastructure attributes and elements of the IT disaster recovery process. Prior research indicated that the infrastructure attributes of the data center should be organized into the following seven attributes: service, application, operating system, computer hardware, networking, utilities, and the physical structure layer. The IT disaster recovery and mitigation is structured into seven elements: IT disaster identification and notification, preparing organizational members, IT services analysis, recovery process, backup procedures, offsite storage, and maintenance procedures.

To populate the matrix, a team of graduate researchers performed an extensive review of over 150 articles. Using the content analysis method, 134 disaster prevention and mitigation techniques were extracted. The techniques were clustered into the most appropriate cells inside the matrix. The resulting framework was refined over multiple iterations. To assess content validity, the matrix was reviewed by a panel of IT researchers who specialize in IT data center management. The panel assessed the completeness of the matrix and ranked the techniques within each cell. The results can be used to improve IT disaster preparedness. This manuscript is organized as follows: first background information on data centers and IT disaster recovery is presented. Next, the research methodology is described and the resulting matrix is introduced, followed by the results, implications and conclusions.

2. BACKGROUND

2.1 Data Centers
As cloud computing increases, so does our dependence on data centers for information service provisioning. Data centers are facilities that house high-performance computers, storage servers, computer servers, networking or other information technology (IT) equipment. They are the building blocks for cloud computing systems. They perform essential duties such as hosting, meta-scale processing, and storage. These data centers host servers and applications that clients use to operate their business [1]. Data centers either support internal clients or act as infrastructure providers (i.e. Google, Microsoft, and Amazon) for external clients. To increase economies of scale and ensure uptime, infrastructure as a service (IaaS) providers are rapidly building geographically-distributed cloud data centers. They support a variety of cloud-based services such as email, web servers, storage, search and instant messaging [2].

2.2 IT Disaster Recovery
Due to its importance in averting disasters and ensuring the continuity of organizations, the concept of IT disaster recovery planning is acquiring an increased amount of attention from IT practitioners and business managers [3]. A disaster recovery plan is a blueprint for recovering from such events and is intended to increase chances of survival and reducing the risk of loss [4]. The purpose of an IT disaster recovery plan is not to simplify IT services that eases restoration, but devise alternative ways of restoring IT services so that service can be brought back online and be sustainable following disaster. IT disaster recovery can be defined as set of actions that an organization follows to improve its ability to resume its IT services after a disaster.

3. CONCEPTUAL DEVELOPMENT
This research develops a matrix of strategies for helping data centers cope with the risk of IT disasters. A comprehensive listing of specific tools and techniques was drawn from contemporary articles from industry and academia. The resulting elicitation was organized along two dimensions – components of data centers (See table 1) and elements of the disaster recovery process (See table 2). For instance, a specific technique might be found to impact one component of a data center, and assist in one step in the IT disaster recovery process. These dimensions were based on constructs which were broken into categories in previous studies. By organizing along these dimensions, it is possible for IT professionals to associate a specific cell with a weakness and locate the best solution. Because the cells are rank-ordered by a team of respected data center professionals, it is easier to identify the best solution out of multiple options.

4. METHODS
Matrix development followed a structured approach in order to increase rigor and build validity. First, a team of graduate student researchers from engineering and information technology performed a comprehensive search of articles relating to disaster recovery for data centers. Using coordinated search terms, over 200 articles were extracted from academic databases and industry outlets. Of these, 114 articles were found to be relevant enough to

Table 1. IT Disaster Recovery Planning

Element	Description
IT Disaster Identification and Notification	IT disaster identification and notification is an element that focuses on processes that have been founded towards the recognition of IT disasters, communication through times of crisis, and advising designated team members and stakeholders. An array of potential disaster scenarios that may arise include both manmade and natural disasters.
Preparing Organizational Members	Preparation of organizational members involves developing a team dedicated towards IT disaster recovery and mitigation, conferring and strategizing with noteworthy non-members, and constructing a priority-based decision structure catered towards the protection of critical assets.
IT Services Analysis	The IT services analysis element is directed towards classifying IT services along with assigning a priority for reactivation, as well as detecting probable threats. IT services should be organized within a scope of reason as to what services are crucial to maintain business continuity and how to identify and neutralize potential risks that will hinder it.
Recovery Process	The recovery process pertains to any sort of procedure that will aid in restoring the data center to a suitable and operable state. Recovery involves establishing tactics with the goal of minimizing downtime and reinstating business continuity in an expedient manner.
Backup Procedures	Backup procedures are adequately designed preparations or blueprints utilized to provide a viable replication of a data center constituent.
Offsite Storage	The element of offsite storage relates the separation and securement of data or resources from the data center facility. This spans from utilizing cloud infrastructure, to consuming warehouse space, relocating resources, and even to instituting an alternative data center.
Maintenance	Maintenance with regards to the data center incorporates testing and sustaining the functionality of resources, documenting the configuration of hardware and software, assessing the disaster recovery plan, and synchronizing the recovery plan with business continuity.

include in the analysis. These articles were used in a content analysis. The purpose of this analysis was to identify and code IT disaster recovery technique and tools. A previously established coding scheme was used for classifying points [3]. It was developed specifically for IT disaster recovery planning involving infrastructure. Each article was reviewed and useful techniques were coded according to two factors: (1) which data center infrastructure layer they impacted and (2) which part of IT disaster recovery they supported. To provide overlap, each articlewas reviewed by at least two researchers. For cases in which there was disagreement over coding, a third researcher broke the tie. Once all the coded units were collected, they were organized into the matrix. The matrix itself was then refined over three

Table 2. Data Center Layers

Attribute	Description
Physical Structure	The physical structure layer for a data center consists of a building or a structure within the same geographic plane. It will also include racks for the hardware, track systems for cables, wiring, building access control systems, and power management systems.
Utilities	The utilities layer consists of a multitude of data center resource systems. These systems include heating, ventilation, air conditioning, power distribution, water supply, fuel reservoirs, waste disposal, fire suppression systems (FM-200), and communications (telecom and internet service provision). The utilities layer also includes standby systems such as power generators, reserve batteries, uninterruptable power supplies, portable chillers, and alternative energy sources.
Networking	The networking layer pertains to all hardware and software that is utilized in a fully functional network. This layer consists of cabling, routers, switches, wireless connection points, virtual and physical firewalls, security protocols, administration, data management, and connectivity access.
Computer Hardware	The computer hardware layer incorporates server systems, hypervisors, storage devices (hard disks, USB drives, compact disks, data tapes), workstations, personal computing components (memory modules, central processing units, and mother boards), as well as sensor systems.
Operating System	The operating system layer consists of any operating system (OS) that functions on any piece of equipment. This would incorporate a server system OS, workstation OS, smart phone OS, and especially virtualization OS (for the hypervisor and virtual machines).
Application	The application layer contains software, data, algorithms, configurable settings, downloadable updates, digital documents, executable files, scripts, hardware firmware, and anything else that involves consolidated hosting.
Service	The service layer is a compilation of examination and load stabilizing tools for data centers to deliver services. This may also include pertinent services such as email, web hosting, third party services for data backup and recovery, and provisioning services in virtualization (hardware, software, and infrastructure-as-a-service).

iterations. For each iteration, the researchers sought to identify redundancies, under-represented topics, and content which was not an integral part of disaster recovery. After three rounds of revision, the result was a matrix consisting of 49 cells and 134 recommendations for coping with the risk of IT disaster. This matrix was then distributed to an expert panel comprised of 5 IT professionals with expertise in disaster recovery and/or data center management. The panel was given two tasks: assess the completeness of the matrix and rank-order the contents in each cell. Following two rounds of feedback and revision, the panel confirmed the content validity of the matrix and agreed to the ranking of disaster recovery techniques within each cell.

5. RESULTS

A collection of 134 notable recommendations were derived from the research. The results were organized into a two dimensional matrix. The row header is formed as the dimensional elements of IT disaster recovery, Table 1. The column header is formed as the attribute layers of the data center, Table 2. When brought together, an easily decipherable matrix helps IT professionals pinpoint to the appropriate disaster mitigation and recovery reference as needed. A blank matrix template can be used as a starting point for data center managers to evaluate their own disaster recovery solutions and build upon areas of identified weakness. This also aids in laying the foundation for a solid plan to present for funding resources in protecting the data center. The following matrix is an organized subsystem of the extracted recommendations. Each subsystem forms an order of priority starting with the physical structure attribute through to the service attribute. This is based on the fact that if there is the elimination of a prior attribute, the proceeding attributes will cease to exist. Incorporated amongst the attribute subsections are comprised of a mixture of the recommendations that are characterized towards the elements of IT disaster recovery. In order to understand how the disaster mitigation and recovery process is achieved, it is necessary to comprehend the criterion of the dimensional elements of recovery first. Afterwards the mitigation and recovery techniques can then be processed and applied as needed.

The data center has been broken down into logical sections, according to the developed matrix, and addressed with disaster mitigation and recovery. A summary of the collected techniques is presented as such.

5.1 Physical Structure

First, there is the physical structure of the data center which houses and protects the core of the business. Therefore, the protection and maintenance of the structure is important. Initiate this by monitoring local meteorological forecasts and news media regularly for potential threats (weather, terrorism, etc.). Assign threat levels to disaster scenarios and create an occupancy evacuation plan. Designate specific emergency action responsibilities to selected members of the organization. Train all of the staff regularly as preparation for potential disasters. The training should take place in the form of conducting building exit strategies, ensuring that the physical structure is secure from further damage, containment of disasters, and establishing emergency protocols. Lastly, be restrictive with building access. Monitor all entry and exit points of the structure. The ultimate protection is having alternate facilities themselves.

5.2 Utilities

Utilities are an essential part of every data center and allow the operability of resources to exist. To start, secure the HVAC system to recirculate air to avoid the intake and dispersion of particulate matter. Monitor the utilities by installing sensors to alert staff of humidity levels, unsafe temperatures, and unauthorized access. Establish teams to recover utilities assuring there are personnel overlaps and redundancies. Update and post utility provider contact information (of all utilities) and prepare staff members on how to report a utility failure or obtain status updates on repairs. Since most key utilities cannot be moved, such as water lines and power lines, establish alternate routes for utilities to service the data center. Maintain adequate fuel supplies for generators and refill fire suppression systems. Review and test backup procedures at the utilities layer on a regular basis.

5.3 Networking

Networking inside the data center consists of a line of interconnectivity between critical hardware components. In order to protect the network assets, identify all networking systems running in the data center and establish priorities of reactivation. Install application level firewalls along with other intrusion prevention systems. This will help identify initial threats within the networking attribute. Also, monitor the behavior of users and hosts by observing for abnormalities. Organize and establish teams to recover networking systems by assuring there are personnel overlaps and redundancies. Once teams have been arranged, backup network configurations and network maps. Consider establishing procedures to recover networking or move the networking to alternative locations. Secure additional hardware equipment (servers, routers, switches) and software licenses to enable the continuity of the data center network operations. Consider virtualization or cloud computing as a method of offsite networking. Finally, review and test backup procedures at the networking layer on a regular basis.

5.4 Computer Hardware

Start by analyzing all of the computer hardware that is present in the data center and address service contracts with vendors regarding the equipment for replacement and repair issues. Provide at least one set of comparable computer hardware to utilize as a replacement in the event of a failure. This could be done through purchasing hot spares or keeping recently retired equipment. Keep backups of physical equipment along with all other backups for the computer hardware at an offsite location. Consider using cloud services as a tool for backing up computer hardware files and configurations. Ensure the cloud system has the sufficient capacity to support the workload of the enterprise.

5.5 Operating System

A data center will house a variety of operating systems on a multitude of computing hardware. Software firewalls should be installed to prevent attacks from taking place against all of the operating systems. Identify all operating systems running in the data center and establish priorities of reactivation, along with the potential risk factors that may arise. Create procedures to recover the array of operating systems within the data center. Assemble a select set of team members to execute and refine the recovery procedures. This will expedite in the recovery of the operating systems and help minimize downtime. Include the selection of alternative environments for operating systems to be executed (either physical or virtual) in the event of a disaster. Consider using virtualization technology since OS templates can be imaged within virtual machines for quick deployment. The virtual machines can even undergo live migration across the infrastructure platforms.

5.6 Application

The application attribute deals with data, executable files, and pertinent configuration files. In order to protect against disaster,start with installing application level firewalls to prevent attacks on applications. Identify all of the applications running in the data center. Establish procedures to recover applications, and include the relocation of the applications to an alternative platform for execution. Institute training events and educate the employees on the appropriate backup procedures for the applications. Ascertain a priority of how items should be recovered in sequence (proprietary software, sensitive or classified documents, expensive or meaningful scientific data). Develop backup copies of configurations at the application attribute and store them in a safe location.

5.7 Service

In order to help mitigate disaster within the service attribute, a disaster response team should be assembled and an appropriate disaster plan must be created. The plan needs to include identifying all of the services offered and establish priorities of reactivation. Establish procedures to recover services or shift services to alternative locations. Devote key staff members to be on call to assist in disaster recovery efforts. Select alternative locations and sources of services to be utilized in the event of a disaster. Training events should be developed and geared towards the inclusion of all of the layers for the data center. Reinforce interface protocols at all levels during training exercises. Review and test backup procedures at the services layer on a regular basis. Finally, establish service level agreements (SLA) for the services provided and monitor these services.

6. Conclusions

Safeguarding data centers is no simple task. Inter-reliant systems and the sheer quantity of hardware and software make administration a complex process. Under such conditions, small problems very quickly escalate into major crises. If affected information services are to be restored, then planning is essential. To assist in this process, this research developed a matrix of techniques for preventing and mitigating IT disasters. The matrix was framed along two dimensions – components of data center and elements of IT disaster recovery. The attributes that compile the matrix are structured in order of reliance on each prior element. This starts with the physical attribute representing the most critical aspect of the data center through to the service layer which would not exist without the prior attributes having formed the foundation. Many specific techniques were identified and organized into the framework. The elements in each cell were ranked by a group IT professionals with expertise in data center management in order to prioritize acquisitions. The matrix can be used as a guide to ensure the adequacy of in-place procedures and guide further development. It is expected that the matrix will be refined in future research.

7. REFERENCES

[1] Stryer, P., *Understanding Data Centers and Cloud Computing.* Global Knowledge Instructor, 2010.

[2] Benson, T., A. Akella, and D.A. Maltz. *Network traffic characteristics of data centers in the wild.* in *Proceedings of the 10th ACM SIGCOMM conference on Internet measurement.* 2010. ACM.

[3] Shropshire, J. and C. Kadlec, *Developing the IT Disaster Recovery Planning Construct.* Journal of Information Technology Management, 2009. **20**(4): p. 37.

[4] Hiatt, C.J., *A primer for disaster recovery planning in an IT environment* 2000: Igi Global.

Administrative Evaluation of Intrusion Detection System

Xinli Wang
School of Technology
Michigan Tech University
Houghton, MI 49931, USA
xinlwang@mtu.edu

Alex Kordas
School of Technology
Michigan Tech University
Houghton, MI 49931, USA
aekordas@mtu.edu

Lihui Hu
Dept. of Computer Science
Michigan Tech University
Houghton, MI 49931, USA
lhu@mtu.edu

Matt Gaedke
School of Technology
Michigan Tech University
Houghton, MI 49931, USA
mdgaedke@mtu.edu

Derrick Smith
School of Technology
Michigan Tech University
Houghton, MI 49931, USA
dedsmith@mtu.edu

ABSTRACT

Due to the complexity of intrusion detection systems and their application in security architectures, there is a need to objectively assess intrusion detection systems in the perspective of system and network administration in order to select a right product which is a good fit to a specific design. In this research, we have developed a methodology to evaluate intrusion detection systems in a simulated environment. The environment is built with a combination of physical and virtual machines. Network traffic is simulated with baseline activities, which is characterized with web browsing and normal user activities, benchmark and actual intrusion attacks. Different tools are employed to measure CPU load, memory need, bandwidth constraint and computer memory input/output. Results show considerable differences among tested intrusion detection systems.

Categories and Subject Descriptors

H.3.4 [**Information Systems**]: Systems and Software—*Performance evaluation*; H.4.m [**Information Systems Applications**]: *Miscellaneous*

General Terms

Experimentation

Keywords

Intrusion Detection System, System Administration, Evaluation, Comparison

1. INTRODUCTION

One problem we must face in the management of information technology (IT) systems is to objectively evaluate existing products in the perspective of system and network administration. For example, there is a great number of intrusion detection systems (IDSs) in both commercial and open source domains [41, 6, 11, 26, 20, 31]. Which one could be a good fit to a specific design of a security management system? Many systems have a similar performance in terms of effectiveness [22, 23]. However, in the practice of IT management, in addition to considering the effectiveness of a product, we need to know its requirements for computing resources, storage space and network bandwidth as well as other factors related to IT management.

Most existing works on IDS evaluation focus on the effectiveness of an IDS [22, 23, 29, 10, 2]. Few researchers mention other aspects of performance such as ease of use and resource requirements [15, 29]. In addition, we can conclude from the existing work on IDS evaluation that the results vary considerably with systems tested, data sets used, environments the systems run in and metrics employed for comparison. Therefore, there is a need to develop an approach to impartially assessing an IDS for the purpose of IT management, which is not deemed to be a trivial task [13, 5, 29]. In addition, we argue that the results of this type of evaluation will also help developers to consider the concerns in IT practice when they design and develop their IDSs.

In this research, we have developed a methodology for evaluating existing IDSs in a simulated environment. We first set up a network with a combination of physical and virtual computers to simulate a small to middle-sized business. Three IDSs were installed and configured on physical machines with identical hardware components. Baseline network traffic, benchmark and intrusion attacks were injected to the network targeted to different machines. Various tools were used to collect data for analysis. Results show significant differences among tested IDSs in terms of CPU usage, memory requirement and bandwidth constraint.

The rest of this paper is organized as follows: Related work is briefly reviewed in Section 2. Then we describe our methodology in Section 3. Section 4 presents our results. Finally, we conclude our work in Section 5.

2. RELATED WORK

Although similar concept and idea of intrusion detection have been there for several decades, the actual research on intrusion detection methods and the development of IDS started with the seminal works by Anderson [4] and Denning [12]. Based on the data used by an IDS, an IDS can be categorized either into a host-based or a network-based system. A host-based IDS analyzes local log data mainly, while a network-based IDS analyzes the data captured from network traffic. Early works are mainly host-based IDSs [24, 25, 32, 7]. There are essentially two approaches to detecting intrusions. One is a misuse or signature-based method and the other is anomaly detection. The signature-based method is also known as knowledge-based method, where known attacks are used to construct rules (signatures of known attacks) and the system processes data by searching for known signatures. Snort [43] and Bro [37] are typical signature-based IDSs. The anomaly detection employs various techniques such as statistical analysis, finite state automaton, data mining algorithms and so forth to simulate "normal" behaviors. Then, given a new packet or a set of new user activities, deviations from the normal behavior are computed. An alert will be generated when the deviation exceeds a predefined threshold. Anomaly detection methods have been the focus of the majority of recent research [47, 36, 17, 26, 20, 21]. The major advantage of an anomaly detector is its capability to catch novel attacks.

A systematic evaluation of IDSs has started with a project sponsored by DARPA (Defense Advanced Research Projects Agency) [22, 23]. Based on previously developed methods [40, 39], simulated data sets are used in the evaluation. Receiver operating characteristic (ROC) curves [14] are employed for comparison between tested IDSs. This evaluation is aimed at providing the developers with insights for them to improve their systems. Although this methodology has drawbacks [28], the simulation data sets and ROC technique have been used by many following researchers for comparison and evaluation of the effectiveness of an IDS [46, 47, 48]. Stolfo et al. [44] propose an alternative method of evaluation that is based on cost metrics. They argue that evaluations based on ROC analysis are often misleading and the use of cost metrics is able to overcome some of the problems of ROC analysis. However, Gaffney and Ulvila demonstrate that ROC analysis is very valuable when it is integrated with decision analysis techniques [16]. Since the effectiveness of an IDS depends on cost metrics and the hostility of an operating environment, integration of ROC analysis and cost metrics with decision analysis techniques will be able to identify an optimal operation point of an IDS running in a specific environment. Based on information theory, Gu et al. propose a new metric to measure the effectiveness of an IDS [18]. This new metric is known as *intrusion detection capability* which is defined as the ratio of the mutual information between IDS input and output to the entropy of the input data.

While most existing works on IDS evaluation are to measure the effectiveness of an IDS, Mell et al. have outlined the issues in IDS evaluation [29]. Fink et al. propose a metrics-based approach to evaluating IDSs for distributed real-time systems [15]. Their metrics can be classified into three categories. Logistical metrics measure the expense, maintainability and manageability of an IDS. Architectural metrics describe how well the intended scope and architecture of an IDS match with deployment architecture. Performance metrics determine the ability of an IDS to fit within the performance constraints of monitored systems. They also mention scoring methods to score and weight each met-

ric. However, the actual scores and weights are not given in their publication. An impersonal scoring method remains open in their work. To avoid the bias induced by simulation data and overcome the lack of testing data, IDS evaluation can be automatically done using the data collected on-site [27]. More recently, comparisons have been conducted between Snort [43] and Suricata [45] to study the effects of multi-threaded implementation of the Suricata system and the performance of running Snort on a multi-core system [10, 2]. Different conclusions are obtained from two tests that are conducted in different environments.

3. METHODOLOGY

Three IDSs from the open source domain were chosen for comparison. A physical network was set up to simulate a real-world computing environment of a small or middle-sized business. Common network intrusions along with baseline and benchmark network traffic were injected into the simulated network. Performance measurements were taken with appropriate tools for comparison.

3.1 Overview of the Chosen IDSs

For this research, we intended to study different types of IDSs, including host-based and network-based intrusion detection systems with signature-based and anomaly detection methods. Snort [43], Ourmon [35] and Samhain [42] were chosen for this purpose.

Snort is a free and open source software system for network intrusion detection and prevention created by Martin Roesch in 1998 [41, 43]. Although anomaly techniques can be integrated, it is essentially a signature-based network intrusion detector [3]. The Boyer-Moore fast string searching algorithm is implemented [8] in the Snort system for pattern search. Snort has been downloaded more than four million times so far and currently has more than 400,000 registered users, which makes it the most widely deployed intrusion detection and prevention system in the world.

Ourmon is a network monitoring and anomaly intrusion detection system [35]. Statistical rules are created to simulate normal network behaviors. This software package is written in Perl, which makes it highly portable between various Linux distributions. Ourmon operates by monitoring network traffic and logging captured data while simultaneously producing graphical printouts of statistics and hosting them on a local web server. This gives administrators the ability to view network activities from a broad aspect which allows an individual to recognize unusual network activities. Due to the fact that the Ourmon system does not utilize predefined rule sets, defining anomalous activities is not trivial. A network administrator must first define a baseline of normal activity. Once the baseline is defined, the administrator can use it as a reference for detecting anomalies occurring on the network and then classify that activity as malicious or normal.

Samhain is a host-based intrusion detection system and file integrity checker with stable releases archived back to as far as 2001 [42]. It consists of an agent on a host that identifies intrusions by checking system state through analyzing system calls, application logs and file system modifications. Samhain is comprised of several components: an integrity checker, a log server, a back-end relational database, and optionally a deployment system and web console. The database can be either Oracle, MySql, or PostgreSQL. The integrity checker functions by the use of extensible modules that can be compiled at the administrator's discretion. By default, it has modules to monitor and analyze log files, registry check on Windows systems and kernel integrity on Linux/BSD, check of SUID/SGID files for rogue SUIDs, optional monitoring of open ports, process monitoring and check of mounted file-systems. With all its built in functionality, Samhain is a solid competitor even against commercial IDS products.

3.2 Network and Hardware Specifications

The network design for this research is depicted in Figure 1. Most of the equipment was chosen from what we had when the experiment was conducted. A switch of Brocade Fastlron Edge GS 648P-POE was used to connect the computers. A Cisco 2651 router was used to connect our local area network (LAN) to the Internet. Two desktop machines were configured to simulate attackers. One ran Backtrack4 and the other ran Windows XP. All of the attacks were initiated from these two computers. To simulate a real-world network, we installed two virtual servers with VirtualBox [34] (Win08Server01 and Win08Server02). Each of them held six Windows XP workstations, which represents 12 workstations in total on the LAN.

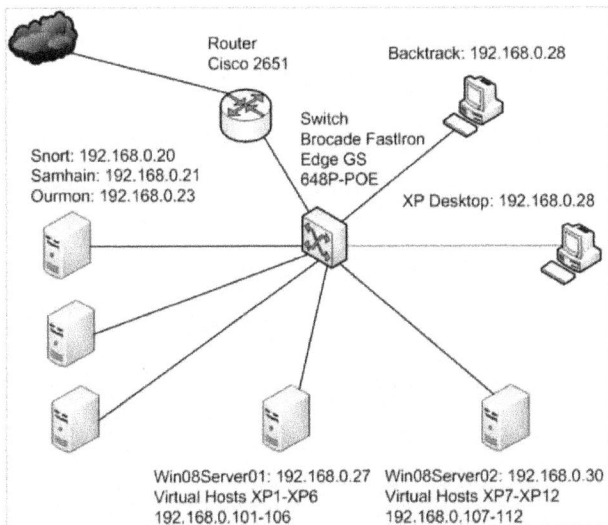

Figure 1: Network diagram

The three IDSs described in the previous subsection were installed on three Fedora 14 systems (shown on the left in Figure 1). For the purpose of comparison, these three machines were built with identical hardware components (Table 1). An exception was that the hard disk on the machine for Ourmon was larger than others. This difference would not affect the comparison results because all hard disks had enough space and they had the same speed.

3.3 Measurements and Experiments

In order to evaluate resource needs for operating an IDS on a computer, memory usage, network traffic and CPU load were measured while the IDSs were in operation. Memory usage represents the amount of system random access memory (RAM) used by the IDS while in operation. Network traffic indicates the impact of an IDS in operation on net-

Table 1: Hardware specifications for IDS machines

Ourmon	**Proc:** AMD Dual Core 5400B 2.8 GHz
	Memory: 1.8 GB RAM
	Hard Disk: 430 GB HDD
	Operating System: Fedora 14
Samhain	**Proc:** AMD Dual Core 5400B 2.8 GHz
	Memory: 1.8 GB RAM
	Hard Disk: 212 GB HDD
	Operating System: Fedora 14
Snort	**Proc:** AMD Dual Core 5400B 2.8 GHz
	Memory: 1.8 GB RAM
	Hard Disk: 212 GB HDD
	Operating System: Fedora 14

work bandwidth. CPU load reflects the computing resource needed to operate an IDS.

The IDSs were properly configured according to corresponding instructions. The whole set of rules coming with a default installation in the open-source domain was used to run Snort. The Ourmon system was properly trained with a dataset of normal network traffic captured when no attacks were injected. A basic installation and configuration was performed for the Samhain system. With these configurations, all of the investigated IDSs were able to detect all injected attacks in our experiment.

Iperf [19] was run on our Backtrack machine to conduct bandwidth benchmarking. At the same time, we used an Nmap [33] SYN scan (with option -sS), the reverse TCP utility in Metasploit [30] and Zeus Botnet to simulate attacks to the network. The attacks were initiated immediately after benchmarking was started. The Nmap probe was started on the Backtrack machine to the entire network shown in Figure 1. The reverse TCP attack was targeted to virtual host number 7. This was just a randomly chosen host to simulate an intrusion to the network. The Botnet was used to push out scripts as well as collect user credentials from our targeted websites. The length of the attacks varied depending on how long it would take to push out our scripts from the Botnet installed on the physical XP Desktop machine. During the experiment, normal web browsing and randomly user activities such as logging to a remote machine were also included in the network traffic.

We were able to acquire bandwidth readings from a memory Input/Output utility included in the Phoronix test suite [38]. During the experiment, the Linux built-in **top** utility was running on each IDS host machine to determine the CPU load and RAM utilization for each IDS process. These readings were taken when the network traffic was relatively stable (see details in Figure 2). The same measurements were taken 6-8 times during a period of around 20 minutes. Averages are used for analysis.

4. RESULTS

The dynamics of network traffic during the 20-minute period of experiment is depicted in Figure 2. In the first few minutes of the experiment, the Samhain system does not affect network traffic very much since it works by checking on log files. However, the Snort system imposes a significant impact on network traffic immediately. The effect of the Ourmon system on network traffic is less than Snort, but stronger than the Samhain system. Network traffic to all IDS hosts and baseline stays relatively stable although small fluctuations exist after about seven minutes from the beginning of the experiment. Then, measurements of memory utilization and CPU load are taken.

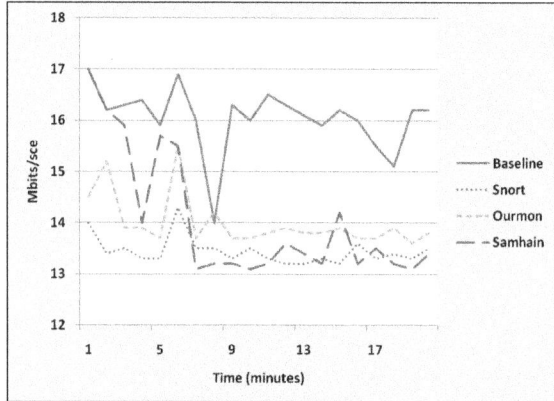

Figure 2: Network bandwidth

All of the three investigated IDSs impose noticeable impacts on network traffic to the host under the condition in our experiment. More specifically, the Snort system constraints network traffic the most. The Ourmon and Samhain systems have relatively lower effect on network traffic. This fact can also be observed from the accumulated amount of data received by each system during the period of experiment (Figure 3). In Figure 3, the numbers represent the total amount of data in gigabytes (GB) transferred to corresponding hosts during the 20-minute period of experiment. From this figure, we can clearly see the accumulative effects of the tested IDSs on network traffic.

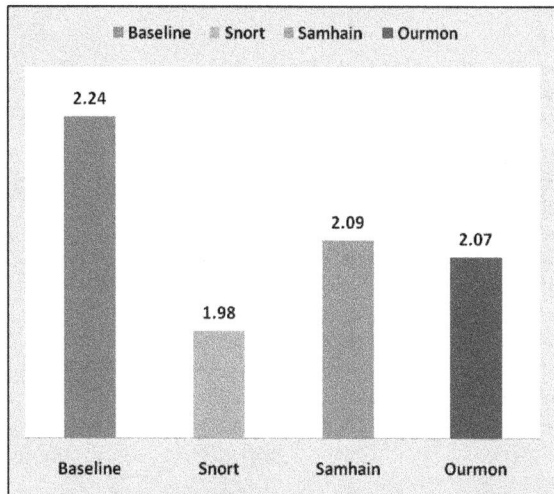

Figure 3: The amount of data transferred in 20 minutes (GB)

Figure 4 shows the amount of system memory occupied by the IDS while in operation. The numbers are in megabytes (MB). Compared with the other two IDSs, Snort demands more memory due to its large set of rules and the pattern search algorithm. The Ourmon system claims the least

memory due to its small set of rules and simpler processing algorithm.

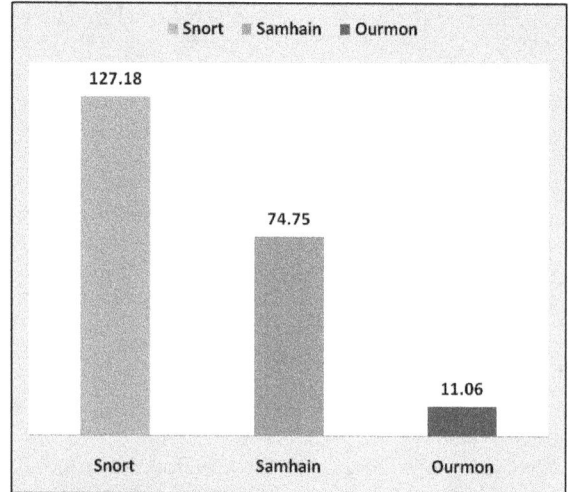

Figure 4: Memory usage in MB

The Samhain system is more CPU-intensive than the other two tested IDSs (Figure 5). This may be due to its relatively expensive algorithms for integrity check and log data analysis. With its efficient pattern search algorithm, the Snort system requires considerably less computing resources.

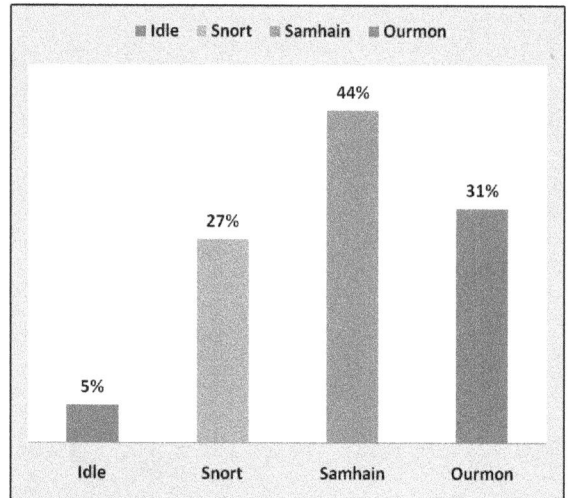

Figure 5: Percentage of CPU load

5. CONCLUSION AND DISCUSSION

We have developed a methodology to impartially assess intrusion detection systems in a simulated environment in the perspective of system and network administration. This environment is a combination of physical and virtual computers. Three intrusion detection systems including Snort, Ourmon and Samhain are chosen for this study. These investigated IDSs are installed on physical computers with identical hardware components for the purpose of comparison. With simulated baseline network traffic, benchmark and actual intrusion attacks, CPU load, network bandwidth constraint and memory demand can be measured using corresponding tools.

Results show that the Snort system imposes noticeably more impacts on network traffic than the other two tested IDSs. It could be a bottleneck on a high speed network. In addition, Snort occupies more system memory than the other two tested systems. However, it generates lower CPU load. The Samhain system imposes the most CPU load among the tested IDSs.

The amount of 127 MBs memory as demanded by the Snort system is probably a small fraction of RAM on a modern computer system. However, when the IDS is collocated with other services, this amount of RAM could be a concern. In addition, the results on Snort imply that Snort may be able to run on a relatively slower computer. However, more RAM memory is needed to host a Snort system. This result agrees well with the recommendation made by Alder et al. citeAlder:Snort. The 44 percent of CPU load demanded by the Samhain system on a Dual Core 2.8 GHz processor could be an issue in some system design, especially in the case where a centralized system needs to process data collected from several other agents.

In the perspective of IT management, other metrics may also need to be measured to comprehensively evaluate an IDS, such as ease of use [9, 1] and the metrics outlined by Fink et al. [15]. However, an impersonal scoring method is in need to obtain unbiased results. One way to develop such an approach is to create a list of survey questions and sample solutions among a large population of IT personnel. This can be done in a separate research on selected systems.

This study focuses on the resource needs of IDSs. However, with proper databases such as the DARPA database [22, 23], our system design can be used to investigate the effectiveness of IDSs by injecting the database into the network. In most cases, the effectiveness of an IDS may be more important in practice. Resources needed to operate an IDS and ease of use will be the second consideration when the effectiveness of IDSs is about the same.

Objective evaluation of existing products in the perspective of IT management is one of the topics in IT research agenda. Here, we provide an example of IDS evaluation. More research is needed to develop the methodology in this respect, such as the metrics we should use and the methods to measure those metrics. Different IT products may need different methods to evaluate impartially to meet the requirements in IT practice.

6. ACKNOWLEDGMENTS

The authors would like to thank the two peer-reviewers. Their comments and suggestions improved the writing of this article. Danny Miller, a faculty member at Michigan Technological University, helped with the equipment acquisition. This work is partially supported by the National Science Foundation under the award number DUE-1140308.

7. REFERENCES

[1] D. A. Adams, R. R. Nelson, and P. A. Todd. Perceived usefulness, ease of use, and usage of information technology: a replication. *MIS Quarterly*, 16(2):227–247, 1992.

[2] E. Albin and N. Rowe. A realistic experimental comparison of the Suricata and Snort intrusion-detection systems. In *Advanced Information Networking and Applications Workshops (WAINA), 2012 26th International Conference on*, pages 122–127, March 2012.

[3] R. Alder, A. R. Baker, E. F. S. Carter, Jr., J. Esler, J. C. Foster, M. Jonkman, C. Keefer, R. Marty, and E. S. Seagren. *Snort: IDS and IPS Toolkit*. Syngress Publishing, Inc., Elsevier, Inc., 30 Corporate Dr., Burlington, MA 01803, USA, 2007.

[4] J. P. Anderson. *Computer Security Threat Monitoring and Surveillance*. James P. Anderson Company, Fort Washington, PA, USA, April 1980.

[5] S. Axelsson. The base-rate fallacy and the difficulty of intrusion detection. *ACM Transactions on Information and System Security (TISSEC)*, 3(3):186–205, August 2000.

[6] S. Axelsson. Intrusion detection systems: a survey and taxonomy. Technical Report 99-15, Department of Computer Engineering, Chalmers University of Technology, Göteborg, Sweden, March 2000.

[7] R. C. Bace. *Intrusion Detection*. Macmillan Technical Publishing, 201 West 103rd Street, Indianapolis, IN 46290, USA, 2000.

[8] R. S. Boyer and J. S. Moore. A fast string searching algorithm. *Communications of the ACM*, 20(10):762–772, October 1977.

[9] F. D. Davis. Perceived usefulness, perceived ease of use, and user acceptance of information technology. *MIS Quarterly*, 13(3):319–340, 1989.

[10] D. J. Day and B. M. Burns. A performance analysis of Snort and Suricata network intrusion detection and prevention engines. In *ICDS 2011: The Fifth International Conference on Digital Society*, pages 187–192, 2011.

[11] H. Debar, M. Dacier, and A. Wespi. A revised taxonomy for intrusion-detection systems. *Annales Des Télécommunications*, 55(7-8):361–378, 2000.

[12] D. Denning. An intrusion-detection model. *Software Engineering, IEEE Transactions on*, SE-13(2):222–232, February 1987.

[13] R. Durst, T. Champion, B. Witten, E. Miller, and L. Spagnuolo. Testing and evaluating computer intrusion detection systems. *Communications of the ACM*, 42(7):53–61, July 1999.

[14] T. Fawcett. ROC graphs: Notes and practical considerations for researchers. *Machine Learning*, 31:1–38, 2004.

[15] G. Fink, K. F. O'Donoghue, B. L. Chappell, and T. G. Turner. A metrics-based approach to intrusion detection system evaluation for distributed real-time systems. In *Proceedings of the 16th International Parallel and Distributed Processing Symposium*, IPDPS '02, page 17, Washington, DC, USA, 2002. IEEE Computer Society.

[16] J. E. Gaffney, Jr. and J. Ulvila. Evaluation of intrusion detectors: a decision theory approach. In *Security and Privacy, 2001. S P 2001. Proceedings. 2001 IEEE Symposium on*, pages 50–61, 2001.

[17] P. Garcia-Teodoro, J. Diaz-Verdejo, G. Macia-Fernandez, and E. Vazquez. Anomaly-based network intrusion detection: techniques, systems and

challenges. *Computers and Security*, 28(1–2):18—28, 2009.

[18] G. Gu, P. Fogla, D. Dagon, W. Lee, and B. Skorić. Measuring intrusion detection capability: an information-theoretic approach. In *Proceedings of the 2006 ACM Symposium on Information, Computer and Communications Security*, ASIACCS '06, pages 90–101, New York, NY, USA, 2006. ACM.

[19] Iperf. Online. http://iperf.sourceforge.net/. Retrieved May 28, 2013.

[20] S. M. Lee, D. S. Kim, and J. S. Park. A survey and taxonomy of lightweight intrusion detection systems. *Journal of Internet Services and Information Security*, 2(1/2):119–131, 2012.

[21] H.-J. Liao, C.-H. R. Lin, Y.-C. Lin, and K.-Y. Tung. Intrusion detection system: a comprehensive review. *Journal of Network and Computer Applications*, 36(1):16–24, 2013.

[22] R. Lippmann, D. Fried, I. Graf, J. Haines, K. Kendall, D. McClung, D. Weber, S. Webster, D. Wyschogrod, R. Cunningham, and M. Zissman. Evaluating intrusion detection systems: the 1998 DARPA off-line intrusion detection evaluation. In *DARPA Information Survivability Conference and Exposition, 2000. DISCEX '00. Proceedings*, volume 2, pages 12–26, 2000.

[23] R. Lippmann, J. W. Haines, D. J. Fried, J. Korba, and K. Das. The 1999 DARPA off-line intrusion detection evaluation. *Computer Networks*, 34(4):579–595, 2000.

[24] T. F. Lunt. Automated audit trail analysis and intrusion detection: a survey. In *Proceedings of the 11th National Computer Security Conference*, pages 65–73, 1988.

[25] T. F. Lunt. A survey of intrusion detection techniques. *Computers and Security*, 12(4):405–418, 1993.

[26] F. Maggi, M. Matteucci, and S. Zanero. Detecting intrusions through system call sequence and argument analysis. *Dependable and Secure Computing, IEEE Transactions on*, 7(4):381–395, 2010.

[27] F. Massicotte, F. Gagnon, Y. Labiche, L. Briand, and M. Couture. Automatic evaluation of intrusion detection systems. In *Computer Security Applications Conference, 2006. ACSAC '06. 22nd Annual*, pages 361–370, 2006.

[28] J. McHugh. Testing intrusion detection systems: a critique of the 1998 and 1999 DARPA intrusion detection system evaluations as performed by Lincoln Laboratory. *ACM Transactions on Information and System Security (TISSEC)*, 3(4):262–294, 2000.

[29] P. Mell, V. Hu, R. Lippmann, J. Haines, and M. Zissman. An overview of issues in testing intrusion detection systems. Technical Report NIST IR 7007, NIST, 2006.

[30] Metasploit. Metasploit home page. Online. http://www.metasploit.com/, Retrieved May 28, 2013.

[31] C. Modi, D. Patel, B. Borisaniya, H. Patel, A. Patel, and M. Rajarajan. A survey of intrusion detection techniques in cloud. *Journal of Network and Computer Applications*, 36(1):42–57, 2013.

[32] B. Mukherjee, L. Heberlein, and K. Levitt. Network intrusion detection. *IEEE Network*, 8(3):26–41, 1994.

[33] Nmap. Nmap home page. Online. http://nmap.org/, Retrieved May 28, 2013.

[34] Oracle. VirtualBox. Online. https://www.virtualbox.org/. Retrieved May 28, 2013.

[35] Ourmon. Ourmon - network monitoring and anomaly detection system. Online. http://ourmon.sourceforge.net/. Retrieved May 28, 2013.

[36] A. Patcha and J.-M. Park. An overview of anomaly detection techniques: existing solutions and latest technological trends. *Computer Networks*, 51(12):3448–3470, 2007.

[37] V. Paxson. Bro: a system for detecting network intruders in real-time. *Computer Networks*, 31(23–24):2435–2463, 1999.

[38] Phoronix. Phoronix test suite. Online. http://www.phoronix-test-suite.com/. Retrieved May 28, 2013.

[39] N. Puketza, M. Chung, R. Olsson, and B. Mukherjee. A software platform for testing intrusion detection systems. *Software, IEEE*, 14(5):43–51, September/October 1997.

[40] N. Puketza, K. Zhang, M. Chung, B. Mukherjee, and R. Olsson. A methodology for testing intrusion detection systems. *Software Engineering, IEEE Transactions on*, 22(10):719–729, October 1996.

[41] M. Roesch. Snort - lightweight intrusion detection for networks. In *Proceedings of the 13th USENIX Conference on System Administration*, LISA '99, pages 229–238, Berkeley, CA, USA, 1999. USENIX Association.

[42] Samhain Labs. The SAMHAIN file integrity / host-based intrusion detection system. Online. http://la-samhna.de/samhain/. Retrieved May 28, 2013.

[43] Snort. Online. http://www.snort.org/. Retrieved May 28, 2013.

[44] S. Stolfo, W. Fan, W. Lee, A. Prodromidis, and P. Chan. Cost-based modeling for fraud and intrusion detection: results from the JAM project. In *DARPA Information Survivability Conference and Exposition, 2000. DISCEX '00. Proceedings*, volume 2, pages 130–144, 2000.

[45] Suricata. Suricata home page. Online. http://suricata-ids.org/. Retrieved May 28, 2013.

[46] K. Wang, G. Cretu, and S. J. Stolfo. Anomalous payload-based worm detection and signature generation. In *Proceedings of the 8th International Conference on Recent Advances in Intrusion Detection*, RAID'05, pages 227–246, Berlin, Heidelberg, 2006. Springer-Verlag.

[47] K. Wang, J. J. Parekh, and S. J. Stolfo. Anagram: a content anomaly detector resistant to mimicry attack. In *Proceedings of the 9th International Conference on Recent Advances in Intrusion Detection*, RAID'06, pages 226–248, Berlin, Heidelberg, 2006. Springer-Verlag.

[48] X. Wang, C.-C. Pan, P. Liu, and S. Zhu. SigFree: a signature-free buffer overflow attack blocker. *Dependable and Secure Computing, IEEE Transactions on*, 7(1):65–79, 2010.

DNS (Do Not Suspect)

Fernando Seror Garcia
3517 N Wilton Ave
60657 Chicago, IL
(773) 373-9894
ferdy89@gmail.com

ABSTRACT

This project investigates the possibility of using the DNS (Domain Name System) protocol to communicate with a zombie host while avoiding detection by an IDS (Intrusion Detection System).

Right now this communication is often made through the IRC (Internet Relay Chatroom) protocol. IRC is used for chat rooms with a known port easily blocked with a firewall and a pattern that raises a lot of alerts on any IDS available. This does not happen with DNS, which is a protocol used for the well-functioning of the whole Internet. If somebody was able to communicate through DNS packets it would result almost invisible and harder to block that IRC.

The purpose of this project is to address the possibility of doing this and if so, to investigate how to make the DNS protocol safer.

Categories and Subject Descriptors: C. 2.2 [COMPUTER-COMMUNICATION NETWORKS]: Network Protocols - *Protocol verification (TCP/IP)*

Keywords:
DNS; IRC; Malware; Botnet

1. INTRODUCTION

The problem I will try to address in this project is to study how zombie computers in a botnet communicate with each other. Traditionally this communication is made through the IRC protocol which is well known and fairly easy to detect, also many times is blocked by a firewall and not effective. I believe this is not going to stop malware developers and I think they might look for other ways to get stealth communication with an infected system.

That way might be through the DNS protocol. This protocol is thought to help humans surf the Internet. It is also meant to make persistent references to computers aside of the IP behind them. It translates a domain into an IP address for the computer to understand, sort of like a phonebook does. It is accepted by all networks in the world, so most of the people do not suspect of the DNS packets. Even those who are aware that DNS might be used with illegitimate purposes do not make an exhaustive scan of the contents of the packets, but rather only the frequency or destination. This is especially true with firewalls and Intrusion

Detection Systems; the configuration and the rule sets currently available do not check for illegitimate communication through DNS.

It might be possible for an attacker to make a full communication through the DNS protocol and not being detected with the security techniques available today, such as antivirus, firewalls or IDS's.

2. IMPLEMENTATION
2.1 Setup

My experiment runs completely on two computers. The first computer works as a DNS server. This one is supposed to be the attacker; actually, the DNS server on it is not a normal one, it just listens to port 53 and uses the DNS protocol in order to communicate with the victims.

The second computer is the target system. It mainly has to be a normal computer with nothing special, although it must have access to the internet and to the first machine. It is also going to need to be running a special piece of software which can communicate through DNS, but I will get to that later.

2.2 Stealth

My goal at this point is to investigate which packets go undetected through a well-protected system, because those are the only ones I am going to be able to use. The idea is to create the most secure environment I can (including antivirus, firewall and IDS) and try to execute the attack against that system. In case I get to penetrate the system, I will assume most of the systems will be vulnerable.

A brief explanation about what differentiates an IDS from a firewall could be this: Imagine your system as a huge gate where packets go in and out. Think about the firewall as the security personnel at the gate and the IDS as a security camera after the gate. The firewall blocks packets based on their origin, destination and port. The IDS analyzes the traffic and raises alerts when certain rules are violated. These rules can be complex, like packet frequency, size or contents. So the IDS could be thought as an upgraded firewall.

For architectural convenience, all the security measures have been included on the victim's computer, such as Wireshark[1] and Snort IDS[2]. Wireshark will let me know if there is anything abnormal

---

RIIT'13, October 10–12, 2013, Orlando, Florida, USA.
ACM 978-1-4503-2494-6/13/10.
http://dx.doi.org/10.1145/2512209.2512222

[1]"The world's foremost network protocol analyzer" http://www.wireshark.org/

[2]"Snort® is an open source network intrusion prevention and detection system (IDS/IPS) developed by Sourcefire. It is the most widely deployed IDS/IPS technology worldwide." http://www.snort.org/

on each packet and Snort will watch for suspicious activity and raise an alert if it finds something.

2.3 My own "DNS" Protocol (Steganography)

After studying several different possibilities about where in the DNS packets (both requests and responses) was I going to hide my messages, I concluded the best both way communication was the following.

The victim will hide his commands as the domain he is asking for. For example, where normally a machine would throw a request for "www.google.com", the victim here will throw one for "COMMAND". It is important to remark here that I just used these commands for comprehension purposes. I could have perfectly used more stealthy queries like the real ones, for example, using http://www.facebook.com as my FLOOD command.

The server will hide his commands as the TXT field in the DNS response package[3]. This also allows me to send more than one parameter, which you'll see is very convenient.

Aside from that, the purpose of the botnet is for the attacker to give order to the victims, not the other way around. However, the DNS protocol (from the OS perspective) makes queries from the client and receives a response from the server. The role of client and server gets swapped in my communication model, as the victim (the one who is going to perform the actions, effectively the server) is going to be sending the queries. Similarly, the attacker (the one asking the victim to do things) is going to send the responses. In order to do this kind of pushing to the victim, I used a technique called long polling[4].

Long polling emulates an open connection between the victim and the attacker. Notice that I couldn't have make it the other way around: installing a working DNS server on a victim is far more complex than a client. Have in mind that it would have to be listening to port 53 (which itself could be suspicious) and get external petitions to that port to be routed to him. That would involve configuring the local network, which makes the problem way more difficult. This way, the OS and the legitimate use of DNS protocol solves this for us.

3. PROTECTION

At this point you may be scared about how insecure most of the systems are. Although there is no way to be 100% safe from malware, there are some things to do in order to avoid illegitimate communication through DNS.

The main point here is the firewall. The firewall allows or denies packets based on their origin or destination. In a normal computer, DNS is just used to translate domains into IPs and normally just one server is used. That means, every other packet with DNS header not addressed to that one server can be considered illegitimate.

Because there are just a bunch of known and trusted DNS servers (like OpenDNS, Google Public DNS, the ISP's ones…) it is easy to configure the firewall to block DNS packets to any other destination. Just that makes it very difficult for malware to misuse DNS. The way to do this may be very different depending on the system. Check the documentation on your firewall to know how.

4. CONCLUSIONS

Definitely, DNS illegitimate communication is possible as shown in this project. While is true that some configuration may block some of these tweaked packets of mine, I have found no clue that suggests that anybody is aware of the possibility of this communication.

After making this study, I can say that DNS communications are far from secure. It should not be much different than HTTP from a security point of view. This is especially true when realizing that are projects out there that allows tunneling of all IPv4 traffic through DNS packets. That is the case of Iodine[5], a free software for Linux-based systems that allows us to bypass every security measure on a network in order to contact an outside computer, as long as DNS communication is unfiltered.

I have found that most DNS communications go unfiltered; no IDS rules take care of them and certainly no firewalls either. The OS should be in charge of securing the packets, the same way it is treating HTTP. Moreover, DNS communications are less frequent that the HTTP ones, so that should not be a problem.

5. ACKNOWLEDGMENTS

To my two advisors on this project, Bill Lidinsky and Jeremy Hajek, as well as other people that have helped with the development of this project, such as IIT Teacher Assistant Ben Khodja and my course partner David Stacey.

6. REFERENCES

[1] Multiple RFCs (Request For Comments): http://www.ietf.org

[2] Security by Default (Spanish blog). About DNS tunneling: http://www.securitybydefault.com/2010/01/tunelizando-dns-otra-opcion-con-iodine.html

[3] Snort (installation and usage): http://www.snort.org/ & https://help.ubuntu.com/community/SnortIDS

[4] Icann (Internet Corporation for Assigned Names and Numbers): http://www.icann.org

[5] OpenDNS: http://www.opendns.com

---

[3] As explained in this RFC1646, there is a TXT field for purposes of sending key-value pairs as plain strings in a DNS response (https://tools.ietf.org/rfc/rfc1464.txt)

[4] Long polling and the push communication method is better explained here https://en.wikipedia.org/wiki/Push_technology#Long_polling

---

[5] More information about Iodine can be found on the project's webpage http://code.kryo.se/iodine/

Securing Insurance Reimbursements with RFID Technologies

Charles Hopkins
East Carolina University
1001 East 5th St
Greenville, NC 27828
252-565-3182
hopkinsc04@students.ecu.edu

ABSTRACT

As RFID enhances many realms of the functional world including: retail, pharmaceutical, aerospace, and defense, it is beginning to show great promise in healthcare. Insurance companies constantly battle fraud among health care providers and new technologies need to be adopted to ensure a lean service-to-reimbursement relationship. This paper will investigate the current state of RFID in health care and demonstrate possible solutions pertaining to not only asset tracking and medication with RFID, but patient tracking and billing reimbursements exchange between insurance companies and practitioners. Fraudulent or not, billing errors among practitioners has continued to be on the rise creating an opportunity for RFID to better structure and secure the health care patient flow.

Categories and Subject Descriptors

C.2.1 [Network Architecture and Design]: Wireless communication
C.3 [SPECIAL-PURPOSE AND APPLICATION-BASED SYSTEMS]: Real-time and embedded systems

General Terms

Design, Theory

Keywords

RFID in Healthcare, RTLS, EHR and RFID

1. INTRODUCTION

Over the last half of a decade, all health care providers from Dentists, Medical Doctors, Mental Health professionals and the like have been striving for a solution to maintain documentation showing meaningful use of treatment, billing management, following the flow of treatment, and documenting treatment fast and efficiently. A typical method of operation for health care providers is to diagnose, gain authorization from a patient's insurance company to treat, build a treatment plan, execute the treatment, and dismiss patient with instances of follow up treatment if necessary. All of these instances with the patients can be broken down into certain billing codes based on the procedure completed and time spent with the patient. In every contact with the patient, paper documentation must be maintained to justify the actual billing and to build a chart to follow care and treatment. The procedure seems straight forward yet lacks

RIIT'13, October 10–12, 2013, Orlando, Florida, USA.
ACM 978-1-4503-2494-6/13/10.
http://dx.doi.org/10.1145/2512209.2512223

efficiency. Obviously, in this day in age, sooner than later this system of care needs to be transformed from paper to a secure and easily managed database system.

An Electronic Health Record (or EHR) system is the next step. Many larger health care providers have transitioned to a functioning EHR system meeting the method of operation stated above; improving efficiency and decreasing paper. EHRs (also known as EMR—Electronic Medical Record system), have increased efficiency with respects to documentation, billing, authorizations, and patient chart management. However, EHRs have merely started the tracking of medical data. As all of health care must follow suite and become "digital" in order continue to provide services, the EHR system needs to graduate from this phase and begin to solve the next problem.

2. PROBLEM

In the medical field, several concerns regarding overbilling have arisen. As the National Health Care Reform Act 2011 was passed, practitioners have become creative in how claims are processed, essentially modifying the way they actually provide care. As the insurance companies keep dropping reimbursement rates, practitioners find ways to bill more codes daily or more periodically. While dropping reimbursement rates and cost of doing business to private practitioners is going up, the doctors *may* deviate from their ethics and overbill. Overbilling being accomplished in two ways: 1) Submitting a claim on a patient where the practitioner never provided any care or procedure and/or 2) Giving a diagnosis that during treatment proves to be more lucrative, entailing more insurance reimbursement. [4] Medical doctors may file claims on a patient they diagnose and bill a diagnostic CPT (billing) code. Whether the patient comes back for a follow up or not, the doctor may contact the patient for follow up and precariously bill another code in order to render more reimbursement, being one way to overbill. If a doctor physically sees a patient for 10 minutes—this represents a code in the ICD9/10 coding standards labeled "Evaluation and Management Codes" (or E and M codes). E and M codes are based on time length and vary in pay rate. A10-minute visit with a doctor could be billed at a 45-minute rate.

Since the Health Care Reform Act of 2011, reimbursement rates from public insurance agencies like Medicare have reduced substantially and it is agreed the national inflation rate for the last few years has risen. Simply put, cost to do business as a hospital has risen and the usual average reimbursement rates have been reduced annually. Although with these facts stated and health care reimbursements being lowered, does not justify a practitioner's behavior in overbilling, but may explain the reasons of improper coding.

3. RFID SOLUTION

As it becomes more evident how helpful RFID technology is in the healthcare setting, how does it relate to patients and billing? As inventory and medication is tracked, what about patients? EHRs are already in place in virtually every practice. RFID may be used subjective-based in addition to object-based; where RFID tags may be added to patients externally with hospital bracelets. In many hospital settings, it is protocol for patients to have bracelets by default. These bracelets are associated to the social security number of the patient and cross-referenced to a database (EHR) with the patients "chart" information and current treatment procedures they are requiring among other demographics. RFID may be added to these bracelets and simply scanned to better track patients and their service provided--simplifying the treatment process. How can Hospitals adopt these technologies? With the EHR already in place in most hospital settings, passive RFID can be added to the patients via mandatory bracelets. These implementations cost roughly $.079 per bracelet for a UHF RFID tag and obliviously scanners costing $550-$1200 throughout the hospital. Another way to add the RFID tags is to use existing Wi-Fi infrastructure. Using the bracelets already in the hospital environment then using active RFID tags within the tags may work with the Wi-Fi. Active RFID tags for this application will cost approximately $50 per bracelet, however, may be reused. In the same way, adding active RFID to patient's bracelets and having them sync with WLAN within the facility. Unpretentiously put, the two scenarios described will work together with the existing EHR increasing efficiency and patient throughput.

In either option, tracking the location of the client is the first part. How does RFID help with billing and efficiency with the EHR? The idea termed "yoking-proof" was presented by Juels where adding one more attribute; adding a Doctor with an RFID name badge and medical tablet device such as an iPad. According to Juels, "We propose the concept of a yoking-proof, namely a proof that a pair of RFID tags has been scanned simultaneously. Our particular aim is to permit tags to generate a proof that is verifiable off-line by a trusted entity, even when readers are potentially untrusted. We suggest that such proofs are a useful tool for maintaining integrity in supply chains, particularly as RFID data will commonly flow across multiple, loosely affiliated organizations." [1] Yoking-proof could be best described as having a RFID badged doctor and an RFID wrist-banded patient temporarily bound together during the treatment process, measuring billable criteria including: location, start time, end time, and date. The interaction is established with the iPad and after complete saved into the back-end database. The interaction is saved the practitioner's queue for the documentation requirements to justify service. The doctor commits to complete the service rendered by adding purpose for treatment, the intervention and treatment procedures, and the outcomes noting complications and effectiveness on a front-end form. The data is added to the EHR for this patient's record.

Recalling the yoking procedure and the data it acquired, the service time is successfully added to the documentation. As mentioned earlier, one of the problems with overbilling is possibly neutralized. Specifically, as one practitioner can bill too much time (knowing or unknowingly) during treatment with basic procedure and documentation; the RFID yoking paradigm cannot lie. The yoking duration is what is inserted in the documentation for billing purposes. In some cases of overbilling, the practitioners' daily billing load is more than 24 hours of service depleting the entire day and of it hours for actual 1-to-1 patient service time. Furthermore, a clinician cannot have an overlapping of patient interaction times, ensuring doctors only see one patient at a time. Yoking will give an accurate snapshot of the doctor's actual billing habits, guaranteeing to meet the billing guidelines set forth by CMS (Centers for Medicare and Medicaid Services). How much money can this save insurance companies?

A doctor may see 20 patients on a given 8 hour day and retaining approximately $1200 in insurance reimbursements. In addition to the 8 hours of service, allocation for time to complete documentation for these patient interactions for the day must be appropriated—adding and additional 2 hours to document. As RFID is implemented, time can be reduced recalling and documenting interactions. After a doctor is "un-yoked", documentation can be executed immediately via the iPad. The major side effect of faster patient visits is more time to spend seeing more patients in a given period of time rendering more billable time. Efficiency in the hospital service setting is greatly improved as more patients are being seen.

4. CONCLUSION

As RFID becomes more acceptable culturally and ethically, this technology will essentially audit all parts of our day-to-day lives. Being that healthcare is based on document-backed service for payments, the practitioners must yield to technology to better guarantee the services rendered is in-fact genuine. The division of health care is changing phase by phase. This myriad of procedures and implementations will take some time to fully apply into the hospital settings and private practices. As health care insurance is becoming nationalized, there must be a way to make the service and reimbursements lean, meaningful, and error free. The stage is set for the next phase of RFID integration into hospitals. RFID shall increase efficiency for the doctors and patients increasing safety, reducing overbilling, and increasing accuracy of patient care. Electronic Health Record databases are in full use, while RFID intensifies the flow of operations. Security measures have been addressed and appear to be undoubtedly remediable as HIPAA compliance is held on the backend with the server, and not on the front end with the face-to-face care.

5. REFERENCES

[1] Juels, A. (2004). "Yoking-Proofs" for RFID Tags, *Proceedings of the Second IEEE Annual Conference, 24(2)*, 381-394. doi: 10.1109/PERCOMW.2004.1276920

[2] Pappu, R. (2010). *The Batteryless RFID Imperative in Healthcare.* [White Paper]. Retrieved from http://rfid.thingmagic.com/whitepaper-download---rfid-in-healthcare/

[3] Turner, P. (2009). Moving Toward a Unified National Health Care Database, *Certification Magazine.* Retrieved from http://certmag.com/print.php?in=3841

[4] Vincent, L. (2012). *Overbilling: A Leading Cause of Healthcare Fraud.* Retrieved from http://www.nursetogether.com/Lifestyle/Lifestyle-Article/itemid/2384.aspx

[5] West, Dr. K. (2009). EMR Doctor's Blog : When Does Efficiency in Documentation Become Misguided and Counterproductive?. Message posted to http://www.happyemrdoctor.com/2010/11/29/emr-doctors-blog-when-does-efficiency-in-documentation-become-misguided-and-counterproductive/

Resource Utilization Prediction:
Long Term Network Web Service Traffic

Daniel W. Yoas
Industrial, Computing, and Engineering Technology
Pennsylvania College of Technology
Williamsport, PA 17701
dyoas@pct.edu

Greg Simco
Graduate School of Computer and Information Sciences
Nova Southeastern University
Ft. Lauderdale, FL 33314
greg@nova.edu

ABSTRACT

Short-term prediction has been established in computing as a mechanism for improving services. Long-term prediction has not been pursued because attempts to use multiple steps to extend short-term predictions have been shown to become less accurate the further into the future the prediction is extended. In each case, the researchers used fine grained sampling for the analysis. This study used course sampling of ten-second intervals and then aggregated them into periods of minutes, fifteen-minutes, and hours. Each of the aggregates was used to calculate the predictions for Hourly, Daily, and Weekly cycles, determine the error rate of the prediction, and establish a confidence interval of 80%. The results then were evaluated to identify the effectiveness of long term prediction and the best cycle to predict the resource utilization most accurately.

Categories and Subject Descriptors

D.4.8 [**Performance**]: Measurements, Modeling and Prediction, Monitors;

General Terms

Design, Experimentation, Human Factors, Management, Measurement, Performance, Reliability, Security, Theory.

Keywords

Prediction methods, Demand forecasting.

1. INTRODUCTION

Computer scientists have been predicting resource management using short-term samples under five seconds [1, 2, 5-8] for years, and time-series analysis is a proven method for scheduling, resource allocation, and load balancing. No research has been conducted into long-term resource utilization, however, so this experiment focused on determining if resource prediction was feasible over the periods of hours, days, and weeks using Naïve, Simple Moving Average (SMA), and Exponential Moving Average (EMA). This type of study is appropriate for Information Technology research since it focuses on the behavior of the system as a whole instead of the behavior of the operating system.

2. RELATED WORK

As more companies rely on public services, the need to provide availability of those services also continues to increase [3, 7]. Researchers have used simulation to provide proof of concept [5, 8] and live trace data to show stability in a real world situation [3, 7]. This provides a foundation for the use of prediction for systems management, but the use of an exact prediction is unreasonable since systems face a degree of randomness introduced by human interaction. However, researchers have found that the use of a confidence interval as a prediction range can be very accurate at determining "normality" of utilization [1, 8].

3. Experiment Setup

The experiment was conducted in two stages. The first used a simulator to determine if a stepped load pattern of web requests would generate predictable network traffic load to and from the web server. The simulation server recorded the network traffic load every ten seconds and then aggregated it into sixty one-minute samples for the hourly predictions and ninety-six fifteen-minute samples for the daily predictions. Naïve prediction was used as a benchmark to determine if either SMA or EMA was more accurate than using the last sample for the Naïve prediction.

Resource utilization was logged on a live web server from January 2012 to July 2012. This provided enough samples to conduct analysis for the weekly patterns of resource utilization in addition to the daily and hourly patterns. Each of the one-hundred sixty-eight samples for the weekly predictions represented a single hour aggregate.

To facilitate this process, the study selected a confidence level of 80% to create binding values both above and below the prediction. Higher levels of 95.5% or 97.7% could have been selected but that would have included almost all of the readings and would impact the ability to consider normal and abnormal system behavior. Mean Average Percentage Error (MAPE) for each of the prediction methods was used to identify the prediction with the least error. MAPE was selected to measure accuracy, since it provides a feeling for the degree of error between the prediction and the actual level of resource utilization.

4. Results

The step input from the simulation opened 600, 450, 300, and 150 connections to generate web requests for each of twenty-one client machines. Each level was used for fifteen minutes before returning to the highest level. Each session generated web requests based on a previously proven pattern of human interaction with web servers [4].

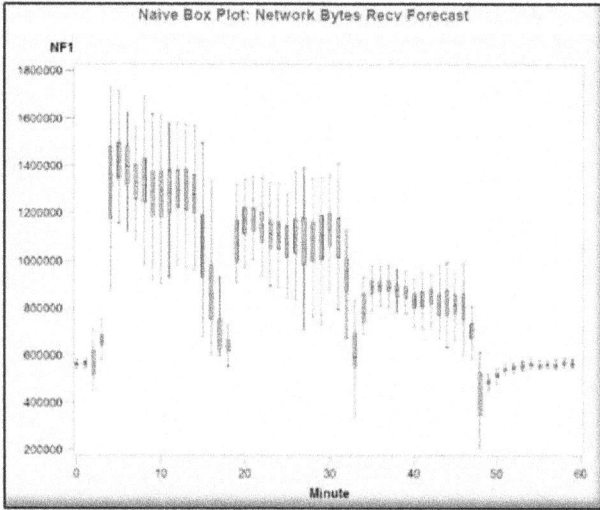

Figure 1: Each Minute during the Hourly Cycle

The pattern resulting from simulated network traffic, as shown in Figure 1, distinctly repeats throughout the fifteen minute request levels. An interesting aspect of the graph shows that the lower the number of requests, the tighter the pattern becomes and therefore, it is more predictable. In every case, with the exception of the minute with the maximum sent bytes for the SMA, both SMA and EMA were better predictors of network traffic than using the Naïve (last sample) prediction. During the lowest utilization, the error rates for SMA were 0.78% (transmission) and 0.57% (receipt) while the highest average prediction error was within 15% of the actual utilization level.

Simulation Web Server Forecasting Statistics			Results by Minute within an Hour					Summary	
			Minimum Mean/STD	~-STD Mean/STD	~Mean Mean/STD	~+STD Mean/STD	Maximum Mean/STD	Mean	STD
Network Bytes Sent (Utilization in Millions)	Naïve	MAPE	0.94	1.53	2.44	3.39	4.47	2.46	0.95
		Utilization	23.22 0.27	21.50 2.48	21.23 0.44	21.18 0.60	21.86 1.08		
		Cycle	17	18	37	8	29		
	MA	MAPE	0.78	1.24	1.97	2.88	5.04	2.04	0.86
		Utilization	21.24 0.25	22.76 0.36	15.92 0.67	20.46 0.81	16.19 4.69		
		Cycle	56	45	49	21	48		
	EMA	MAPE	0.83	1.25	2.04	2.79	3.72	2.05	0.77
		Utilization	23.22 0.27	20.63 0.32	20.72 0.49	21.42 0.69	21.85 1.09		
		Cycle	17	53	36	13	29		
Network Received (Utilization 100K)	Naïve	MAPE	0.72	1.79	6.81	12.36	22.14	7.23	5.11
		Utilization	5.61 0.08	4.87 0.13	11.72 0.79	12.94 1.39	8.81 1.76		
		Cycle	0	49	20	13	16		
	MA	MAPE	0.57	1.44	5.61	9.43	15.83	5.58	3.76
		Utilization	5.61 0.08	4.87 0.13	13.28 1.80	12.72 1.44	8.81 1.76		
		Cycle	0	49	4	14	16		
	EMA	MAPE	0.61	1.49	5.87	9.99	17.86	5.96	4.18
		Utilization	5.61 0.08	4.87 0.13	6.47 0.75	11.15 1.27	8.81 1.76		
		Cycle	0	49	18	30	16		

Figure 2: MAPE Values for Hourly Network Traffic

Simulation Web Server Forecasting Statistics			Results by 15 Minutes within a Day					Summary	
			Minimum Mean/STD	~-STD Mean/STD	~Mean Mean/STD	~+STD Mean/STD	Maximum Mean/STD	Mean	STD
Network Bytes Sent (Utilization in Millions)	Naïve	MAPE	0.51	0.67	1.28	1.83	4.90	1.27	0.65
		Utilization	21.83 0.30	21.84 0.33	21.89 0.44	21.78 0.54	21.64 1.52		
		Cycle	54	50	17	46	64		
	MA	MAPE	1.10	1.37	2.13	2.87	4.75	2.12	0.75
		Utilization	21.83 0.30	21.92 0.34	21.92 0.62	21.45 0.77	21.64 1.52		
		Cycle	54	49	84	83	64		
	EMA	MAPE	0.63		1.29	2.00	5.36	1.29	0.74
		Utilization	21.79 0.33		21.48 0.77	21.73 0.59	21.64 1.52		
		Cycle	18		23	69	64		
Network Received (Utilization 100K)	Naïve	MAPE	0.72	2.71	4.45	6.06	22.14	4.32	1.61
		Utilization	10.33 0.74	8.75 0.43	8.67 0.57	8.71 0.40	10.34 0.57		
		Cycle	0	34	38	42	16		
	MA	MAPE	0.57	4.02	5.18	6.75	15.83	5.24	1.48
		Utilization	10.33 0.74	5.82 0.19	10.28 0.69	5.83 0.24	10.34 0.57		
		Cycle	0	19	33	7	16		
	EMA	MAPE	0.61	2.44	3.95	5.59	15.83	4.11	1.45
		Utilization	10.33 0.74	5.85 0.24	5.82 0.19	5.83 0.19	10.34 0.57		
		Cycle	0	3	19	47	16		

Figure 3: MAPE Values for Daily Network Traffic

The trace results showed strong patterns for the daily and weekly predictions. The daily trace results were just as dramatic as the hourly simulation result, having an average error rate of

about 1% during the quietest times. The usage was predictable to within a 5% error rate even during the highest usage of the web server. Keep in mind that this only addresses the direct prediction and doesn't include the use of a confidence interval to identify the likely range of that prediction.

5. Conclusions and Future Research

This overview provides samples to show that an understanding of normal utilization could flag the periodic abnormalities for further investigation. In many of the cycle periods, even for the periods having a very poor prediction rate, there are clearly defined ranges of utilization. The accuracy of the prediction and level of error from that prediction will change with the cycle selected and will need to be selected based on the characteristics of the service's usage.

Network managers will also need to define appropriate confidence levels for their system, but once done, the basic forecasting methods can be used to predict utilization levels. Some possible uses for long-term prediction include:

- long-term resource management for distributed systems,
- ability to identify an abnormal state for graceful degradation prior to system failure,
- balance virtual machine with opposite resource demands, or
- a tripwire to increase the scrutiny of an Intrusion Detection/Prevention system.

6. References

[1] Abusina, Z.U.M., S.M.S. Zabir, A. Ashir, D. Chakraborty, T. Suganuma, and N. Shiratori (2005) *An engineering approach to dynamic prediction of network performance from application logs.* Int. J. Netw. Manag. **15**, 151-162 DOI: 10.1002/nem.554.

[2] Andreolini, M. and S. Casolari (2006) *Load prediction models in web-based systems.* Proceedings of the 1st international conference on Performance evaluation methodolgies and tools, 27 DOI: 10.1145/1190095.1190129.

[3] Andreolini, M., S. Casolari, and M. Colajanni (2008) *Models and framework for supporting runtime decisions in Web-based systems.* ACM Trans. Web **2**, 1-43 DOI: 10.1145/1377488.1377491.

[4] Barford, P. and M. Crovella (1998) *Generating representative Web workloads for network and server performance evaluation.* SIGMETRICS Perform. Eval. Rev. **26**, 151-160 DOI: 10.1145/277858.277897.

[5] Dinda, P.A. (2002) *A Prediction-Based Real-Time Scheduling Advisor.* International Parallel and Distributed Processing Symposium (IPDPS'02) **1**, 0010b-0010b DOI: 10.1109/IPDPS.2002.1015480.

[6] Krithikaivasan, B., Y. Zeng, K. Deka, and D. Medhi (2007) *ARCH-based traffic forecasting and dynamic bandwidth provisioning for periodically measured nonstationary traffic.* IEEE/ACM Trans. Netw. **15**, 683-696 DOI: 10.1109/tnet.2007.893217.

[7] Sharifian, S., S.A. Motamedi, and M.K. Akbari (2010) *An approximation-based load-balancing algorithm with admission control for cluster web servers with dynamic workloads.* J. Supercomput. **53**, 440-463 DOI: 10.1007/s11227-009-0303-8.

[8] Wolski, R. (2003) *Experiences with predicting resource performance on-line in computational grid settings.* SIGMETRICS Perform. Eval. Rev. **30**, 41-49 DOI: 10.1145/773056.773064.

Security Mechanisms for Multi-User Collaborative CAx

Francis Mensah
Brigham Young University
265 CTB
Provo UT, 84602
+1 801-800-3375
fn.mensah@byu.edu

Chia-Chi Teng
Brigham Young University
265 CTB
Provo UT, 84602
+1 801-422-1297
ccteng@byu.edu

ABSTRACT

Advances in computing technologies have provided the needed tools to transform traditional single user architecture Computer Aided Applications (CAx) to multi-user collaborative CAx architectures that supports simultaneous concurrency. To allow for a successful deployment in a corporate enterprise environment, the multi-user CAx architecture will require reliable security mechanisms to ensure protection of intellectual property. In this paper we propose mechanisms for securing user access and communications in a multi-user collaborative CAx software system. The proposed security solution is currently under development and is being tested on a collaborative multi-user version of a popular commercial CAD application.

Categories and Subject Descriptors

C.2.4 [Distributed Systems]: Client Server. D.4.6 [Security and Protection]: Access Controls Authentication Cryptographic controls Information flow controls

General Terms

Design; Reliability; Security; Verification.

Keywords

Collaboration; CAx; Security; Multi-user

1. INTRODUCTION

CAx systems have historically been implemented based on single user architectures, meaning a single designer works on a single instance at a time [5]. Although this architecture has worked sufficiently well in the past it does have many draw backs including time inefficiency especially when it involves geographically dispersed designers.

The drawbacks of single user CAx architectures coupled with the increasing trend of globalization of the world economy, increased competition, and pressures to reduce product development time call for a new approach toward engineering design and development technologies. In line with this trend research work has gone into seeking techniques and tools that will allow the design of engineering parts through the use of collaborative tools [1][3][6][4].

The transition from single user CAx architecture to a multi-user collaborative architecture, though brings enormous amount of benefits, also comes with some prices. One such price is the security risks that are introduced as a result of using networking technologies which potentially exposes the system to malicious entities within or without the network. Product design data represents the intellectual property of an organization and is of critical importance and significant worth and must be protected at all cost from falling into the wrong hands.

In this paper we propose the design and implementation of security mechanisms that will ensure that all network communications between clients and servers in a collaborative multi user CAx environment meet the requirements of integrity, confidentiality, authentication, non-repudiation without compromising availability. The proposed security solution is currently being tested on an ongoing multi-user CAx project, called v-CAx, at the Mechanical Engineering department of Brigham Young University. Figure 1 shows an overview of the architecture of v-CAx.

2. SECURITY DESIGN FOR MULTI-USER CAx (v-CAx)

This section describes how selected existing security technologies and standards have been employed in designing a framework for ensuring security in the v-CAx application. The framework works to achieve authentication and authorization of users and confidentiality of communicated data. The shaded portions of Figure 1 show the security framework components of v-CAx.

2.1 Authentication

Authentication in v-CAx is implemented as a combination of two mechanisms also known as multi-factor authentication. The first is through the use X.509 certificates when the NX-Client attempts to initiate a connection to the v-CAx server. During the Transport Layer Security (TLS) protocol handshake the v-CAx server authenticates itself to the NX-Client and vice versa through the exchange of certificates. This first lap of authentication will be successful if and only if the certificate presented by the client is trusted by the server and the certificate presented by the server is trusted by the client. The connection will be dropped immediately if the trust conditions are not met.

Integration of the v-CAx server with a directory server, in this case Microsoft Active Directory, is responsible for the second lap of authentication. With user authentication records stored in Active Directory the v-CAx server, on successfully completing the first round of authentication with the NX-Connect client, now further validates user supplied credentials with Active Directory. On successful validation the user is now granted access to the v-CAx application.

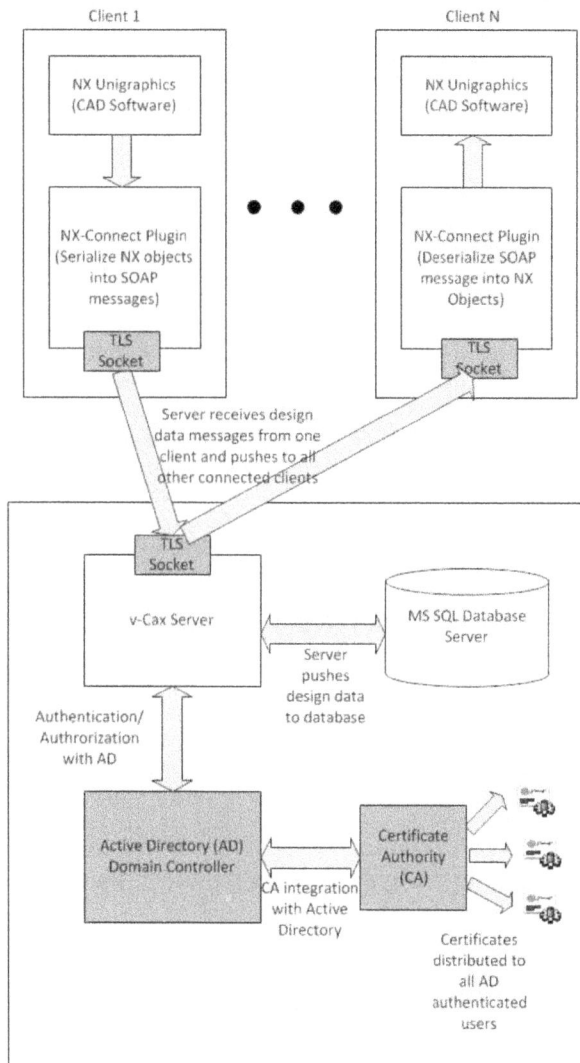

Figure 1 v-CAx Architecture with security framework implementation

2.2 Authorization

After a user is successfully authenticated the authorization mechanism ensures that the user has access to engineering design data that the user's security clearance permits. The mechanism also regulates the operations that can be performed on design part based on defined roles to which the user is assigned. The authorization mechanism is a hybrid access control model making use of features from the Mandatory Access Control (MAC) and Role-Based Access Control (RBAC) models as described by [2]. User authorization data is stored in Active Directory and is retrieved upon successful authentication. From this time on any operation the user seeks to perform on any design part within the application is validated using the authorization data of the user.

2.3 Confidentiality

Using the TLS protocol ensures that all messages communicated between NX-Connect clients and the v-CAx server are encrypted. In the event of a message being intercepted in transit it cannot be deciphered. The certificates needed by the TLS protocol are automatically managed and distributed through an integration of the Certificate Authority and Active Directory. The framework has been designed such that an authorized user who logs in to the designated Active Directory domain automatically receives a certificate to use to authenticate to the v-CAx server and for subsequent encryption.

3. CONCLUSION AND FUTURE WORK

This paper has presented security mechanisms for a collaborative multi-user CAx application, v-CAx, for ensuring confidentiality, authentication and authorization. These security mechanisms were designed as an integration of v-CAx with Microsoft Active Directory among other technologies and standards. Active Directory is a proven enterprise security infrastructure especially in terms robustness, scalability, and extensibility, and it is expected that its integration with v-CAx will provide the needed security objectives as mentioned in this paper. By implementing these mechanisms the security of the application is increased and can be considered as a trusted platform for engineering collaborative work. These mechanisms, however, do not exhaust all the security requirements of the v-CAx platform. It is expected that future work regarding the security of v-CAx will include other aspects of security including non-repudiation or auditing as well message integrity checks.

4. REFERENCES

[1]   Bidarra, R. et al. 2001. Web-based collaborative feature modeling. *Proceedings of the sixth ACM symposium on Solid modeling and applications. ACM.* (2001), 319–320.

[2]   Kim, S. et al. 2011. A Feature-Based Modeling Approach for Building Hybrid Access Control Systems. *2011 Fifth International Conference on Secure Software Integration and Reliability Improvement.* (Jun. 2011), 88–97.

[3]   Ramani, K. et al. 2003. CADDAC: Multi-Client Collaborative Shape Design System with Server-based Geometry Kernel. *Journal of Computing and Information Science in Engineering(Transactions of the ASME) 3.2.* (2003), 170–173.

[4]   Red, E. et al. 2013. Emerging Design Methods and Tools in Collaborative Product Development. *Journal of Computing and Information Science in Engineering.* 13, 3 (Apr. 2013), 031001.

[5]   Red, E. et al. 2010. v-CAx : A Research Agenda for Collaborative Computer-Aided Applications. *Computer-Aided Design and Applications.* 7, (2010), 387–404.

[6]   Rouibah, K. and Ould-Ali, S. 2007. Dynamic data sharing and security in a collaborative product definition management system. *Robotics and Computer-Integrated Manufacturing.* 23, 2 (Apr. 2007), 217–233.

A Grounded Theory Analysis of Modern Web Applications - Knowledge, Skills, and Abilities for DevOps

Soon K. Bang, Sam Chung, Young Choh, Marc Dupuis
Information Technology & Systems, Institute of Technology,
University of Washington - Tacoma
Box 358426, 1900 Commerce St, Tacoma, WA 98402
1-253-692-5886
{imageup2, chungsa, ychoh, marcjd}@uw.edu

ABSTRACT

Since 2009, DevOps, the combination of development and operation, has been adopted within organizations in industry, such as Netflix, Flickr, and Fotopedia. Configuration management tools have been used to support DevOps. However, in this paper we investigate which Knowledge, Skills, and Abilities (KSA) have been employed in developing and deploying modern web applications and how these KSAs support DevOps. By applying a qualitative analysis approach, namely grounded theory, to three web application development projects, we discover that the KSAs for both Software Development and IT Operator practitioners support the four perspectives of DevOps: collaboration culture, automation, measurement, and sharing.

Categories and Subject Descriptors

K.6.3 [**Management of Computing and Information Systems**]: Software Management - *Software development*

Keywords

Grounded Theory, Knowledge, Skills and Abilities, DevOps

1. INTRODUCTION

The arrival of cloud computing allowed us to merge together software development, deployment, and operation in what is known as DevOps. DevOps is a combination of development and operations [1]. Consequently, diverse stakeholders are involved in DevOps, including business analysts, software developers, software testers, and quality assurance personnel for development, and system administrators, database administrators, network administrators, web masters, and security officers for operations. Because of these diverse roles, DevOps has four perspectives: 1) a culture of collaboration between all team members, 2) automation of build, deployment, and testing, 3) measurement of process, value, cost, and technical metrics, and 4) sharing of knowledge and tools [2].

IT practitioners have used configuration management tools such as Chef[1], Puppet[2], Salt[3], Amazon OpsWorks[4], etc., to support

DevOps. However, the current DevOps approach is limited to the usage of proprietary configuration tools focused on automation of operations.

Instead, we propose a new approach to support DevOps - Knowledge, Skills, and Abilities (KSA) for DevOps. KSA has been used by the Department of Defense to identify the better candidates from a group of people qualified for a position [3]. For this purpose, we first describe grounded theory [4] in the context of several KSAs that have been used to develop and deploy modern web applications and apply it to the artifacts of modern web application development projects. Based upon this analysis, we then discover how the KSAs can support the four perspectives of DevOps and argue that a new theory - modern web application development with KSAs approach support the four perspectives of DevOps.

2. GROUNDED THEORY

Grounded theory is an inductive qualitative analysis approach which involves generating a theory from given source data [4]. Grounded theory consists of five steps. First, all data are collected from the test cases. Second, discrete codes are assigned to the collected data. Third, after assigning discrete codes to the artifacts of the three web applications, these codes are then grouped into concepts. Next, the relationships between concepts are examined and classified into categories. Finally, based upon these categories, a new theory is proposed.

We applied grounded theory to modern web application development. Modern web applications consist of many different artifacts in addition to source code, such as design documents in Unified Modeling Language (UML), Burn Down Charts (BDCs) and logs, Data Flow Diagram (DFD), Dependency Injection (DI), many cloud configuration files, etc. We first assign the names of the tools as the discrete codes to the data since the abilities to generate the data are proved by showing how the tools are used. For example, if we use a scrum management tool, Microsoft Team Foundation Service, we are able to generate BDCs. Then, we group the discrete codes into specific concepts by identifying which tools are employed to support which skills. For example, both Microsoft Team Foundation Service and Google Spreadsheet template are grouped into Scrum project management skills. Based upon the grouped concepts, we classify the concepts into categories – knowledge that can be earned through exercising the

RIIT'13, October 10-12, 2013, Orlando, Florida, USA.
ACM 978-1-4503-2494-6/13/10.
http://dx.doi.org/10.1145/2512209.2512229

---

[1] Opscode chef, http://www.opscode.com/
[2] Puppet Labs, https://puppetlabs.com/
[3] SaltStack, http://saltstack.com/
[4] AWS OpsWorks, http://aws.amazon.com/opsworks/

skills and a perspective of DevOps that the knowledge can support. Then, we propose a new theory which modern web application development with KSAs approach support four perspectives of DevOps from the relationship between KSAs and DevOps.

3. ANALYSIS

We will examine data from three real life cases: a Point of Delivery (POD) Web Application for an Aerospace Manufacturer, a Membership Management Web Application for a Smart and Secure Computing Research Group (SSCRG), and an Online Ordering Web Application for Asia Ginger Teriyaki Restaurant.

To perform a grounded theory analysis, four steps are performed. During the first step, we collect data from the three case studies. Many diverse data are collected.

At step 2, we assign discrete codes to the collected data of each web application. UML diagrams can be created by using Sparx's Enterprise Architect v10.0 CASE Tool or MS Visual Studio Architecture Edition. MVC directories are automatically generated if MS ASP .NET MVC 4 template is chosen. MS Threat Modeling Toolkit is used to draw a DFD based upon the given use case and misuse case. All used tools are identified and assigned to the data.

At step 3, we group the discrete codes into concepts. For example, MS Team Foundation service is used to manage the web application project with Scrum [5] concept or skill. Enterprise Architect CASE tool is used to document software architecture of each application. To use the CASE tool, a set of guidelines for documentation is required. 5W1H Re-Doc [6] is used.

Table 4: Concepts and Categories

	Two-Phase Categorization	
Concepts	Knowledge	Perspectives
- Scrum	- Agile development methodology	- Collaboration - Automation - Measurement - Sharing
- 5W1H Re-Doc	- Architecture Documentation	- Collaboration - Sharing - Measurement
- MVC Architectural Pattern	- Architectural pattern Separation of concerns	- Collaboration - Automation
- Dependency Injection	- Separation of concerns	- Collaboration - Automation
- Unit Testing	- Behavior-Driven Development	- Automation
- Mock Objects	- Behavior-Driven Development	- Automation
- Cloud – SaaS	- Architecture Documentation Agile development methodology	- Collaboration - Sharing
- Cloud - PaaS	- Cloud computing	- Automation
- MS Threat Modeling and Risk Analysis	- Threat modeling and risk analysis	- Automation - Measurement

At step 4, we construct categories that highlight the relationship between concepts. We use a two-phase categorization by first categorizing the concepts to knowledge that software developers and IT operators have learned. For example, Scrum is one of the agile development methodologies, which is a software development process with agility on requirement changes. The categories for each concept are shown in Table 4.

Then, the knowledge is categorized to the four properties of DevOps at the second categorization phase, which is shown in Table 4. For example, the Agile software development methodology supports the four perspectives of DevOps: 1) *collaboration* between all team members by means of daily scrum meetings, sprint retrospectives, reviews, and planning meetings; 2) *automation* of build, deployment, and testing; 3) *measurement* of process and technical metrics by scrum burn down chart, and 4) *sharing* of knowledge by product and sprint backlogs.

4. DISCUSSION

Finally, we propose a theory from Table 4: **KSAs support the four perspectives of DevOps**. Through the four steps of grounded theory analysis, we first discover what tools are used in creating the artifacts of the modern web application development projects, which skills are exercised to use the tools, what knowledge are studied to understand the concepts of the skills, and then how the knowledge are related to the four properties of DevOps.

Based upon this analysis, we propose a new theory that modern web application development with the Knowledge, Skills, and Abilities approach supports the four perspectives of DevOps. Future work is needed to discover how we can educate and train software developers and operators to be equipped with these KSAs to support DevOps.

5. REFERENCES

[1] Michael Hüttermann, September 2012, *DevOps for Developers*, Apress.

[2] Jez Humble & Joanne Molesky, August 2011, *Why Enterprise Adopt Devops to Enable Continuous Delivery* Cutter IT Journal, Vol. 24, No. 8.

[3] Department of Homeland Security, *Common Terms on Job Opportunity Announcements*, DOI= http://www.dhs.gov/common-terms-job-opportunity-announcements.

[4] Wellons, J., J. Johnson, 2011 *A Grounded Theory Analysis of Introductory Computer Science Pedagogy*, Journal on Systemics, Cybernetics and Informatics, vol.8 2011.

[5] Deemer, Pete, et al., 2010, *The Scrum Primer* DOI=http://assets.scrumtraininginstitute.com/downloads/1/scrumprimer121.pdf

[6] Sam Chung, Daehee Won, Baeg, M.H., Sangdeok Park. Jan. 2009, *Service-oriented reverse reengineering: 5W1H model-driven re-documentation and candidate services identification.* Service-Oriented Computing and Applications (SOCA), 2009 IEEE International Conference

[7] A. Freeman, 2012, *Pro ASP.NET MVC 4, (4th Ed.)*, Apress, New York

[8] Bellware, Scott. June 2008, *Behavior-Driven Development.* Code Magazine.

[9] Peter Mell, Timothy Grance. September 2011, *The NIST Definition of Cloud Computing.* National Institute of Standards and Technology Special Publication 800-145, 7 pages.

[10] MSDN, *Threat Modeling*, DOI= http://msdn.microsoft.com/en-us/library/ff648644.aspx

Sitemap Explorer: Browser Integrated Web Navigation

Jack Zheng
Southern Polytechnic State University
Marietta, GA USA 30060
(678) 915-5036
jackzheng@spsu.edu

ABSTRACT

A fundamental issue is still not addressed in current web navigation designs is the consistency of navigation models across different websites. In addition, almost all of the current designs are static and passive; users have to adapt their navigation behaviors to each model and follow it all the time on a particular website. This research presents a new browser integrated web navigation model which features a browser add-on called Sitemap Explorer to dynamically discover and load sitemap files and visualize them to users in a model of their own choices. The solution provides a consistent and personalizable client interface for the complex and unpredictable web, and offers rich functionalities and flexibility for users to easily manage and adapt web navigation to their needs. For more information, visit https://code.google.com/p/sitemap-explorer

Categories and Subject Descriptors

H.5.3 and H.5.4 [**INFORMATION INTERFACES AND PRESENTATION**]: Group and Organization Interfaces, Hypertext/Hypermedia – *Web-based interaction, Navigation*

General Terms

Algorithms, Design, Human Factors, Languages.

Keywords

Sitemap, Web Navigation, Browser Add-on

1. INTRODUCTION

People use web browsers as the major tool for information navigation and seeking on the Internet today. A good navigation mechanism is a key factor of web usability [3] that can improve the information seeking effectiveness. Web usability guidelines are offered to guide developers to develop better web interfaces, but they still have not effectively addressed two major issues:

1. Navigation models and designs are inconsistent across websites. Navigation designs are often quite different in terms of style, interaction, content structure, etc. These differences create difficulties for normal users when visiting an unfamiliar site [5]: users don't like to be "forced to learn a

special way of doing things" [6]. Sitemaps are one example of the differences evident in user interaction design, resulting in user confusion [6].

2. Current navigation models are website specific but not user oriented. Because web navigation designs are typically static and fixed, users cannot customize or personalize the structures or interfaces. Personalization or customization on interface and content structure is a common expectation for the purpose of ease-of-use [1]. Fixed navigation structure also does not provide rich functions for personal information management such as sorting, indexing, user annotation, organization, and categorization.

Traditional web navigation and information seeking research focuses on an analysis of information architecture, using tools like card sorting and usability testing to determine the findability of information by users. Web usability studies also suggest general user interface and interaction guidelines (such as [4, 6]): 1) visualizing the structure of information space, as, for example, a site map; 2) providing easy and flexible access to the navigation information; 3) providing context cues; 4) providing navigation trace/history.

This research study examines a drastically different approach to address the issues of navigation and findability using a model that focuses on cross-site consistency and personalization. The center piece of the design is a browser-integrated web navigation tool called Sitemap Explorer. A browser-integrated navigation tool is either a built-in component or an add-on of a browser [2]. Two major related research questions are:

1. Does a browser-integrated navigation tool such as Sitemap Explorer assist users in web navigation and information seeking?

2. What are the desired features of such a tool in terms of personalization and information management?

2. Sitemap Explorer

Our preliminary work suggests that a general solution lies in separating sitemaps from the website for navigation purposes and consistently displaying and controlling sitemap structures across all websites. Inspiration for this research derives from Nielsen [6] who suggests that better awareness of the user's navigation probably requires some amount of integration with the Web browser. In accordance with this notion of improving the user experience with sitemaps, this research has developed a new navigation model, in which navigational information (e.g., a sitemap) is separately presented and managed by a web browser add-on. The new model consists of three components:

RIIT'13, October 10–12, 2013, Orlando, Florida, USA.
ACM 978-1-4503-2494-6/13/10.
http://dx.doi.org/10.1145/2512209.2512230

1. Sitemap Explorer: a client-side user interface component which was prototyped as a Firefox browser add-on. This is the core part of the model.

2. Sitemap description file: a structured expression of sitemaps and other navigation information.

3. Sitemap location and dynamic discovery: a protocol to allow the client side Sitemap Explorer to find and load sitemaps. It can be a central sitemap repository with related services provided through a cloud service, or it can be placed on each website.

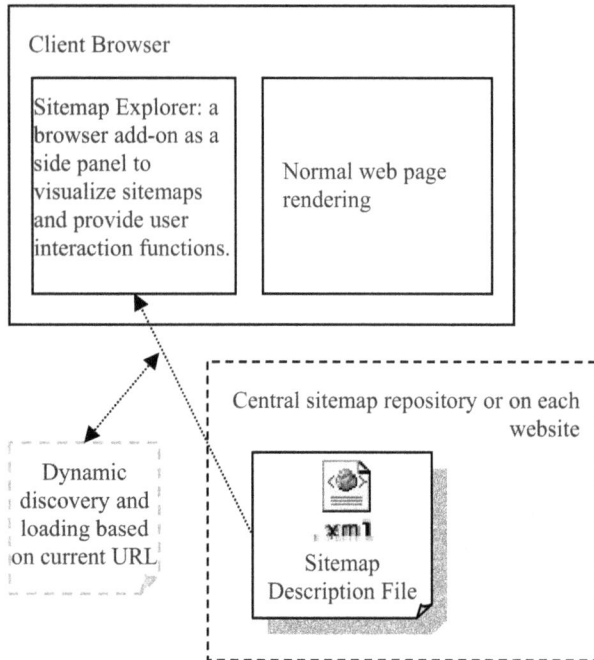

Figure 1: Browser Integrated Web Navigation Model

3. Prototype

A prototype is being developed as a Firefox browser add-on using popular web technologies of HTML, CSS, and JavaScript. Figure 2 shows a screenshot of the add-on. The add-on is showing a sitemap for an academic department website. The sitemap is visualized in a tree structure and can be searched within the structure.

4. Conclusion

Browser-integrated navigation systems have a number of advantages if implemented well. They provide navigation consistency, easy and flexible access, and a greater level of personalization and customization. More research on this type of navigation system will provide more navigation assistance to users.

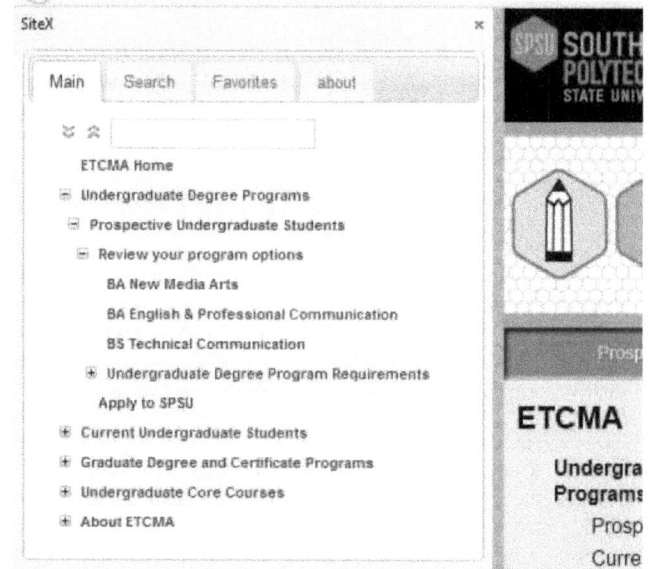

Figure 2: Sitemap Explorer Prototype (FireFox Addon) Screenshot

5. REFERENCES

[1] Blom, J.O. and Monk, A.F. 2003. Theory of Personalization of Appearance: Why Users Personalize Their PCs and Mobile Phones. *Human-Computer Interaction.* 18, 3 (2003), 193–228.

[2] Levene, M. 2010. *An Introduction to Search Engines and Web Navigation.* John Wiley & Sons.

[3] Palmer, J.W. 2002. Web Site Usability, Design, and Performance Metrics. *Information Systems Research.* 13, 2 (Jun. 2002), 151–167.

[4] Proctor, R.W. 2002. Content Preparation and Management for Web Design: Eliciting, Structuring, Searching, and Displaying Information. *International Journal of Human-Computer Interaction.* 14, 1 (2002), 25–92.

[5] Silver, M. and Ward, S. 2004. Browser-Based Applications: Positive or Negative Transference? *Proceedings of the American Conference on Information Systems 2004.* (Dec. 2004).

[6] Site Map Usability: 2002. *http://www.useit.com/alertbox/20020106.html.* Accessed: 2010-01-02.

Design and Evaluation of Face Tracking User Interfaces for Accessibility

Norman H. Villaroman
Brigham Young University
Information Technology Program
Provo, Utah
normanhv@byu.edu

Dale C. Rowe Ph.D.
Brigham Young University
Information Technology Program
Provo, Utah
+1 (801) 422 6051
dale_rowe@byu.edu

Richard G. Helps Ph.D.
Brigham Young University
Information Technology Program
Provo, Utah
+1 (801) 422 6305
richard_helps@byu.edu

ABSTRACT

Some individuals have difficulty using standard hand-manipulated computer input devices such as a mouse and a keyboard effectively. However, if these users have sufficient control over their face and head movement, a robust face tracking user interface can bring significant usability benefits. Using consumer-grade computer vision devices and signal processing techniques, a robust user interface can be made readily available at low cost, and can provide a number of benefits, including non-intrusive usage. Designing and implementing this type of user interface presents many challenges particularly with regards to accuracy and usability.

Continuing previously published research, we now present results based on an analysis and comparison of different options for face tracking user interfaces. Five different options are evaluated each with different architectural stages of a face tracking user interface — namely user input, capture technology, feature retrieval, feature processing, and pointer behavior. Usability factors were also included in the evaluation. A prototype system, configured to use different options, was created and compared with existing similar solutions. Tests were designed that ran on an Internet browser and a quantitative evaluation was done. The results show which of the evaluated options performed better than the others and how the best performing prototype compares to currently available solutions. These findings can serve as a precursor to a full-scale usability study, various improvements, and future deployment for public use.

Categories and Subject Descriptors

H.5.2 [**Information Interfaces and Presentation**]: User Interfaces – *Evaluation/methodology, Input devices and strategies*
K.4.2 [**Computers and Society**]: Social Issues – *Assistive technologies for persons with disabilities.*
I.5.5 [**Image Processing and Computer Vision**]: Implementation – *Interactive systems.*

Keywords

Face Detection, Face Tracking, Accessibility, Depth, Perceptual User Interface, Consumer Devices, Assistive Technology

1. INTRODUCTION

Some users with physical limitations may find it very difficult, if not totally impossible, to use a mouse and keyboard as standard input devices. For users who have the capability to move their heads and faces with relative ease, face tracking user interfaces can provide an alternative input method to enable them to use computers more effectively.

While various techniques and implementations have been presented in research and in the industry, performance comparisons between different solutions can be difficult because there is great variability in test methods, environment (e.g. screen resolution), and user interface design, among other things.

Our research attempts to solve some of these problems. In previous works, we presented a logical and architectural organization of this type of user interface and presented different design and implementation options.[1, 2] In this work we generalize and update that organization. We also present our comparative performance analysis of an implementation of each approach. To be able to make meaningful comparisons between prototypes and existing solutions, we also designed and implemented tests that can be used for comparison. These tests will be presented in this paper in a summarized form. The details of the testing framework will be released in a more complete publication in the future.

2. BACKGROUND

Face tracking user interfaces are not new, with some directly related research published as early as 1994. [3] The application SINA (http://dmi.uib.es/~ugiv/sina/) from Varona et al. detected and tracked the position of the nose from image features for cursor control along with detecting and employing eye winks (from color distributions) for control commands (e.g. mouse click). [4] The earlier application *Nouse* (http://nouse.ca) of Gorodnichy et al. tracked the nose and eyes as well and used multiple blinks as control commands [5]. They also proposed and implemented a visual feedback mechanism whereby a small image follows the cursor and shows how the system is interpreting the current state of the user's head pose [6]. Morris et al. used skin color to detect the face and the nostrils, producing a system that they admit is vulnerable to noise from similarly colored regions [7]. Chathuranga et al. implemented a system where the nose is tracked for cursor control and where speech recognition is used for selection [8]. The Camera Mouse (http://www.cameramouse.org/) uses correlation to track user-defined and automatically updating templates to track a small region in a video sequence [9]. For the same application, Tu et al. used a 3D model fitted to 2D features (using Least Mean Squared Error) to track a face using normalized correlation [10].

This research builds on the previous work by providing a formal analysis and comparison of various design and implementation options of the entire interface. The advancement of technology provides new hardware and software options both for design and implementation and thus also provides new opportunities for evaluation.

Commercial systems offer an alternative to research designs. Two of these are the HeadMouse Extreme (Origin Instruments, http://www.orin.com) and the SmartNav (NaturalPoint, http://www.naturalpoint.com). Both track a reflective dot placed on the user's face. HeadMouse Extreme emulates a hardware mouse with a video input, tracker, and logic embedded in the hardware. Since it emulates a standard mouse no external software needs to be installed. The SmartNav also tracks a reflective dot but the input simulation is done through the Windows API.

The technologies mentioned above are good but do not completely satisfy the design requirements we wish to have in such a user interface. (see Section 3.1) For example, the HeadMouse Extreme and the SmartNav require the user to wear or put on an accessory. CameraMouse requires another person to start tracking for normal operation. Other technologies that were evaluated proved to have limited robustness in their ability to detect and track face features. The above technologies represent some common and recommended assistive technology options (from interviews with the staff of the Utah Center for Assistive Technology) and are used here for comparison in this research.

3. RESEARCH APPROACH

3.1 Design Requirements
Our hypothesis is that, assuming sufficient performance can be achieved, a vision-based face tracking user interface provides several usability improvements over existing solutions. These benefits include non-intrusive and assistance-free usage (i.e. the user does not have to wear anything and can operate the user interface independently), and can emulate mouse functionality just by head and face movement. In addition low-cost consumer devices should replace expensive, specialized hardware. To formalize this, design requirements were set which are summarized as follows.

- Face detection and tracking happen automatically
- Input should be controllable by head and face movements that do not require the movement of the torso.
- Normal usage (including starting and stopping) should not require the intervention of a helper
- Operation should be unobtrusive and does not involve having to wear a device or a paraphernalia
- Operation should be robust to some variance in the location of the user's face relative to the screen
- Can be used with a wide variety of existing technology and applications
- Calibration of the system is not required or is minimal
- Simple input operations should not require multiple or prolonged attempts
- Costs should be minimal and, if possible, use commercial-off-the-shelf equipment.

These requirements guided the design and implementation of the prototypes.

3.2 Generalized System Architecture
Face tracking system design can be discussed using the generalized architecture shown in Figure 3-1. This structure will be used to discuss the various systems investigated in this report.

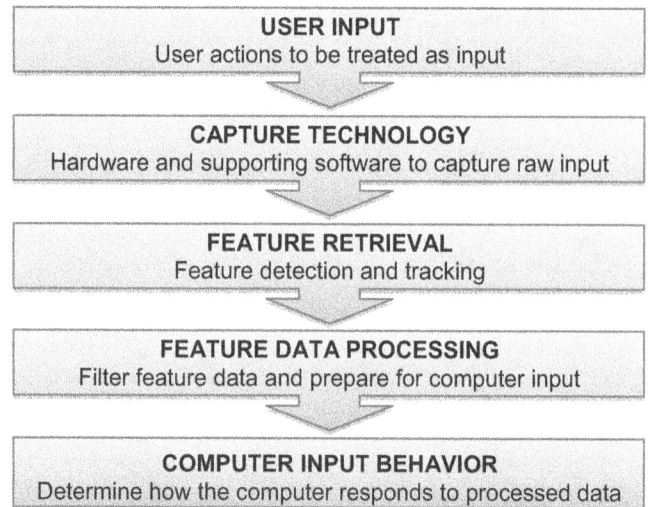

Figure 3-1 Input stages of face tracking user interfaces

3.2.1 User Input
The movement and position of a user's face provide the input for the user interface. Pointer control, traditionally provided by mouse movement and clicking, is replaced by face-oriented alternatives. Face gestures can also be used to trigger selection and other commands. For pointer control, three different options were evaluated (see Figure 3-2).

Point from 2D Location uses a 2D point in the captured feature that represents the location of the feature as the main input source. **Point from 2D Rotation** uses the pitch and yaw orientation to locate the interaction point. **Head Pose Pointing** uses the location and orientation of the head in 3D space and calculates where it is pointing to determine a calculated point on the screen.

Figure 3-2 User Input options (left to right) - Point from 2D Rotation, Point from 2D Location, and Head Pose Pointing

3.2.2 Capture Technology
Various devices can provide the raw data for a face tracking user interface. While many commercial and specialized devices are available, only two classes of vision-based consumer devices fit the design requirements for evaluation in this study. They are non-intrusive, relatively cheap, and readily available.

Webcams provide 2D image data, are low cost, and are readily available. **3D Consumer Depth Sensors** provide depth data of a scene usually with registered color data. While different devices can provide 3D data (e.g. multi-view cameras, time-of-flight, etc.), the recently developed LightCoding™ technology by PrimeSense (http://www.primesense.com/) provides an alternative that is low cost and effective. This technology has been used in commercial products such as Microsoft Kinect, ASUS Xtion, etc.

The availability of these devices and their supporting software make the inclusion of such devices for this study an easy choice.

The hypothesis relative to depth sensors is that depth data can enhance the accuracy of a face tracking engine, which would thus provide increased robustness for a user interface.

3.2.3 Feature Retrieval

Feature retrieval is the core of an effective user interface. This is most important and can be a significant modifier to overall system robustness. Unreliable feature retrieval can make the user interface unusable. The identified feature is represented by a feature vector. The feature vector can be collected using detection, tracking and, optionally, pose estimation algorithms. There is much research in this area of computer vision. We used existing face detection and tracking implementations in this research.

We chose the following implementation of face detection and tracking algorithms - **MS Face Tracking SDK**, **Seeing Machines faceAPI**, **Fanelli's Discriminative Random Regression Forests** [11], and the classic **Haar Cascade Classifier** [12]. These were chosen because they provide a usable library, they easily integrate with consumer devices, and they provide automatic face detection and tracking out of the box.

Other applications and implementations were considered but they lacked the availability, functionality, or performance required for our user interface. These include, among others, Nouse [5], Camera Mouse[9], faceShift (faceshift.com), SINA [4], SHORE (Fraunhofer IIS) scale invariant feature transform (SIFT) [13], local binary pattern, iterative closest point [14], and various template matching algorithms.

3.2.4 Feature Data Processing

Feature data from the tracking engine typically needs to be both transformed into a suitable format for the interface and to be filtered to remove noise. Removing the noise is essential to provide stable pointer performance and is best done on the feature data points [1]. Some relevant filtering algorithms include mean/median filters, mean-shift, [4] particle filters, and the Kalman filter. In this study, only two good candidates were implemented—the average filter and the Kalman filter.

Average or moving average filters are easy to implement and are computationally efficient, but include outliers in the data, which can be problematic. Weighted average filters improve performance. The classic Kalman filter was found to give good results for smoothing pointer movement. The Kalman filter can operate on a simple time-discrete linear model and is relatively resilient to outliers and Gaussian noise in general. As a recursive Bayesian method, it provides an efficient way of estimating the true state of an object by recursively predicting the next state and updating it with new observations if there are any. The filter was implemented with the OpenCV computer vision library.

3.2.5 Computer Input / Pointer Behavior

Three options were evaluated for the way the computer translates the processed feature data into relevant input—**velocity**, **differential** and **location** pointer modes. These three are shown from left to right in Figure 3-3.

Determining pointer movement by velocity uses the feature data together with an interaction zone to calculate how much the pointer will move from its current location. The interaction zone is a limited subsection of the image which contains the body part of interest (e.g. face). The location pointer mode also requires an interaction zone and uses that to directly translate to a screen location by scaling.

Depending on the other options used (e.g. face tracking engine), an interaction zone may not be available. In such a case a good option is to use a differential pointer—where the next pointer location is calculated based on the change from the previous pointer location. This is similar to how standard computer mice work. This option presents certain usability advantages over options with interaction zones because depending on how the interaction zone is defined (e.g. head orientation limits, a region from the first frame in the tracking sequence, etc.), the interaction zone may not be well-behaved, thus detracting from the user experience. With a differential pointer, the need for a reliable interaction zone is eliminated and the user can easily adjust where the pointer is relative to his head orientation.

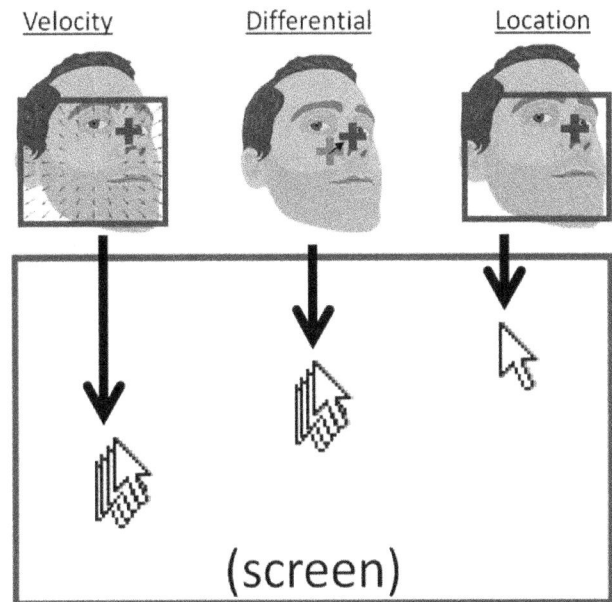

Figure 3-3 Computer input / pointer behavior options

3.3 Testing

As we evaluated the different design and implementation options in a face tracking user interface as well as existing applications that attempt to achieve similar objectives, we realized the necessity of having a test framework to quantify the performance of each solution. The solutions that have been presented in various research work or that are available publicly operate under different environments and were evaluated using different methodologies, thus making effective comparisons challenging.

We therefore designed a set of tests to evaluate the performance of each option enumerated in Section 3.2. The designed tests overcome some of the challenges of differences in operating environment by being executed as a client-side application (using HTML and Javascript) within an Internet browser—offline or online. Where appropriate, the controls in these single page applications use pixels as the basis for sizes to take into account differences in screen resolution where the environment forces a particular range of resolutions. A brief description of this test framework is included here. A more detailed discussion is deferred to a later publication.

3.3.1 Pointer Control

We selected the primary objective of the face tracking user interface for this project as pointer control. The pointer control test measures the speed with which a user can point to and select a set of numbered buttons in order. (see Figure 3-4) The nine clickable buttons are numbered left-to-right, top-to-bottom, providing a natural order but requiring a mixture of long and short traverses between targets. To avoid having the result be bloated by inaccurate selection (i.e. a user may click several times as he tries to place the pointer over the target), we also count how many "clicks" missed their mark.

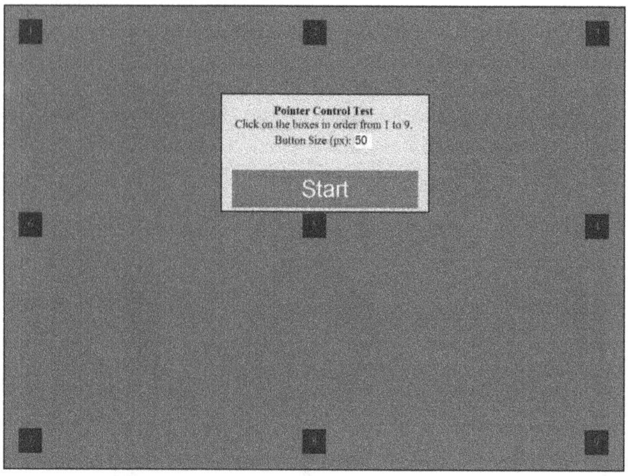

Figure 3-4 Screenshot of the pointer control test

3.3.2 Pointer Spread

The pointer spread test measures the noise generated by the user interface. In it, the user tries to point to a cross-hair target. The test starts with a click on the target. The user then remains as stationary as possible for five seconds while the test runs. Data is gathered at 50 ms intervals (thus making it independent of the update frequency of the user interface) giving 100 samples for every test run.

Some simple statistical data of how far the pointer traveled away from the target is given together with the raw data as shown in Figure 3-5.

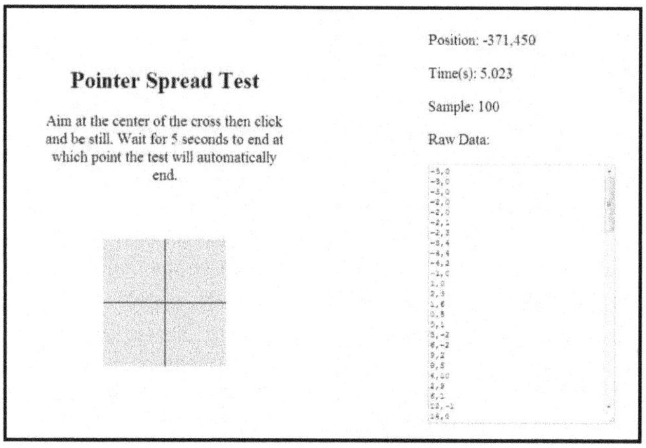

Figure 3-5 Screenshot of the pointer spread test

3.3.3 Typing

Text entry is a basic computer input operation and a typing test that measures how fast a set of words can be typed accurately provides an indicator that can be used to compare with other text entry solutions that may be using different modalities or are in different environments.

In this test, accuracy is forced so the user cannot proceed to the next word until he types the word properly. This provides a time

penalty for errors. In user interfaces that control the pointer and rely on a virtual keyboard for text entry, performance difficulties become apparent because the keys are relatively small and are close together. A fixed-size frame of size 800x300px is provided as a placeholder for the resizable on-screen keyboard used to make sure that the keys are the same size on each run.

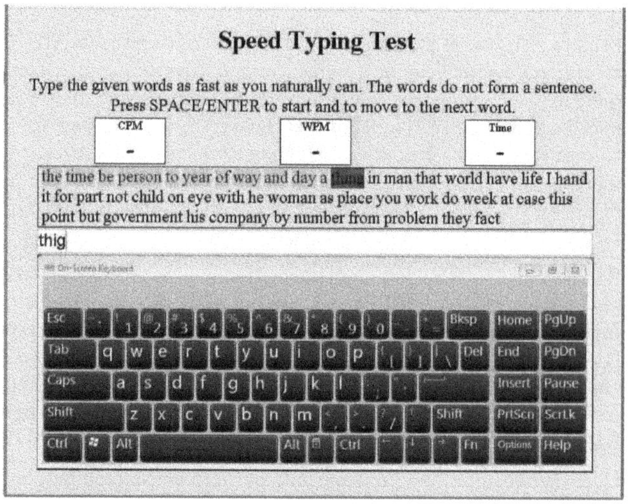

Figure 3-6 Screenshot of an ongoing typing test

3.4 Experimental Setup

The prototypes for the user interface were developed on a personal computer that is running Windows 7 and is powered by an Intel® Core™ i5-2500 (3.3 GHz) quad-core CPU and 8GB of memory. Testing was done on a few different machines including a laptop with a dual-core Intel® Core™ 2 T5300 (1.73 GHz) CPU and 2GB of memory. The prototypes were written in C++. A 2.0 MP Logitech QuickCam Pro 9000 USB camera was used (in 640x480 mode) where a webcam was needed. A Kinect for Windows was used where a depth sensor was needed.

For testing, a 23" screen set to a resolution of 1920 x 1080 was used. The user's face is positioned about 2 feet from the screen. Each test was done ten times after a series of practice rounds. Since the purpose of these tests was to focus on the comparative performance of the technologies involved, rather than user variability, and to reduce variance caused by human factors, only one user performed all the tests. However it should be noted that the system was tried by a number of different users, though they did not perform all the prescribed tests. Clearly future research can and should investigate the effect of multiple users on the system performance.

4. RESULTS

The following shows a summary of the results obtained.

4.1 Input Stages

To avoid having to test all the different combinations of options, it was assumed for simplicity that the different architecture stages (see Figure 3-1) are independent of each other and so the options in each stage were tested with all the options in the other system stages held constant.

4.1.1 User Input

In addition to the three options evaluated, the tests were also performed to provide a comparative baseline for performance analysis. The pointer control test was used to evaluate these options and the results are shown in Table 4-1.

The results show firstly that a hand-held mouse is much faster than the head movement options. It is also apparent that using feature location in 2D space to control the pointer gives the best control of the three head-movement options. This also shows that the technology used to estimate head rotation is not as accurate (shown in the results for 2D Rotation and Head Pose Pointing). Also it shows that although Head Pose Pointing has significant human usability benefits its performance is less viable with the technology used.

Table 4-1 User input results (pointer control test)

(sec)	From 2D Location	From 2D Rotation	Head Pose Pointing	Standard Mouse
Average	33.9	43.1	57.8	7.3
Std Dev	3.5	4.7	7.4	0.3
Min	27.4	35.5	47.2	6.9
Max	39.6	49.4	66.7	7.8

4.1.2 Capture Technology

The four different face tracking engines that we tested use either a regular webcam or a consumer depth sensor. The results of the evaluation of these face tracking engines are shown in Table 4-2. As far as the capture technology is concerned, note that MS Face Tracking used both the color data and depth data of a Kinect, Random Forest (Fanelli's random regression Forests) used just the depth data of a Kinect, and the other two used a regular webcam.

Table 4-2 Comparison of face tracking engines

	MS Face Tracking	faceAPI	Random Forest	Haar Cascade
Pointer control (s)	22.0	22.3	105.0	>120.0*
Spread-Std Dev (horizontal| vertical)	10.6 | 9.0	12.7 | 6.3	29.9 | 34.2	77.1 | 40.6
Speed (fps)	24	30	9	16
CPU-Tracking	22%	14%	25%	21%
CPU-Not Tracking	22%	2%	25%	19%
Memory Usage	134MB	99MB	127MB	23MB

*The subject was unable to complete the speed pointing test

The results here are interesting in that while depth data does make face tracking more robust for estimating orientation, as used by the MS Face Tracking SDK, [15] (see also Section 4.1.3) the depth data is not essential to provide a robust engine for a face tracking user interface. With the right algorithms, a regular webcam may be sufficient, which has the advantage of eliminating the cost and bulk of a Kinect sensor. Fanelli's Random Regression Forests, though remarkable in its ability to perform pose estimation from depth, is also indicative of the noise that is present in the depth data produced by the Kinect sensor.

4.1.3 Feature Retrieval

The results in Table 4-2 show a number of things about feature retrieval. Using feature tracking where previously generated feature data is used to make the next estimate more accurate significantly improves performance. The Haar Cascade classifier performs quickly enough to be able to detect the location of a face per frame but the resulting sequence of location was very noisy.

The results show that MS Face Tracking and faceAPI are comparable in their performance in face tracking user interfaces (particularly with a user input that is based on a point from 2D location). Though the details are not shown here, MS Face Tracking outperformed faceAPI in the pointer control test 43.1s to 66.0s using point from 2D rotation. This means that, in part because of the use of depth data, the former's ability to estimate orientation is better than the latter.

4.1.4 Feature Data Processing

Vision-based systems are subject to noise from multiple sources.[1] In addition to any smoothing or noise reduction schemes used in the different input stages of a face tracking user interface, the feature data obtained can be further processed. We evaluated two filtering schemes (Average and Kalman) and compared them to the same system without them. Table 4-4 shows the results of these options when evaluated using the pointer spread test and the pointer control test.

Table 4-4 Comparison of feature data filters

	None	Average	Kalman
Point spread (horizontal | vertical)	10.6 | 8.9	7.9 | 3.4	3.5 | 4.5
Pointer control (s)	22.0	33.9	22.1

These results show a number of interesting things. While the average filter did help in reducing noise in the generated points, this does not necessarily make the pointer easier to control. Direct filtering may have unintended adverse consequences to control. As with the average filter, it was observed that the resulting delay would make the pointer hard to place on a target, causing it to go past the target and bounce back, even when the user's head has stopped. We implemented a technique to mitigate this effect. This technique involved the use of the Kalman filter, the results of which are in the same table. Even though the pointer control results between the Kalman filter and no filtering (None) are similar, missed clicks with the Kalman filter were significantly lower.

4.1.5 Computer Input / Pointer Behavior

Three options were evaluated for the way the processed feature

Table 4-3 Comparison of best performing prototype with existing solutions

Test		faceUI	Head Mouse	Smart Nav	Camera Mouse	Standard Mouse
Speed Pointing (s)	Avg	19.2	14.9	18.3	20.8	8.1
	σ	1.8	1.2	1.0	1.5	0.7
	Min	16.8	13.5	16.8	18.2	7.4
	Max	22.7	17.0	19.9	22.6	9.7
Spread, σ (horizontal | vertical)		3.2 | 3.1	1.6 | 1.2	2.8 | 1.9	6.7 | 3.0	0.0 | 0.0
Speed Typing	cpm	39.6	53.4	52.1	25.8	98
	wpm	9.6	13.2	12.8	6.0	23.4

data is converted to computer input. (see Section 3.2.5) In terms of performance, a location and a differential pointer only differ in the way they calculate the pointer location, providing different implementation and usability conditions, however, they are otherwise substantially similar. Thus, in our evaluation, we only evaluated the performance of the location and the velocity pointer.

Table 4-5 Evaluation of pointer options using the pointer control test

Pointer Control	Location	Velocity
Average (s)	29.0	49.4
Std Dev	2.9	6.1
Min	23.4	37.5
Max	32.7	59.7

The results show that for the users involved, using a location pointer is better than the velocity pointer. We are not, however, discounting the possibility that this may only be an indication of the user's affinity towards one interaction style over the other, thus possibly minimizing the validity of any generalization from this result. But there is a suggestion that it can be generalized in that a velocity pointer requires more movement to place the pointer on a target—because of the need to orient the head back to neutral position (forward-facing) to stop pointer movement. The velocity pointer may be particularly helpful where the control space has significantly lower resolution than the target screen space. [4, 5]

4.2 Comparison with Other Solutions

Finally, we present an evaluation of our best performing prototype, comparing it with other available solutions. We call this prototype *faceUI* in the results. This includes the use of point from 2D location as user input, a regular webcam, the faceAPI face tracking engine, the Kalman filter, and a location pointer. The other solutions we compared it with include SmartNav, HeadMouse Extreme, CameraMouse, and a standard mouse. The results are shown in Table 4-3.

The results show that faceUI performs better than CameraMouse and is comparable to, but behind SmartNav and HeadMouse. Since SmartNav and HeadMouse both require a dot placed on the user's head (see 2) they both do not meet the requirements outlined in Section 3.1. There is yet more work to be done to get this prototype to a solution that beats some of the best solutions available.

5. CONCLUSION AND FUTURE WORK

In this work we provided a generalized architecture for a perceptual user interface. Using this framework, we investigated the feasibility and advantages of different options that can be used in each option. We implemented these options and evaluated them using a general testing framework that we designed and implemented, and that can be used to evaluate and compare various user interfaces that attempt to control a pointer. We have also learned various techniques in solving problems associated with perceptual user interfaces. We have found the test framework we used effective in comparing the performance of various forms of our prototype and the other solutions.

Future work includes further developing and publishing the test framework we used so it can be used by others working on alternative user interfaces. As technology improves and as new techniques are learned, the prototype will be improved so that it will be robust enough to be offered to the public.

6. REFERENCES

[1] VILLAROMAN, N. H. and ROWE, D. C. Improving accuracy in face tracking user interfaces using consumer devices. In *Proceedings of the 1st Annual conference on Research in information technology* (Calgary, Alberta, Canada, 2012). ACM,57-62

[2] VILLAROMAN, N. H. Face tracking user interfaces using vision-based consumer devices. In *Proceedings of the 14th international ACM SIGACCESS conference on Computers and accessibility* (Boulder, Colorado, USA, 2012). ACM,297-298

[3] HUNKE, M. and WAIBEL, A. Face locating and tracking for human-computer interaction. In *Signals, Systems and Computers, 1994. 1994 Conference Record of the Twenty-Eighth Asilomar Conference on*, 1994).1277-1281 vol.1272

[4] VARONA, J., MANRESA-YEE, C. and PERALES, F. J. Hands-free vision-based interface for computer accessibility. *Journal of Network and Computer Applications*, 31, 42008), 357-374.

[5] GORODNICHY, D. O. and ROTH, G. Nouse 'use your nose as a mouse' perceptual vision technology for hands-free games and interfaces. *Image and Vision Computing*, 22, 122004), 931-942.

[6] GORODNICHY, D. *Perceptual Cursor - A Solution to the Broken Loop Problem in Vision-Based Hands-Free Computer Control Devices*. 2006.

[7] MORRIS, T. and CHAUHAN, V. Facial feature tracking for cursor control. *Journal of Network and Computer Applications*, 29, 12006), 62-80.

[8] CHATHURANGA, S. K., SAMARAWICKRAMA, K. C., CHANDIMA, H. M. L., *et al.* Hands free interface for Human Computer Interaction. In *Information and Automation for Sustainability (ICIAFs), 2010 5th International Conference on*, 2010).359-364

[9] BETKE, M., GIPS, J. and FLEMING, P. The Camera Mouse: visual tracking of body features to provide computer access for people with severe disabilities. *Neural Systems and Rehabilitation Engineering, IEEE Transactions on*, 10, 12002), 1-10.

[10] TU, J., TAO, H. and HUANG, T. Face as mouse through visual face tracking. *Computer Vision and Image Understanding*, 108, 1–22007), 35-40.

[11] FANELLI, G., WEISE, T., GALL, J., *et al.* Real Time Head Pose Estimation from Consumer Depth Cameras. In *DAGM'11* (Frankfurt, Germany, 2011).

[12] VIOLA, P. and JONES, M. Rapid object detection using a boosted cascade of simple features. In *Computer Vision and Pattern Recognition, 2001. CVPR 2001. Proceedings of the 2001 IEEE Computer Society Conference on*, 2001).I-511-I-518 vol.511

[13] LOWE, D. G. Object recognition from local scale-invariant features. In *Computer Vision, 1999. The Proceedings of the Seventh IEEE International Conference on*, 1999).1150-1157 vol.1152

[14] WEISE, T., BOUAZIZ, S., LI, H., *et al.* Realtime performance-based facial animation. *ACM Trans. Graph.*, 30, 42011), 1-10.

[15] SMOLYANSKIY, N. *Face Tracking SDK in Kinect For Windows 1.5*. http://nsmoly.wordpress.com/2012/05/21/face-tracking-sdk-in-kinect-for-windows-1-5/ (Last Accessed: Jun 2013).

Formalizing the Design of Embedded Software Using Sequence Diagrams and Abstract State Machines

Abdel Ejnioui
University Of South Florida
3433 Winter Lake Road
Lakeland, Florida 33803
1-863-667-7708
aejnioui@usf.edu

Carlos E. Otero
Florida Institute of Technology
150 West University Boulevard
Melbourne, Florida 32901
1-321-674-8000
cotero@fit.edu

Abrar A. Qureshi
University of Virginia's College at Wise
One College Avenue
Wise, Virginia 24293
1-276-328-0100
aqureshi@uvawise.edu

ABSTRACT

The latest specification of the Unified Modeling Language (UML) 2.x revised completely the structure and elements of sequence diagrams by expanding their modularity via interaction fragments. These fragments are based on a set of operators that can simplify the diagram's structure or alter the order of events in the diagram. Unfortunately, the new revision introduced a significant degree of ambiguity in the interpretation of these diagrams. This ambiguity is exacerbated by the fact that different styles of sequence diagrams can be used for different purposes of modeling and analysis. To address this ambiguity, this paper presents a formal model in operational semantics based on Abstract State Machines (ASM) to define the semantics of sequence diagrams. Specifically, update rules are devised for ASMs to handle important behaviors present in most embedded software operating in distributed or parallel environments. The approach in this paper assumes that lifeline processes in a sequence diagram act as autonomous agents that communicate by exchanging messages among each other in asynchronous and distributed manner. This formal model can be readily extended to define the semantics of the remaining operators including information about time intervals and constraints.

Categories and Subject Descriptors

F.3.2 [Logics and Meanings of Programs]: Semantics of Programming Languages – *operational semantics*.

General Terms

Design, Theory.

Keywords

UML, Sequence diagrams, Abstract state machines.

1. INTRODUCTION

With the advent of model-driven engineering, the latest UML 2.x standard adopted by the Object Management Group (OMG) is gaining importance in the software engineering community [1]. UML offers software designers a variety of diagrams for modeling software systems from different perspectives. Among these diagrams, dynamic diagrams such as sequence and state

diagrams can describe system behavior at various levels of abstraction. Sequence diagrams have been extended in UML 2.x to increase their expressiveness by allowing different types of flows such as branching, iterations, and interleaving via interaction fragments. In essence, sequence diagrams provide a visual notation to represent message interactions between objects or processes in a system. These and other modeling capabilities are essential when designing embedded (real-time) software, which tend to require formal and rigorous design processes to ensure its correctness before construction begins.

To increase their modularity, the newly adopted standard allows these diagrams to contain interaction fragments, which can be grouped into combined fragments to compose complex interaction expressions [1]. A combined fragment consists of an operator, one or more interaction fragments or operands, and possibly interaction constraints. Operators of combined fragments can be used to express different behaviors and can be generally divided into three groups: (i) operators that make the sequence diagrams more compact such as *alt*, *opt*, *break* and *loop*; (ii) operators that alter the order of events in the combined fragment such as *par*, *strict*, *critical*; and (iii) operators that alter the way a trace can be named as valid or invalid such as *neg*, *assert*, *ignore* and *consider* [2]. The OMG standard characterizes the semantics of sequence diagrams as the generation of valid and invalid traces where a trace is a sequence of event occurrences [2]. While the addition of combined fragments increases the expressiveness of sequence diagrams, it makes their interpretations quite difficult. This is complicated by the fact that sequence diagrams can be used for different modeling purposes. For instance, diagrams used to model asynchronous distributed systems can be interpreted differently from those used to model synchronous reactive systems. These vague semantics are a consequence of the ways in which the OMG specification describes interactions in sequence diagrams. Automating the analysis, simulation and verification of these diagrams remains a challenge in the face of these vague semantics. To address this problem, several semantics were proposed in the past to narrow the scope of the original semantics using formal denotational or operational semantics in most cases [2, 3]. While most formal semantics are denotational, very few operational semantics were proposed for this problem. This paper proposes a theoretical model based on abstract state machines to formalize the semantics of sequence diagrams. These semantics are intended for asynchronous distributed systems.

2. RELATED WORK

As stated above, formal semantics proposed in the past for sequence diagrams can be separated into two categories:

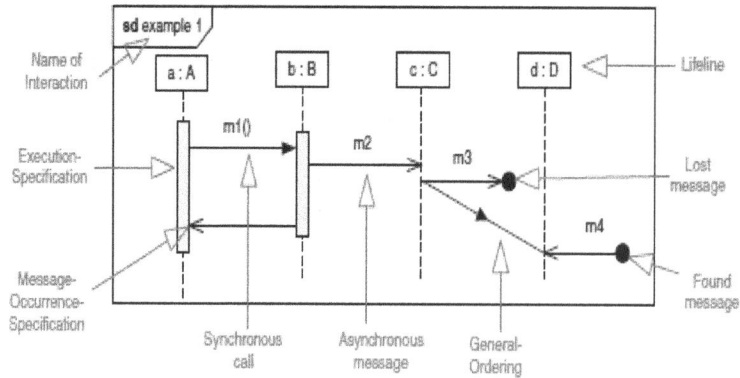

Figure 1. Sequence diagram example [3].

2.1 Denotational Semantics

One of the earliest formal semantics proposed for sequence diagrams in UML 2.x is a trace-based semantics based on the OMG specification, which defines the set of valid and invalid traces [4]. The semantics defines a partial order for plain interaction embedded in trace semantics of combined fragments. In [5], the authors develop a denotational semantics for interaction traces using partially ordered multisets for modeling concurrency based on Pratt's framework. These semantics can distinguish between positive and negative traces. In [6], the authors propose semantics based on event structures for sequence diagrams using a two-level hierarchical logic. The top level, or communication logic, describes inter-object interactions whereas the low level, or home logic, described intra-object behavior. In [7], the authors develop a scheme to translate a sequence diagram into a colored Petri net. Using basic operators in sequence diagrams, they use templates to represent an operator in a sequence diagram as a subnet of colored Petri nets. In [8], the authors propose semantics based on multivalued nets for sequence diagrams. Multivalued nets are a special algebra based on high-level Petri nets. The benefits of using these nets stems from the simplicity of constructing a multivalued net by applying a set of well defined operators. Finally in [9], the authors propose semantics that formalize sequence diagrams with combined fragments in terms of linear temporal logic (LTL) templates. Simple LTL formulas can be composed to express combined and nested combined fragments in a complex sequence diagram.

2.2 Operational Semantics

In [10], the authors develop a formal model that translates sequence diagram interactions into a special class of automata showing features of finite state, Büchi and counter automata. These translations support basic as well as complex operators in UML 2.0 sequence diagrams. However, in [11], the authors propose ASMs to formalize liveness-enriched sequence diagrams where each interaction is represented by a single ASM. To deal with synchronization and location difficulties, the basic ASM model is refined to insure liveness properties as defined in [12].

This paper presents a formal operational semantics based on ASMs where each lifeline is viewed as an independent agent proceeding through the interactions on its lifeline. Each agent is modeled by an individual ASM. Contrary to the semantics in [11], the semantics proposed in this paper remain faithful to the OMG specification by avoiding synchronization altogether in dealing with combined fragments, and relying on solely inter-agent message exchange to coordinate agent progress over lifelines in the sequence diagram.

3. SEQUENCE DIAGRAMS

Sequence diagrams are two-dimensional graphic representations of interactions where these interactions occur as message exchanges between objects. A lifeline emanates downward from an object to represent interaction events between the lifeline of an object and other object lifelines in the diagram. An event instance consists of sending, receiving, creating or destroying a message where a message is represented by a horizontal arrow between two instances on different lifeline. Figure 1 shows a basic sequence diagram [3].

To expand their modularity, sequence diagrams are allowed to contain interaction fragments, which can be combined with other interaction fragments. A combined fragment contains an operator and operands. In this paper, we address the semantics of the alt, par and opt operators shown in Figure 2:

- Based on the OMG specification [1], the *alt* operator represents a choice of behavior where at most one of the operands will be chosen. The chosen operand must have an explicit or implicit guard expression that evaluates to true at this point in the interaction. If none of the operands has a guard that evaluates to true, none of the operands are executed and the remainder of the combined fragment is executed.

- The *opt* operand designates that the combined fragment represents a choice of behavior where either the (sole) operand happens or nothing happens. An *opt* operand is semantically equivalent to an *alt* combined fragment where there is one operand with non-empty content and the second operand is empty [1].

- The *par* operand designates that the combined fragment represents a parallel merge between the behaviors of the operands. The occurrence specifications of the different operands can be interleaved in any way as long as the ordering imposed by each operand as such is preserved [1].

4. ABSTRACT STATE MACHINES

ASMs are a formalism that expresses behavior in terms of pseudocode over abstract data [13]. As formal concepts, ASMs bridge the gap between the difficult-to-understand, but verifiable, formal methods applied in system design and difficult-to-verify,

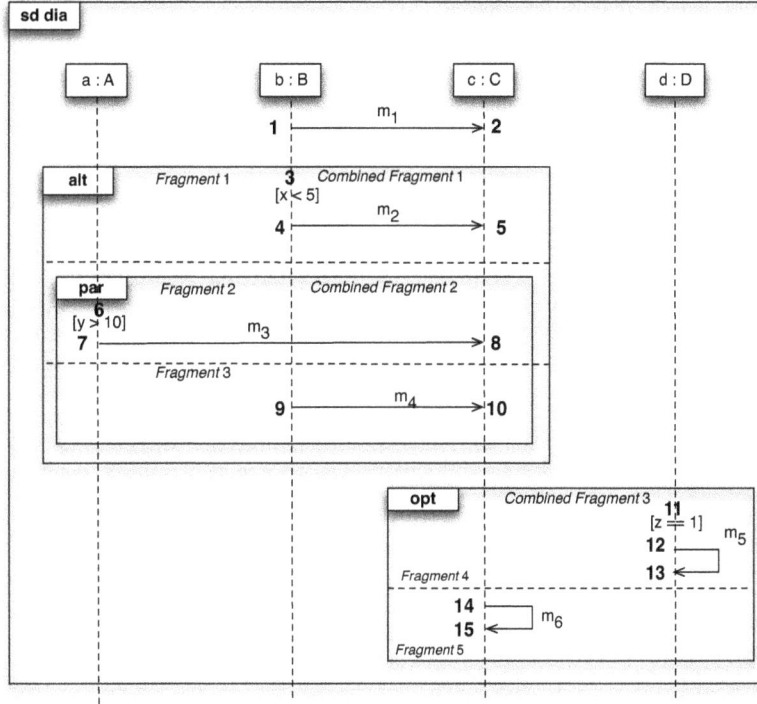

Figure 2. Sequence diagram showing alt, par and opt combined fragments.

informal algorithmic approaches used in system design and specification. In its basic form, an ASM is a program or algorithm together with a collection of states and update rules. ASM algorithms can be sequential in the case of *Basic ASMs* or recursive in the case of *Turbo ASMs* [14]. Groups of ASMs can act in a synchronous or asynchronous distributed manner in the case of *multi-ASMs*. In addition, ASMs support non-deterministic behavior and unbounded parallelism [14]. In essence, ASMs embody transition systems where the states can be viewed as multi-sorted first-order structures.

5. INTERACTION SEMANTICS

The OMG standard specifies the semantics of sequence diagrams in terms of interactions [1]. These interactions take place between lifelines representing various agents in the sequence diagram. Each agent proceeds along its lifeline by executing the interaction occurrences it encounters from top to bottom on its lifeline. These interaction occurrences can be message occurrence or execution. In these semantics, we assume an environment in which the agents interact with each other in asynchronous and distributed fashion. As such, the message occurrences considered in these semantics are primarily asynchronous messages. However, minor modifications to the proposed semantics are sufficient to include synchronous messages occurrences in the proposed semantics ASM Signature

A sequence diagram D is defined as $\langle A, M, F \rangle$ where A, M, and F are respectively the set of agents, messages and fragments in D. Each agent can proceed downward from location to location on its lifeline. In asynchronous distributed environments, agents communicate with each other by exchanging messages that can be stored in their own respective buffers. As such an agent $a \in A$ owns a buffer B_a, which can store messages received from other agents in A. The locations are numbered as integers from left to right and top to bottom. A location, $l \in L$ where L is the set of locations in D, can represent one of the following events: SEND

for sending a message event, RECEIVE for receiving a message event and EVALUATE for evaluating a guard expression. A guard, $g \in G$, where G is the set of guards in D. The following functions can be associated with locations:

- *LocationEvent*: $L \rightarrow \{$SEND, RECEIVE, EVALUATE$\}$ returns the type of event associated with a location.

- *NextLocation*: $L \rightarrow L$ returns the location next to a given location on the same lifeline.

- *Fragment*: $L \rightarrow F$ returns the fragment containing a given location.

- *CombinedFragment*: $L \rightarrow CF$ where CF is the set of combined fragments in D. This function returns the combined fragment containing a given location. Note that $CF \subseteq P(F)$ where $P(F)$ is the power set of F.

The following functions can be associated with a fragment $f \in F$:

- *Agents*: $F \rightarrow P(A)$ returns the set of agents involved in a fragment $f \in F$.

- *FirstLocation*: $F \times A \rightarrow L$ returns the first location of an agent in a fragment.

- *LastLocation*: $F \times A \rightarrow L$ returns the last location of an agent in a fragment.

A combined fragment $cf \in CF$ can be defined as $\langle o, K, ecf \rangle$ where o is an operator; K, where $K \subseteq F$, is the set of fragments contained in cf; and ecf is the enclosing combined fragment containing cf. As specified in UML 2.x, the operator $o \in O = \{$*alt, opt, break, loop, par, strict, critical, neg, assert, ignore, consider*$\}$). ecf is intended to cover the case of embedded combined fragments. The following functions can be defined on cf:

- *Operator*: $CF \rightarrow O$, which returns the operator of a combined fragment cf.

- *Agents*: $CF \rightarrow P(A)$ where $P(A)$ is the power set of A. This function returns the set of agents involved in a combined fragment cf.

- *Fragments*: $CF \rightarrow P(F)$ returns the set of fragments contained in a combined fragment cf.

- *FirstFragment*: $CF \rightarrow F$ returns the first (topmost) fragment in a combined fragment cf.

- *LastLocation*: $CF \times A \rightarrow L$ returns the last location of an agent in a combined fragment cf.

5.1 Update Rules

We assume each agent owns an ASM. This ASM proceeds downward along its own lifeline by keeping track of its current location at any time. Since there is more than one agent proceeding along its lifeline in D, a number of ASMs will be firing their update rules at each step. An agent always uses its current location to determine what action to take.

5.1.1 General Update Rules

In every location l, the ASM of an agent updates its state as follows:

```
case Operator(CombinedFragment(l))
        alt: DoAlt; skip
        opt: DoOpt; skip
        par: DoPar; skip
        else: DoDefault
```

Based on the reached location, an agent decides the update rules to execute. The else option represents the case where the current location is outside any fragment in D.

5.1.2 The Par Update Rules

These rules are applied when an agent reaches a location inside a *par* combined fragment.

DoPar

```
If LocationEvent(l) = SEND
        ParSend
If LocationEvent(l) = RECEIVE
        ParReceive
```

It is assumed that the first agent, which reaches the first location in a *par* combined fragment cf elects itself as a coordinating agent. For simplicity, we assume that no more than one agent is the first to enter a *par* combined fragment. This agent decides which fragment f in cf to enter by informing the other agents in cf of its decision. Entering fragments in a random fashion leads to interleaved event traces for the par operator.

ParSend

```
If B = ∅
    cf := CombinedFragment(l)
    ∀ f ∈ Fragments(cf)
        choose randomly a fragment f in cf
        ∀a ∈ Agents(f), Bₐ := Bₐ ∪ {enter(f)}
    ∀a ∈ Agents(cf), Bₐ := Bₐ ∪ {exit(cf)}
Else if enter(f) ∈ B
    If f ≠ Fragment(l)
        l := FirstLocation(f, self)
        send message m to recipient agent r
        Bᵣ := Bᵣ ∪ {send(m, r)}
```

```
    If l = LastLocation(f, self)
        B := B \ { enter(f)}
    Else
        l := NextLocation(l)
Else if exit(cf) ∈ B
    l := NextLocation(LastLocation(cf, self))
    B := B \ {exit(cf)}
```

If the buffer of an agent is empty, it assumes that it is the first to reach the *par* combined fragment cf. In this case, this agent randomly picks the fragments in cf. For each fragment f in cf, it inserts an *enter(f)* in the buffer of each agent involved in f, including its own buffer. At the end, it inserts an *exit(cf)* message in the buffer of each agent involved in cf, including itself. On the other hand, if an agent, including the coordinating agent, discovers an *enter(f)* message in its buffer, it assumes that it was sent by the coordinating agent in which case it jumps to the first location in f, sends the message to a recipient agent r, and inserts a *send(m, r)* message in the buffer of r. If an agent reaches the last location in f, it removes the *enter(f)* message from its buffer. Finally, if an agent, including the coordinating agent, finds an *exit(cf)* message in its buffer, it exits cf by jumping to the location next to the last in cf, after which it removes the *exit(cf)* message from its buffer. Note that *self* indicates the current agent referring to itself.

ParReceive

```
If enter(f) ∈ B
    If f ≠ Fragment(l)
        l := FirstLocation(f, self)
    If send(m, r) ∈ B
        receive message m from source agent s
        B := B \ {send(m, r)}
        If l = LastLocation(f, self)
            B := B \ { enter(f)}
        Else
            l := NextLocation(l)
  Else if exit(cf) ∈ B
    l := NextLocation(LastLocation(cf, self))
    B := B \ {exit(cf)}
```

If the buffer of a recipient agent is empty, it waits until it receives a message in its buffer from a source agent, in which case it performs the same steps in *ParSend*.

5.1.3 The Alt Update Rules

These rules are applied when an agent reaches a location inside an *alt* combined fragment.

DoAlt

```
If LocationEvent(l) = SEND
        AltSend
If LocationEvent(l) = RECEIVE
        AltReceive
If LocationEvent(l) = EVALUATE
        AltEvaluate
```

It is assumed that a guard expression is associated with only one agent in the *alt* operator. As such, only that agent performs its evaluation. It is also assumed that a fragment in the *alt* combined fragment contains at most one guard expression. These two assumptions are based on an asynchronous distributed environment. To avoid ambiguity and ensure progress of the agents through an *alt* combined fragment, an implicit guard is always assumed in a fragment that does not contain an explicit guard. Finally, it is also assumed that if an agent a does not have any location inside the *alt* combined fragment cf, meaning $a \notin Agents(cf)$, it is disregarded from consideration in cf. The guards in the combined fragment *cf* are all grouped in the set G_{cf} where each guard g_a is owned by some agent *a* in *Agents*(*cf*).

AltEvaluate

```
If B = ∅
    cf := CombinedFragment(l)
    G_cf := G_cf \ {g}
    If g = true
        f := Fragment(l)
        ∀a ∈ Agents(cf): B_a := B_a ∪ {enter(f)}
        l := NextLocation(l)
    Else
        If G_cf = ∅
            ∀a ∈ Agents(cf):
                B_a := B_a ∪ {exit(cf)}
        Else if |G_cf| = 0 and g = else
            ∃ a ∈ Agents(cf) with g_a = else:
                l_a := EvaluateLocation(g_a)
Else if enter(f) ∈ B
    l := FirstLocation(f, self)
Else if exit(cf) ∈ B
    l := NextLocation(LastLocation(cf, self))
```

If an agent, which has reached a location containing a guard to evaluate in an *alt* combined fragment, has an empty buffer, it proceeds to evaluate the guard. An empty buffer means that this agent is the first to enter the *alt* combined fragment. This gives a green light to any agent in other fragments ready to evaluate a guard to do so. If the evaluation of the guard is true, the evaluating agent inserts an *enter*(*f*) message in the buffer of each agent involved in the *alt* combined fragment *cf*, after which it proceeds to the next location. Note that *f* is the current fragment where the evaluation took place. On the other hand, if the evaluation of the guard returns false, the agent checks whether the set G_{cf} is empty or not. If the set is empty, it inserts an *exit*(*cf*) message in the buffer of each agent in *cf* indicating to the remaining agents that they must leave *cf* since no guard in *cf* is true. If the set G_{cf} is not empty, the agent checks whether the last remaining guard in the set G_{cf} is an *else* guard. If it is, it finds the agent associated with the *else* guard and moves it to the location of the *else* guard in *cf*. Note that *EvaluateLocation*(*g_a*) returns the location of the else guard in *cf* and assigns it to the location l_a of the agent owning the guard g_a. On the other hand, if an agent discovers an *enter*(*f*) message in its buffer, it means that another agent has evaluated a guard expression in some fragment *f* and its evaluation result is true. This instructs this agent to refrain from evaluating its guard and jump instead to the first location in *f*. Finally if an agent finds an *exit*(*cf*) message in its buffer, it knows that all guards were evaluated to false and all agents must exit the *alt* combined fragment *cf*.

AltSend

```
If enter(f) ∈ B
    If Fragment(l) ≠ f
        l := FirstLocation(f, self)
    Else
        send message m to some agent r
        B_r := B_r ∪ {send(m, r)}
        If l = LastLocation(f, self)
            B := B \ {enter(f)}
            cf := CombinedFragment(l)
            ll := LastLocation(cf, self)
            l := NextLocation(ll)
        Else
            l := NextLocation(l)
Else if exit(cf) ∈ B
    l := NextLocation(LastLocation(cf, self))
```

```
    B := B \ {exit(cf)}
```

If a message sending agent finds an *enter*(*f*) message in its buffer, it knows that another agent wishes it to jump to fragment *f* in which case it does so. Once inside *f*, it sends its message *m* to some recipient agent *r* and inserts a *send*(*m*, *r*) in *r*'s buffer. If it has reached the last location in *f*, it removes the *enter*(*f*) message from its buffer and jumps to the location next to the last location in *cf*. Otherwise, it merely proceeds to the next location in *f*. On the other hand, if this message sending agent finds an *exit*(*cf*) message in its buffer, it indicates that another agent evaluated a guard and the evaluation returned a false in which case it informs others to leave fragment *f*. This message sending agent gets out of *cf* altogether and removes the *exit*(*cf*) message from its buffer.

AltReceive

```
If enter(f) ∈ B
    If Fragment(l) ≠ f
        l := FirstLocation(f, self)
    Else
        If send(m, r) ∈ B
            receive message m from some agent s
            B_r := B_r \ {send(m, r)}
            If l = LastLocation(f, self)
                B := B \ {enter(f)}
                cf := CombinedFragment(l)
                ll := LastLocation(cf, self))
                l := NextLocation(ll)
            Else
                l := NextLocation(l)
Else if exit(cf) ∈ B
    l := NextLocation(LastLocation(cf, self))
    B := B \ {exit(cf)}
```

An agent *r* receives a message from a source agent *s* using the same steps in *AltSend* with the exception it does not so until it sees a *send*(*m*, *r*) in its buffer. Although an agent can get out of *cf*, it can be brought back to some fragment *f* via the *enter*(*f*) message if another agent decides so based on the result of its guard evaluation.

5.1.4 The Opt Update Rules

In an *opt* combined fragment, it is assumed that an implicit guard is present if there is no explicit guard available. The *opt* operator can be viewed as an *alt* operator with only one operand or fragment. As such, the update rules of sending message or receiving message agents can be identical to those in the *alt* operator. However, the update rules of a guard evaluating agent can be slightly modified to handle the *opt* operator.

DoOpt

```
If LocationEvent(l) = SEND
        OptSend
If LocationEvent(l) = RECEIVE
        OptReceive
If LocationEvent(l) = EVALUATE
        OptEvaluate
```

In this case, *OptSend* and *OptReceive* are similar to *AltSend* and *AltReceive*.

OptEvaluate

```
If g = true
    cf := CombinedFragment(l)
    f := Fragment(l)
    ∀a ∈ Agents(cf), B_a := B_a ∪ {enter(f)}
    l := NextLocation(l)
Else
```

```
cf := CombinedFragment(l)
∀a ∈ Agents(cf), Bₐ := Bₐ ∪ {exit(cf)}
l := NextLocation(LastLocation(cf, self))
```

The agent evaluating a guard in an *opt* combined fragment will be the only agent doing so based on the requirements stated above. As such, there will be no other guards to be evaluated by other agents. The other agents in the *opt* combined fragment will be either sending or receiving messages. In this case, the guard evaluating agent will never find messages from other agents in its buffer. It will be the only agent sending messages to other agents. If the evaluation of the guard returns true, this agent inserts an *enter(f)* message in the buffers of each other agent in the *opt* fragment *cf* after which it proceeds to the next location in *f*. Note that *f* is the current fragment in which the guard evaluation took place. However if the guard evaluation returns false, the agent inserts an *exit(cf)* message in the buffer of the remaining agents in *cf* after which it gets out of *cf*.

6. CONCLUSION

This paper introduces a formal semantics for sequence diagrams based on ASMs. The proposed work provides an approach for formalizing designs that rely on sequence diagrams and contributes significantly to the design verification process typically employed in most embedded software projects. Although the focus of these semantics is to model sequence diagrams for asynchronous distributed environments, they nevertheless follow closely the original semantics described in the OMG specification. In this environment, the paper considers lifeline processes as autonomous agents communicating by exchanging messages where each agent stores the messages it receives from others in its own buffer. In addition, the paper assumes that guard expressions may not be applied to an entire fragment, but rather can be attached only to individual lifelines. While the paper presents appropriate update AMS rules for the alt, *par* and *opt* operators, work is underway to extend these rules to model the remaining operators. Furthermore, time intervals and constraints will be considered in future extensions of the AMS model proposed in this paper.

7. REFERENCES

[1] Object Management Group. 2011. Unified Modeling Language (UML) Specifications, available at http://http://www.omg.org/spec/UML/2.4.1/Superstructure/PDF/.

[2] Micskei, Z. and Waeselynck, H. 2008. UML 2.0 sequence diagrams' semantics. Technical Report 08389. University of Toulouse.

[3] Micskei, Z. and Waeselynck, H. 2011. The many meanings of UML 2 sequence diagrams: a survey. *Software System Modeling*, 10, 4, (Oct. 2011), 489-514.

[4] Störrle, H. 2003. Semantics of interactions in UML 2.0. *IEEE Symposium on Human Centric Computing, Languages and Environments* (Arlington, Virginia, USA, Apr. 2002), 129-136.

[5] Cengarle, M., Knapp, A. 2004. UML 2.0 interactions: semantics and refinement. *International Workshop on Critical Systems Development with UML*. (Lisbon, Portugal, Oct. 2004), 85-99.

[6] Küster-Filipe, J. 2006. Modelling concurrent interactions. *Theoretical Computer Science*, 351, 2 (Feb. 2006), 203-220.

[7] Fernandes, J. M., Tjell, S., Bæk Jørgensen, J., and Ribeiro, O. 2007. Designing tool support for translating use cases and UML 2.0 sequence diagrams into a coloured Petri Net. *International Workshop on Scenarios and State Machines* (Minneapolis, Minnesota, USA, May 2007). 1-10.

[8] Eichner, C., Fleischhack, H., Meyer, R., Schrimpf, U., and Stehno, C. 2005. Compositional semantics for UML 2.0 sequence diagrams using Petri nets. *Software Design Languages Forum* (Grimstad, Norway, Jun. 2005), 133-148.

[9] Shen, H., Robinson, M., and Niu, J. 2008. Formal analysis of sequence diagram with combined fragments. *International Conference on Software Paradigm Trends* (Rome, Italy, Jul. 2012), 44-54.

[10] Knapp, A. and Wuttke, J. 2006. Model checking of UML 2.0 interactions. *Lecture Notes in Computer Science: Models in Software Engineering*, 4634 (2007), pp. 42-51.

[11] Cavarra, A. and Küster-Filipe, J. 2004. Formalizing liveness-enriched sequence diagrams using ASMs. *Lecture Notes in Computer Science*, 3052 (2004), pp. 62-77.

[12] Grosu, R. and Smolka, S. A. 2005. Safety-liveness semantics for UML 2.0 sequence diagrams. *International Conference on Application of Concurrency to System Design* (St. Malo, France, Jun. 2005), pp. 6-14.

[13] Börger, E. and Stärk R. 2003. *Abstract State Machines: A Method for High-Level System Design and Analysis*. Springer-Verlag, Berlin Heidleberg, Germany.

[14] Gurevich, Y. 1995. Evolving algebras 1993: Lipari guide. In *Specification and Validation Methods*, In E. Börger, Ed. Oxford University Press, Oxford, U.K., 231-243.

Automated Webpage Evaluation

Ryan Tate, Gregory Conti, Edward Sobiesk

Army Cyber Center

U.S. Military Academy

West Point, New York 10996 USA

ryan.tate@usma.edu, gregory.conti@usma.edu, edward.sobiesk@usma.edu

ABSTRACT

Webpage evaluation and metrics have historically focused on page-level characteristics or on key words. We introduce an automated technique for graphically measuring specific elements on a webpage. Our technique provides a means to increase the fidelity of webpage analysis and introduces a novel metric focused on the number of pixels that certain elements occupy in a browser window. We implemented the technique as a Firefox extension and successfully tested it on Alexa's top 25 U.S. websites. The technique is fully automatable and consistently measures a customizable set of elements as they appear to users in the Firefox web browser. Importantly, the application allows for communication with and the incorporation of other browser-based tools or extensions. We discuss design considerations and creative solutions to technical implementation challenges. The application provides for a wide range of research opportunities that may require a new level of fidelity in webpage analysis and comparison.

Categories and Subject Descriptors

D.2.8 [**Software**]: Metrics - *product metrics.*

H.3.5 [**Information Storage and Retrieval**]: Online Information Services – *data sharing, web-based services.*

K.6.5 [**Management of Computing and Information Systems**]: Security and Protection - *invasive software.*

General Terms

Measurement, Security, Human Factors, Standardization

Keywords

web measurement, web content analysis, interfaces, interface design, user experience, webpage analysis

1. INTRODUCTION

Research techniques for evaluating webpage content on the World Wide Web (WWW) usually focus on the entire page, on metadata, or on key phrases. As webpages become more complex and increasingly integrate content from multiple sources, there must be reliable and automated means to measure specific HTML elements or content categories within the page. Such a capability can assist researchers and organizations in learning about common patterns within webpages, similarities of particular content embedded within webpages, usage characteristics, invasive advertising, the correlation of specific content with

RIIT'13, October 10–12, 2013, Orlando, Florida, USA.

2013 ACM 978-1-4503-2494-6/13/10

http://dx.doi.org/10.1145/2512209.2512220

various rankings, and other research questions at a finer level of detail than simply considering the entire webpage, specified metadata, or key word searches.

This paper introduces an automated technique we developed for graphically measuring specific webpage content at a (customizable) granularity below page level. Our technique is implemented as an extension that runs in the Mozilla Firefox web browser. It is fully automated and works consistently on most popular webpages. Importantly, the tool uses a creative procedure that allows for communication with and the incorporation of other browser-based tools or extensions. The tool provides for a wide range of research opportunities that may reach a new level of fidelity in webpage analysis and comparison.

In this paper, we discuss the significant considerations involved with our automated technique and we describe and document the resulting application we created that measures specific content within a webpage. We also cover critical technical challenges we encountered in building the application as well as creative solutions to these challenges. We then demonstrate the application's operation. We conclude with related work and several straightforward, feasible adaptations that would make the application of value for many diverse purposes.

2. DESIGN CONSIDERATIONS

Designing an application to consistently measure specific elements within a webpage requires a clear picture of what is a useful metric for elements on a page, a clear definition of what constitutes measurable content on a page, and the technical means to accurately measure such content. We implemented a Mozilla Firefox browser extension that satisfies these requirements by determining the number of pixels that a browser displays for selective HTML content elements. The important first step toward developing that application was clearly determining an appropriate metric.

2.1 Graphical Content Measurement

There exist many methods to measure a webpage. They include page load time, popularity, user satisfaction, byte size, diversity of content, colors, motion, etc. In general, a good metric for this task should be contextually specific, quantifiable, and can be consistently inexpensively measured [1]. Our application proposes such a metric.

Our recommended metric for measuring webpage elements is computing the number of pixels that a web browser displays for each (HTML) element. While sounding simple, in today's web environment automating the computation of this metric's results actually involves many complex issues, as will be seen as we describe the actions and techniques of our application. Our metric of computing the number of pixels per element quantifies how much of a valuable, limited resource (the browser window) a particular element consumes. It is feasible to determine this number when operating from within a browser which must determine how to (consistently) display the many diverse HTML elements it receives from various sources.

Webpages are primarily a visual presentation of information. One of the most important questions a web designer must answer is how much screen space to allocate to each element of a page. The larger any particular element appears, the greater the percentage of the presentation it occupies. Larger elements, such as a featured passage or featured advertisement, generally occupy more of a user's attention. Measuring elements by counting the number of pixels that they occupy in the browser is therefore contextually specific and quantifiable. In today's multi-source web environment, though, an automated calculation of element displayed pixel count is not entirely straightforward.

There must be a distinction between the pixels of the measurable content -- the message, such as an image or the words of a paragraph -- and the effects of style-rendered pixels immediately surrounding an element, such as border and padding. Pixels that fit within the context of a webpage's message are the pixels of an HTML element that lie inside all padding, border, and margin. Style-rendered pixels, on the other hand, are typically solid-colored "whitespace" pixels that provide a means to spatially arrange and emphasize certain elements on a webpage. This aligns with the classic distinction between style as in Cascading Style Sheets (CSS) and content in HTML design. For example, an identical image may appear on multiple webpages with different border and margin settings. Content pixels notably incorporate adjustments to height and width such as font size: they describe the pixels that users actually see and process. Based on this situation, it is important to define which elements count as content.

2.2 Defining Webpage Content

Ask a group of web users to define the content of a webpage and an inconsistent definition will inevitably emerge. What constitutes 'content' is relative to purpose. Therefore, a metric calculating content should allow for the measurement of selective or customizable categories of content. Our application is powerful enough to accurately describe certain sets of elements on a webpage such that one can automate tracking of them while easily redefining content categories. In some cases, this may amount to identifying certain HTML tags, such as all images.

Another method is to use CSS selectors for more precision. CSS selectors describe elements on a webpage by using HTML tag type, height and width attributes, background color, id or class attributes, and other descriptors. No matter the means, the end state is the ability to describe exactly which elements of a webpage are content such that our application can count the pixels of each. As will be shown in the next subsection, piggybacking on web browser capabilities can make this task much simpler.

2.3 Importance of the Web Browser

A webpage content measuring tool must determine how to display particular elements on the screen based on HTML and other code and how to classify elements based on CSS selectors. Building an application that is able to parse HTML, CSS, Javascript, and other webpage technologies, classify elements based on selectors, resolve overlap, boundary, and padding conditions, and finally count the pixels of each element is a significant undertaking. All

of these tasks are essentially the job of web browsers. Despite very clear and accepted WWW standards, however, web browsers frequently display the same code differently. To remain contextually specific, it is important to capture content as users will actually see it. Using a popular existing web browser ensures that our application remains updated as standards and practices change. Therefore, we chose to make the web browser part of the application.

One option is to display a webpage within a browser while using an external program to capture elements on the screen. However, clearly defining the boundaries of elements and differentiating style from the true content would be difficult. We instead decided to build a browser extension (add-on). Our tool extends the popular Mozilla Firefox web browser because it brings portability across operating systems and is open-source with excellent documentation. By extending the browser, the browser itself becomes a key building block that makes creation of the tool much simpler. Browsers parse and analyze the HTML, CSS, and script code composing a webpage in order to properly render the page. Firefox exposes the various methods and properties associated with its rendering of webpages and their elements to extension code - making our application easier to build. Many of these HTML rendering methods are standardized across various popular browsers thanks to the World Wide Web Consortium (W3C) Document Object Model (DOM). In the next section, we describe how to use DOM methods to overcome difficult technical challenges to measuring webpage elements.

3. IMPLEMENTATION HIGHLIGHTS

Design considerations significantly guided implementation, but building the application brought significant technical challenges requiring creative solutions. Foremost, programmatic identification of content elements was difficult given the wide range of HTML code in practice on the web. Obtaining automatic and accurate measurements of displayed pixels for each content element required some modifications to built-in capabilities to separate rendered style and account for embedded windows (iframes). Dynamic and multi-sourced webpages presented a challenge in determining when a page was completely loaded. Integration with other extensions required working around the protections browsers enforce between different extension codebases for security and other purposes. And finally, the testing and debugging demanded a means for the programmer to visually confirm results.

Building a Firefox (or any browser) extension requires some initial understanding of an extension file structure but primarily involves Javascript use and a basic knowledge of the W3C DOM. The Mozilla Developer Network has tutorials and a repository of references available at https://developer.mozilla.org/en-US/docs/Building_an_Extension. The important tools for accessing a webpage document and the necessary browser methods are available through Mozilla's DOM API or XPCOM API. Using the DOM, an extension is able to access and dynamically change the content, structure, and presentation of a webpage much like Javascript embedded within a page but more so. In this section, we will focus on the important DOM methods necessary to implement the critical parts of the application. The source code of our tool is available at http://www.rumint.org/gregconti/publications/awe1.zip.

The basic algorithm for the application is to find and learn the position and sizes of all content elements displayed in the browser once a webpage fully loads. Key steps involve obtaining programmatic access to content elements, measuring their size and position on the screen, determining when to obtain and measure elements, integrating with other browser tools, and testing and debugging. Below, we describe creative ways to overcome the technical challenges these steps presented.

3.1 Identifying and Describing Content Elements

Research objectives will dictate which elements of a webpage will be treated as the measurable content. This aspect of the process is not automatable. A good technique is manual inspection of several different webpages of interest in order to identify patterns and common elements of interest. In most cases, this will be fairly straightforward. Consider Figure 1 as an example of a generic webpage as it would appear in a browser window. Research may require the ability to measure the images or Flash objects on a page, for example.

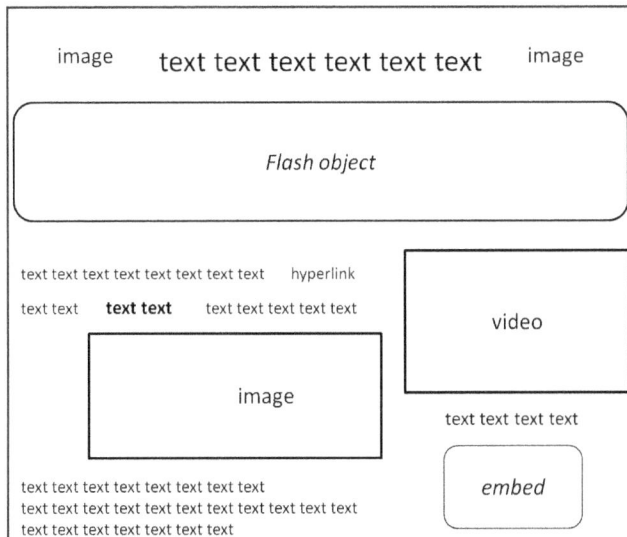

Figure 1. The appearance of a generic webpage with various HTML elements displayed in a browser window.

Existing tools like Mozilla Firefox's DOM and Style Inspector assist the researcher in identify particular elements. With a right-click on the webpage, the tool highlights selected elements within the page's HTML code in a window below the display of the page, revealing an element's tag name and other attributes and property values. The simplest method to classify elements as content is by tag type, but any programmatic method of distinguishing HTML elements using the DOM API is possible. One could view the DOM tree created from Figure 1 using the Firefox DOM and Style Inspector. In the DOM, an HTML document is basically a navigable and manipulatable tree of HTML elements. The tree reflects the structure of the HTML code for the webpage. It is possible to programmatically navigate the tree using DOM API methods on each element, such as childNodes and parentElement. The DOM tree includes more than HTML elements; it also allows access to text nodes.

In Figure 1, the paragraph below the Flash object has three types of text: plain text, a hyperlink, and bolded text. A browser renders each passage of text according to its parent (containing) HTML element in the DOM tree. These HTML elements dictate, for example, if the text should be block or inline and bold or italics. In every case, the text itself is a child of those elements

known as a text node. The difference between an element and a text node will be important for classifying text. Text displayed on the screen may appear inside paragraph, heading, bold, list item, and many more HTML tags. In practice, web designers use nearly all block-level and inline tags as container elements for text. Rather than listing every possible text containing tag as content, it is simpler to just consider all DOM text nodes as content and selectively eliminate undesired parent element tag types. This method has important implications for measuring text as content, which we discuss in the next subsection. After the researcher determines which elements or nodes to consider as content, the next step is to describe them such that the application may locate them within the DOM tree of any webpage.

The simplest method of describing content elements for an application is to identify elements by HTML tag name. The most straightforward approach is to traverse a document's tree with a recursive depth-first algorithm, beginning with the document (root) node and using the childNodes method. An element in the DOM is essentially an object that has many accessible properties which an application can evaluate in order to classify it as content. A more precise approach to obtaining content nodes is to pattern match specific elements using CSS selectors. A DOM element method called querySelectorAll returns a depth-first, pre-order search of all elements matching a comma separated list of CSS selectors. Describing content in terms of a combination of CSS selectors is a proven technique for many other works and all browsers support CSS selectors to be able to apply style rules. It is possible to describe content using CSS selectors based on HTML tag type, class name, or even certain properties. Either tree traversal with element property inspection or the obtaining of a list of elements from querySelectorAll provides access to the desired content on a webpage. The next step is to measure the pixels of each element in the content list.

3.2 Measuring Content Pixels

The content our application identifies includes any image, video, embed, or object element and any displayed text. Object and embed tags may include Flash that appears on a webpage. The first four elements each have HTML tag names (such as IMG) which our application uses to identify those elements as content while traversing a webpage's document tree. Most HTML elements occupy a rectangular space on a page which the browser has calculated. Measuring displayed text requires some additional manipulation of the document. In both cases, measuring the true content pixels of an element in a webpage (as opposed to style pixels) depends on several important definitions.

First, there must be a consistent means to classify exactly which pixels count as content and which do not. For example, HTML and CSS code may render an image on the browser window along with a border and a large margin. The basic premise is to draw a rectangle around the 'true content' pixels of each content element. Next, text on a webpage may appear in conjunction with significant whitespace depending on whether it falls inside a block-level or inline tag. And last, there must be a method for determining how to classify pixels from different elements on a webpage that may overlap and obscure each other.

3.2.1 Minimum Bounding Rectangles

Not every pixel rendered in a web browser will become the focus of a user's attention. Web browsers may render padding, border, and margin to almost any HTML element using the CSS box model. These three properties allow web designers to creatively decorate or emphasize certain elements as well as spatially arrange them. Figure 2 shows the same generic webpage as Figure 1, but emphasizes the effects of padding, border, and margin which a browser renders based on CSS, style rules, scripting, or other methods. The markup in Figure 2 helps to show the effects of the CSS box model and where each element's pixels actually begin and end.

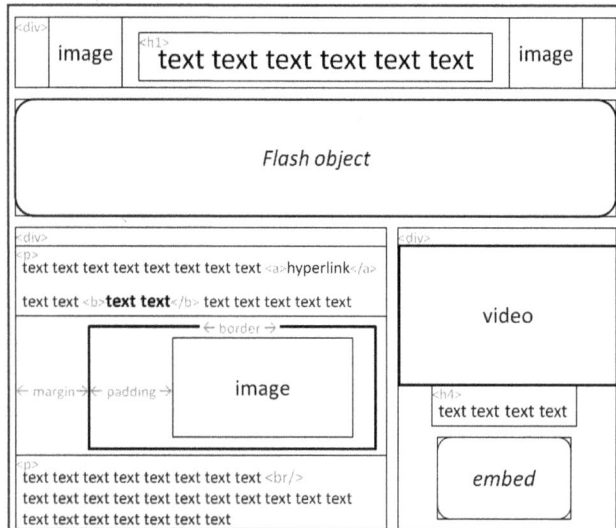

Figure 2. The generic webpage shown in Figure 1 with select markup of HTML element tag names. A thin border around many of the elements indicates an element's boundary. While each element has padding, border, and margin (possibly 0 pixels), only those of the large image element are annotated.

Our application discounts the pixels of all padding, border, and margin because they are aspects of style - not the element itself. For example, a web browser may display an image with a large border, but the file itself has no border. Moreover, the same image may appear on different pages with differing style renderings and some browsers may even display those style rules differently. The style of a webpage plays an important role, but we distinguish it from the content of a page. This definition of content narrows the selected pixels to those that form the actual message that users take away from the page – the message contained in the words and images of the page. The result is essentially a minimum bounding rectangle that surrounds an image or object element but not its padding. Figure 3 depicts these content rectangles (in blue) for elements in the same webpage as Figures 1 and 2.

Determination of an element's minimum bounding rectangle is simple for most HTML elements because the element method getBoundingClientRect provides an element's left, top, width, and height within a browser window. A window is a browser window object (a frame) that displays a webpage document once the document is loaded. The getBoundingClientRect element method includes any border and padding the browser renders along with the element. It is possible to remove those attributes by first obtaining the final computed list of style rules from the window method getComputedStyle. The list contains the number of padding and border (and scrollbar) pixels for all elements. iframes, which are separate documents with their own windows displayed within the main browser window, complicate the absolute positioning of their elements. Many webpages use iframes to display external content or for other reasons, and often

even nest them. Since bounding rectangle measurements are relative to a document's window, absolute element rectangle positions – and whether they are completely visible – depend upon the determination of each iframe's offset within the main window. Offset calculations must accumulate the offset values of each iframe, to include recursively calculating all nested iframes and applying the final offsets to their elements. Elements may also overlap and occlude each other for other reasons.

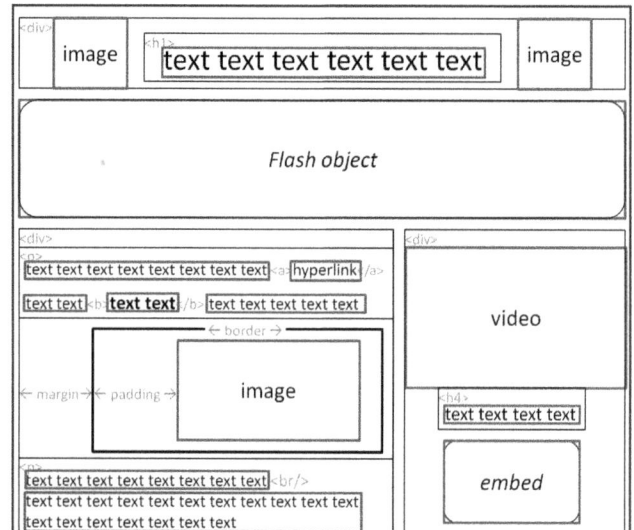

Figure 3. This figure depicts our application identifying content (blue) regions from the generic webpage of Figures 1 and 2. Content includes image, video, embed, object elements and displayed text. Content regions are based on bounding rectangles which ignore padding, border, and margin.

The complexity of HTML and CSS may result in the overlap or occlusion of other elements. It is necessary to determine how much of a bounding rectangle is actually visible. This begins with finding the bounding ancestor element. Our application accomplishes this by evaluating each ancestor element in a bottom-up algorithm using each element's parentElement method, stopping when one of the ancestor's own bounding rectangles restricts it or when reaching the HTML body or iframe element. Restriction is based on the overflow property or, if desired, the edge of the browser window. Those restrictions essentially reduce the size of the bounding rectangle. An element's opacity, visibility, z-index, and display properties may also affect the visibility of an element's rectangle. The z-index property can cause overlap between elements, for example.

Webpage designers usually avoid accidental overlap between elements, but it happens by design or browser inconsistencies as well. Default HTML element stacking order provides that elements appearing last in the code will appear on top unless they are positioned outside the normal flow and given a different stack order (z-index). For implementation simplicity, we assumed the default stack order of elements by traversing the document tree in a depth-first manner. In the case of overlap between like elements (i.e. content-content), this assumption does not affect the correct classification of overlapping pixels. However, there is a problem where content and non-content elements stack according to a different order. A solution is to clear or reclassify all pixels of non-content elements encountered during a stack order traversal of a document's elements.

3.2.2 Recording Content Pixels

To record the final content bounding rectangles, our application uses an HTML canvas that it dynamically inserts over the main document. The canvas element allows web designers to draw and animate graphics, such as rectangles. The canvas functions as a built-in 2D hashtable of pixels. Automated drawing of the final bounding rectangles of each content element essentially labels the content pixels in their absolutely positioned locations and assists with visually confirming the results. The overall calculation of content pixels amounts to a single pass over the canvas while counting pixels within the labeled rectangles. The final measurement of all content is basically the sum of the areas of all blue rectangles in Figure 3.

3.2.3 Capturing Text

Figure 3 depicts the inclusion of text pixels as content. As Section 3.1 introduced, capturing text as content is more complicated than capturing a bounding rectangle around other HTML elements. To capture the text of a document, a creative and effective technique is to insert an arbitrary span element into the document as the immediate parent of all text node descendents of the root body element. DOM methods createElement, insertBefore, and appendChild provide the means to achieve the desired effect. For example, an h1 tag containing text becomes the grandparent of the text node – with a span taking its place as the immediate parent. With a few steps to ensure the span does not alter browser text rendering, spans create an anchor for obtaining a bounding rectangle for any passage of text.

Since the span is an inline element, it helps minimize whitespace pixels when calculating the number of pixels that text actually occupies in a browser window. Inserted spans should include a special class attribute that will classify them as content and have the padding, margin, and border set to 0px through inline style (inline style rules take precedent). It is also helpful to surround each contiguous set of non-whitespace text (text that is not a carriage return or newline, for example) with its own span. This may result in several inserted spans within a single, original text-containing element, but this further reduces whitespace and makes measurements more accurate to 'true content.' Not every text node is content; the application should ignore text nodes within elements such as style and video that are not normally visible in the browser. These additional measures assist in more accurately measuring the number of pixels of the text and prevent the possible double-counting of text that appears inside multiple elements.

3.3 Initiating Measurements

The web is dynamic. Designers competing for user attention create flashing, animated, and interactive webpages. Many popular websites use various scripts. This environment complicates the decision of when to measure a webpage because the measurements may change over time. It may change by design, through user interaction, scripting, or simply because of lags in page loading. The researcher may be interested in the change of measurements over time or with user interaction, but for simplicity our application currently measures a webpage at a single point in time shortly after page load.

Browser extensions are able to listen for certain events associated with webpages, such as a document "load" which indicates when a document and all of its resources have fully loaded. However, this event may fire before embedded documents (iframes) load, as they depend upon user or location parameters that dynamic pages

detect in various ways. Our application measures a webpage five seconds after the base document's "load" event. We empirically confirmed the 5 second delay was sufficient for every webpage in our dataset to fully load all iframe documents and for scripted elements to "settle" (excluding user interaction).

3.4 Integration with Other Browser Tools

Integration of another developer's external application may provide the best means of determining content or for further sub-classifying content. There are thousands of browser extensions that fulfill various purposes, but fundamental browser security demands a separation that makes communication between them difficult. An innovative solution is to modify elements of the document by dynamically inserting an arbitrary class attribute to elements in a live document and therein share information between extensions. Since all extensions have access to the document HTML code and its current state, this technique safely bridges the security barrier. For example, we modified Adblock Plus [2], a popular ad blocking extension, to label advertising elements as a particular type of content by inserting a unique class name for those elements in the live document. Our content measuring application included this class name in the list of CSS selectors describing the content and added those elements to the tracking canvas with a different color to distinguish them as a unique subclass of content.

3.5 Testing/Confirmation

Using an HTML canvas to track content pixels provides the key ability to visually confirm that rectangles align properly with content elements. It is also possible to insert arbitrary properties and values into elements of a document, such as the dimensions of bounding rectangles, to permit a manual inspection of values when viewing a document's source code.

4. DEMONSTRATION AND ANALYSIS

We evaluated our tool using Alexa's top 25 U.S. websites and found, through manual confirmation, that it accurately measured content elements (as defined in Section 3). We placed a corpus of screenshots and archived websites online at http://www.rumint.org/gregconti/publications/awe2.zip. Figures 4 and 5 demonstrate how the tool works on two popular webpages using the definition of content in Section 3. Thin blue rectangles surround each content element and the figure captions list the total number of pixels for each page.

As discussed above, it is possible to further subcategorize content. Red rectangles surround a subcategory of content in Figure 5. We modified, with permission, the code-base of Adblock Plus version 2.2.1, a popular open source ad blocker available at http://adblockplus.org. Rather than blocking them as Adblock Plus normally would, our modified version of Adblock Plus labeled advertising elements using the technique discussed in Section 3.4. Figure 5 demonstrates the ability of using external tools to guide content classification and the potential of creating subcategories of content to provide greater fidelity with webpage research. Our Adblock Plus example also illustrates the power of integration because our application can seamlessly adjust when Adblock Plus updates its list of ad sites.

Our application currently has some restrictions which follow the simplifying assumptions we made in building it. For example, we excluded CSS background images from our definition of content because they frequently overlapped multiple elements and are rendered in the browser through style rules rather than HTML elements. This is evident in Figure 4 where the Amazon logo image, implemented as a CSS background-image, has no bounding rectangle. CSS background images were the single dominant challenge that our application ignored, but a more robust algorithm could improve upon this shortcoming. Despite its limitations, Figures 4 and 5 demonstrate the potential power our application offers in providing a greater fidelity in analyzing and comparing webpages.

5. RELATED WORK

Our application does not replace traditional usability and user experience evaluation techniques, but potentially enhances them. Automated website measurement tools have partially resembled our own efforts. Commercial and open-source software as well as research tools provide an automated means to accomplish certain aspects of our tool. Ivory et al developed an automated tool that functions like a web browser and calculates 11 page-level metrics useful in comparing webpages and designs [3]. Those metrics provide a statistical analysis of webpage content like word count, body text %, page size in bytes, image % in bytes, and image count. This work most closely resembles our own, but our use of an existing browser provides a more accurate measurement platform. Other software programs allow users to manually measure pixels on a screen between two points, and several browser extensions (add-ons) allow users to manually highlight a single element in the browser. Frietas developed a Firefox extension that allows users to manually measure any element in pixels [4] and Firefox's DOM and Style Inspector tool assists in identifying elements on the screen; but neither tool can measure multiple elements automatically.

6. CONCLUSION AND FUTURE WORK

There are many useful metrics for comparing webpages on the World Wide Web, but they measure a page holistically, fail to measure pages within the context of the message that users see, or use methods that are not automatable. Our technique provides a means to increase the fidelity of webpage analysis and introduces a novel metric focused on the number of pixels that certain elements on a page occupy in a browser window. This method is customizable, provides user context in measuring the pixels that users actually see in a popular web browser, and is fully automatable. Several feasible extensions of the application will suit this technique for many different research objectives.

Promising future research areas include subcategorization of content, integration with other external tools, and general improvement of the application. We have demonstrated the utility of classifying content into various categories in Figure 5. Content may be more accurately measured through a content-specific weighting scheme, such as through element opacity. Measurements may also be taken over time to capture the dynamic nature of webpages. Finally, more accurate measurements demand the lifting of several simplifying assumptions discussed in Section 3. Our technique can potentially provide greater fidelity in research which may lead to increased understanding of common practices on the web and improved user experiences. As an automated tool, our application has the potential to improve search engine rating schemes and inform users of global trends with respect to certain elements on a webpage. Finally, a promising area of future work includes opportunities for a more general application of our metric as an automated tool for other purposes.

Figure 4. A screen capture of the Amazon homepage using our application to measure page content as defined in Section 3. There are 418,641 content element pixels out of 633,270 total pixels in this browser window.

Figure 5. A screen capture of the NY Times homepage using our application to measure page content as defined in Section 3 and a subcategory of content as discussed in Section 3.4. There are 361,571 content element pixels out of 633,270 total pixels in this browser window. 94,278 of the content pixels are the subcategory of advertising elements that Adblock Plus identified (shown with red rectangles).

7. REFERENCES

[1] Andrew Jaquith. 2007. Security Metrics: Replacing Fear Uncertainty, and Doubt. Addison Wesley, 2007.

[2] Wladimir Palant. 2007. Adblock plus Firefox extension. Available from http://adblockplus.org/en/firefox

[3] Melody Y. Ivory, Rashmi R. Sinha, and Marti A. Hearst. 2001. Empirically validated web page design metrics. Proceedings of the SIGCHI conference on Human factors in computing systems, March 2001, Seattle, Washington, pp 53-60.

[4] Kevin Freitas. 2011. MeasureIt Firefox extension. Available from https://addons.mozilla.org/en-US/firefox/addon/measureit/

The views expressed in this paper are those of the authors and do not reflect the official policy or position of the United States Military Academy, the Department of the Army, the Department of Defense, or the United States Government.

Implementation of SHA-1 and ECDSA for Vehicular Ad-Hoc Network using NS-3

Sinan Nacy
Rochester Institute of Technology
Sector 906, Street 48, House 16
Baghdad, Iraq
+964 790-138-7055
ssn2252@rit.edu

Tae Oh
Rochester Institute of Technology
152 Lomb Memorial Drive
Rochester, NY 14623
585-475-7642
thoics@rit.edu

Jim Leone
Rochester Institute of Technology
152 Lomb Memorial Drive
Rochester, NY 14623
585-475-6451
Jim.Leone@rit.edu

ABSTRACT
VANET, the Vehicular Ad-Hoc Network, treats cars as nodes in a mobile network. Not surprisingly, VANET must be very secured since one of the network characteristics allows the network to be open to public. The digital signature used in VANET is the standard, ECDSA, or Elliptic Curve Digital Signature Algorithms. ECDSA provides network security by employing a digital signature for messages being transmitted over the network. An ECDSA developed in C++ is described here. VANET messages were sent using the NS-3 network simulator. Two scenarios were created to test the code and the differences before and after implementing the digital signature.

Categories and Subject Descriptors
C.2.0 [Computer-Communication Networks]: General—Security and protection; C.2.1 [Computer-Communication Networks]: Network Architecture and Design—Network communications, Wireless communication.

Keywords
VANET, Digital signature, Security, ECDSA

1. INTRODUCTION
Vehicular Ad Hoc Network (VANET) is a emerging technology that creates a mobile network by using moving vehicles as nodes. In VANET, messages are transferred between vehicles as well as roadside units. As with any other emerging technology, standards and protocols for VANET have to be created and tested before being adopted. The implementation of such a technology in a real world scenario will increase the safety of drivers and help police, fire, EMT and other emergency vehicles in life-critical situations. As with any network, VANET security is considered the number one issue when discussing the challenges associated with such a new technology. Because the VANET network is open to public, eavesdropping on data will be a major concern as data can be altered while being transferred between the nodes. Any digital security implementation must be sufficiently efficient to allow anticipated (message) traffic to occur without degradation to the network's real-time capabilities.

RIIT'13, October 10–12, 2013, Orlando, Florida, USA.
Copyright © 2013 ACM 978-1-4503-2494-6/13/10…$15.00.
http://dx.doi.org/10.1145/2512209.2512221

The NS-3 network simulator provides a convenient test-bed with which to test an algorithm's efficiency. The process involved the use of a Secure Hash Algorithm (SHA-1) to create a unique key for each message. The ECDSA then generates a two key pair signature using the SHA-1 key that incorporates ECDSA domain parameters. The signature is sent to the destination along with the message. The receiver verifies the signature using SHA-1 key for the message, ECDSA domain parameters and the two key pair. If the output of the verification process matches one of the key pairs, then the signature is verified; otherwise, the message was corrupted on transmission.

As for the organization of the paper, related works is discussed in Section 2 and the problem statement was covered in Section 3. The implementation is explained in Section 4 and the results are discussed in Section 5. Finally, the paper is concluded with conclusion and summary in Section 6.

2. RELATED WORK
In this section, several previous and enhancement of SHA-1 and ECDSA are described. The sub-sections are divided into different categories of security development and the sub-section starts with utilizing NS-3 to develop a layer 2 technology that is related to VANET implementation.

2.1 Applications of NS-2/NS-3 Network Simulator
Arbabi and Weigle developed a simulator in NS-3 to model customized onboard and roadside units.[1] Chen, and et al. used NS-2 network simulator tool in other layer 2 areas to model Dedicated Short Range Communication (DSRC) technology using IEEE 802.11 protocols.[2] However, the more accurate DSRC technology is an improvement to the IEEE 802.11 PHY and MAC modules.

2.2 Signature Security in VANET
Biswas et al. proposed a scheme for securing broadcast messages from RSU to OBU in VANET that uses a mechanism called legacy warrant, which is a modification to the original proxy signature.[3] Daihoon, Jaeduck and Souhwan proposed an identification and key exchange scheme that is based on group signature.[4] Aslam and Zou proposed a security architecture that is based on revised Blind signature scheme, which provides one-way link-ability.[5]

2.3 Authentication Security in VANET
Giorgio, Panos, Jean-Pierre and Antonio proposed a new scheme mechanism to manage credentials in VANET that depends on the

pseudonymous authentication concept, which the authors of the article term Baseline Pseudonym (BP).[6] Fan, Hsu, and Tseng proposed an efficient pseudonym PKI mechanism that is based on bilinear mapping which improves the certificate revocation and certificate tracing, implementation cost, management cost, and performance of the message authentication.[7] Studer, Shi, Fan and Perrig proposed a new VANET key management scheme that is based on Temporary Anonymous Certified Keys (TACKs). The scheme provides strong security, and privacy for key management in VANET.[8]

Manvi, Kakkasageri, and Adiga proposed an Elliptic Curve Digital Signature Algorithm (ECDSA) based message authentication for VANET.[9] The operation process in the scheme takes the following steps:

1. The source vehicle will generate a pair of keys: a private key, and a public key.
2. The public key is available to all the vehicles in the network.
3. The source vehicle creates a hash to the message using a hash function.
4. The hash value is encrypted using the vehicle's private key, and then send to its destination.
5. The destination vehicle receives the message, decrypts it using the sender's vehicle public key, and gets the hash value.
6. The destination vehicle generates a hash value to the message using the same procedure that the sender's vehicle used to generate the hash, and then it compares the two hashes. If the two hashes are identical, then that means the message was not modified while transmission. Otherwise, the message was altered. Using this scheme, strong authentication and message integrity are maintained.

Hsin-Te et al. developed a comprehensive message authentication scheme that makes use of the Diffie-Hellman key establishment protocol, and the Hash Message Authentication Code (HMAC).[10] Their protocol enables the authentication of the message in intra- and inter-roadside units range, and the handoff inside different roadside units. Vighnesh and et al. has proposed a novel sender authentication scheme to enhance the security of VANET. The scheme uses hash chaining to authenticate vehicles by hashing an input a number of times.[11] Behera, Mishra, Navak and Jena proposed a security protocol that uses a cryptographic technique called Elliptic Curve Digital Signature Algorithm (ECDSA) to provide message authentication and privacy for VANET users.[12]

Biswas, Misic, and Misic proposed a safety message authentication scheme for VANET that uses ID-based proxy signature and verification mechanism. The scheme provides strong security and high performance.[13] Tat, Lucas, Siu, and Victor proposed a Multiple Level Authentication Scheme (MLAS) that has six basic modules. The scheme makes use of tamper-proof devices.[14]

2.4 Other Areas of VANET Security
Yan, Choudhary, Weigle and Olariu proposed a novel position security system to enhance the security in VANET that makes use of on-board radar to detect neighbor vehicles and confirms with them their coordinates. It provides both global and local position security.[15] Fonseca et al. proposed a driver protection framework consisting of four different features, 1) extended

location service, 2) cross-layer addressing, 3) link layer callbacks and 4) pseudonymity-enhanced packet forwarding schemes.[16]

Yi and Moayeri developed a framework for security and application oriented network design that has two basic schemes: application aware control scheme, and unified routing scheme.[17] Ching-Hung, Yueh-Min, Tzone-I and Hsiao-Hwa created a decentralized IVC (Inter Vehicle Communication) scheme without the need of infrastructure called a Dynamic Establishment of Secure Communication in VANET (DESCV) that provides random wireless connections between vehicles.[18]

Gosman, Dobre and Cristea have proposed a security protocol designed for VANET environment that guarantees the integrity of the data in the messages against different attackers.[19]

Samara, Al-Salihy and Sures proposed a simple, scalable, and flexible design for VANET certifications that includes new methods for efficient certificate management.[20]

Wasef, Rongxing, Xiaodong and Xuemin developed new complementary security mechanism to prevent Denial of Service attack (DoS).[21]

The IEEE standard 1609.2 is used to define secure message format and identifies security mechanism and algorithms for use in a Wireless Access in Vehicular Environment (WAVE). Rabadi proposed the use of implicit certificates in the WAVE standard because the size of implicit certificate is shorter than explicit certificate.[22]

Trusted Platform Module (TPM) is a security hardware component. It can handle software attacks on VANET. Moreover, it maintains the data integrity in the network. Based on this TPM, Sumra, Hasbullah, Ahmed and Ab Manan proposed a new 'chain of trust' model that is built within vehicles to manage a variety of attacks and preserves the message integrity in the vehicular network.[23]

Mershad and Artail developed a new system that makes use of the Roadside Units (RSUs) that have Internet connectivity and provides information to VANET users. The system is called secuRe and Efficient dAta aCquisiTion in VANETs (REACT). The system provides a novel privacy and security mechanism.[24]

Rawat, Bista, Yan and Weigle proposed a new algorithm to secure the communication between vehicles with the help of trust measured for given period using probabilistic approach.[25]

3. PROBLEM STATEMENT
VANET is an emerging technology and is still under development. The primary security issue in VANET is checking the integrity of messages exchanged among vehicles. In the paper, implementation of security algorithms in modeling and simulation for VANET are discussed. Our modeling and simulation could be used in many VANET research activities and streamlines the security protocol development for VANET. Our implementation provides a new security approach to secure the messages using ECDSA. The following steps described the functionality of our implementation:

1) The sender node will create a hash value for its message using SHA-1 algorithm.

2) The node will then create a digital signature for the message using ECDSA.

3) The receiver node will calculate the hash value for the message and verify the digital signature.

4) If the digital signature is verified, the receiver node will assume that the message came from its original sender.

4. OUR IMPLEMENTATION

The main tool used to implement the project is NS-3 in a Linux environment. We have developed and implemented a C++ code that provides ECDSA digital signature inside NS-3. We also added a SHA-1 code to our work since ECDSA requires a hashing function. We have used a simulation in NS-3 that provides VANET functionality. A Controller class controls the scenarios in the VANET simulation.

The ECDSA signature scheme is used by two entities: a signer X, and a verifier Y. The signer X will sign the message M and send it to the verifier Y. The verifier Y will receive the message M and verify it. In fact, any entity can verify the signature if it has X's public key. Sometimes third party can be involved to verify the signature of the message.

Entity X should use the key deployment procedure to establish a key pair. Entity Y should be able to obtain X's public key. And X will use the key pair in order to control the signing operation while Y uses the public key required to control the verification step. When X wants to send a message M, it should sign the message using its key pairs and generate a signature S. Entity X will create a message using M and S, and send it to Y. When Y receives the message, it applies the verifying operation using X's public key in order to verify the message authenticity. If the output of the verifying operation is valid, then Y will know that the message M is authentic. In other words, it came from the sender X.

4.1 ECDSA Domain Parameters

ECDSA algorithm requires that the private, and public keys used for digital signature generation and verification be generated with respect to a set of domain parameters. The domain parameters can be the same to a group of users and may be public. Domain parameters can remain fixed for an extended time period. [26] [27] [28] The ECDSA domain parameters are:

- q or p, the size of the underlying field,
- a, elliptic curve parameter that is used to define the equation of the curve,
- b, elliptic curve parameter that is used to define the equation of the curve,
- $G = (Gx, Gy)$, a point on the elliptic curve, and is called a base point,
- n, the order of the base point G,
- h, the order of the elliptic curve divided by the order n, and is called the cofactor.

4.2 ECDSA Private Key/Public Key

ECDSA key pair consists of private key d, and public key Q. Each key pair is associated with a specific set of domain parameters. The private key d, the public key Q, and the domain parameters are mathematically related to one another via the relation $Q = dG$, where dG is the sum of d copies of the base point G. It is also know as elliptic curve scalar multiply of G by d. The sum operation is done using elliptic curve arithmetic. The private key d can be used for a limited period of time (i.e. the cryptoperiod). On the other hand, the public key Q can be used as long as the digital

signature that is generated using the associated private key is still in use because the digital signature needs to be verified. [26] [27] [28]

ECDSA private key and public key are only used in the generation and the verification of the ECDSA digital signature. They should not be used for other purposes (e.g. key establishment). [26] [27] [28]

4.3 ECDSA Key Generation

In order for an entity to generate the key pair, it must make sure that the domain parameters are valid. Each key pair is associated with a specific set of domain parameters [26] [27] [28]. Generating the key pair is done as follows:

1. Select a random integer d in the interval $[1, n\text{-}1]$.
2. Compute $Q = dG$.

The results are d and Q, where d is the private key, and Q (Qx, Qy) is the public key.

4.4 ECDSA Signature Generation

An entity can sign a message m using the key pair and the domain parameters. The output from the signing operation is a signature, and is represented by (r, s) [26] [27] [28]. An entity does the following to sign a message:

1. Select an integer k, where $1 \leq k \leq n\text{-}1$.
2. Compute $kQ = (x1, y1)$.
3. Compute $r = x1 \pmod{n}$. If $r = 0$ then go to step 1.
4. Compute $k^{-1} \pmod{n}$. Note: $k^{-1} \pmod{n}$ is computed using the inverse theory in Appendix A.
5. Compute SHA-1(m), and convert this string to an integer H(m).
6. Compute $s = k^{-1} (\text{H}(m) + dr) \pmod{n}$. If $s = 0$, then go to step 1.

The signature for the message is (r, s).

4.5 ECDSA Signature Verification

To verify a signature (r, s) on a message m, the receiver obtains a copy of the sender's domain parameters, and its public key Q [26] [27] [28]. The receiver does the following:

1. Verify that r and s are integers, and in the interval $[1, n\text{-}1]$.
2. Compute SHA-1(m), and convert this string to an integer H(m).
3. Compute $w = s^{-1} \pmod{n}$. Note: $s^{-1} \pmod{n}$ is computed using the inverse theory in Appendix A.
4. Compute $u1 = \text{H}(m)w \pmod{n}$, and $u2 = rw \pmod{n}$.
5. Compute $X = (x1, y1) = u1G + u2Q$.
6. If $X = 0$, reject the signature. Otherwise, compute $v = x1 \pmod{n}$.
7. Accept the signature if $v = r$.

The signature to the message m is verified if $v = r$.

5. SIMULATION RESULTS

The code was implemented inside the Controller class. Two scenarios were created and ran the simulation twice for each scenario. The first run is before implementing our code, and the second run is after implementing our code. Then we compared between the two runs for each scenario.

5.1 Scenario 1

In this scenario, we have a bi-directional highway with 1000 meters of roadway. There are two lanes on each direction. The width of the lane is 5 meters. The median width is 5 meters. The highway has 20% of trucks, and 80% of sedan vehicles. A broken car has stopped in the middle of the highway, at the location (x = 500 meters, direction = 1, lane = 0).

The broken vehicle broadcasts warning/safety messages asking for help, and revealing its location every 5 seconds. A police car has been created in the scenario, and will start moving from the beginning of the highway. The police car is faster than any regular car, and has a higher wireless transmission range. It listens to broadcast messages and sends a unicast for each received message. The police car will start to decelerate once it gets closer to the broken car, and will eventually stop nearby.

Figure 1 shows the output result from the gnuplot after 2 minutes and 20 seconds from running the simulation. The police car has reached the broken car after 50 seconds, and stopped in the second lane of the highway. As you can see in the Figure, the police car has made congestion behind it.

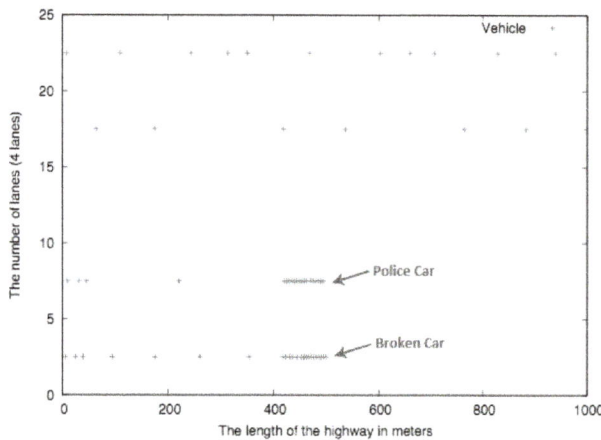

Figure 1. Scenario 1, before implementing ECDSA on broadcast messages.

In Figure 2, we have used the same scenario, with the exception of implementing the ECDSA code on the broadcast messages.

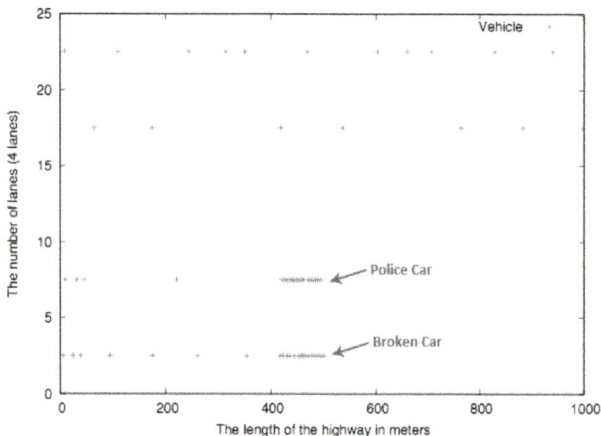

Figure 2. Scenario 1, after implementing ECDSA on broadcast messages.

Figure 3 represents the number of packets received, dropped, and the police acknowledgment for receiving a packet. The number of packets is the same before and after implementing the ECDSA code,.

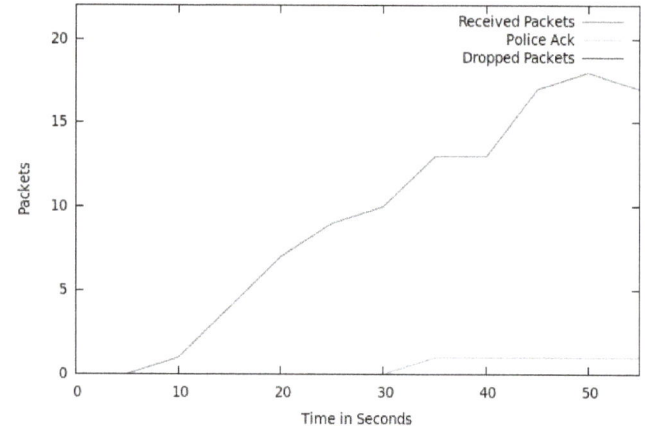

Figure 3. Scenario 1, the number of packets on the network.

Comparing between the results from Figure 1, and Figure 2, we found that there are no major differences between the two output results. There could be a minor delay time in mille seconds, but there is no problem. As for Figure 3, the number of packets is the same before and after implementing the ECDSA code. For this scenario, we conclude that, implementing the ECDSA does not affect the work of our simulation environment; instead, it makes our implementation more secure, robust, and reliable.

5.2 Scenario 2

In this scenario, we have a bi-directional highway with 1400 meters of roadway. There are three lanes on each direction. The width of the lane is 5 meters. The median width is 5 meters. The highway has 20% of trucks, and 80% of sedan vehicles. A broken car has stopped at the location (x = 850 meters, direction = 1, lane = 0). The broken vehicle broadcasts warning/safety messages asking for help, and revealing its location every 5 seconds. A police car has been created in the scenario, and will start moving from the beginning of the highway. The police car is faster than any regular car, and has a higher wireless transmission range. It listens to broadcast messages and sends a unicast for each received message. The police car will start to decelerate once it gets closer to the broken car, and will eventually stop nearby.

In Figure 4, we can see the output result from the gnuplot after 2 minutes and 35 seconds from the time of the simulation. The police car has reached the broken car at location x=850 after 1 minute, and stopped in the second lane of the highway. As you can see in the Figure 4, the police car is starting to make congestion on the highway. The third lane on the highway is open, but because two lanes are closed the traffic is being directed to the third lane. As a result, congestion will occur on the highway.

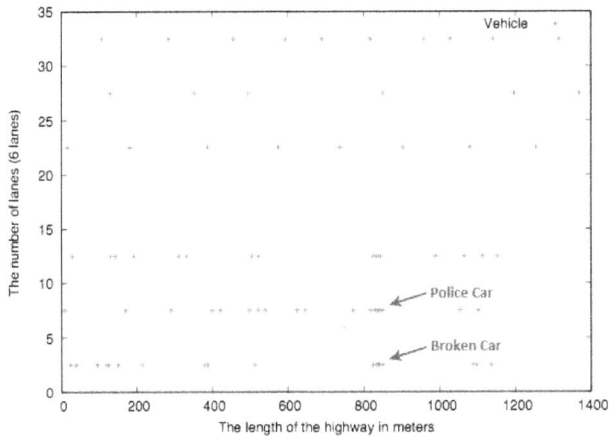

Figure 4. Scenario 2, before implementing ECDSA on broadcast messages.

In Figure 5, we have used the same scenario, with the exception of implementing the ECDSA code on the broadcast messages.

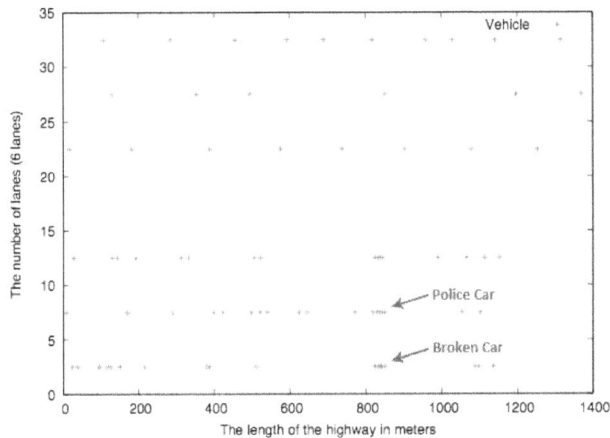

Figure 5. Scenario 2, after implementing ECDSA on broadcast messages.

Figure 6 represents the number of packets received, dropped, and the police acknowledgment for receiving a packet. The number of packets is the same before and after implementing the ECDSA code, that's why we have only added one figure.

Comparing between the two results from Figure 4, and Figure 5, there are no major differences between the two output results. Just like the first scenario, there could be a minor delay time in mille seconds. As for Figure 6, the number of packets is the same before and after implementing the ECDSA code. As a result, we conclude that, implementing the ECDSA does not affect the work of our simulation environment, and does not cause any delay; instead, it makes our implementation more secure, robust, and reliable.

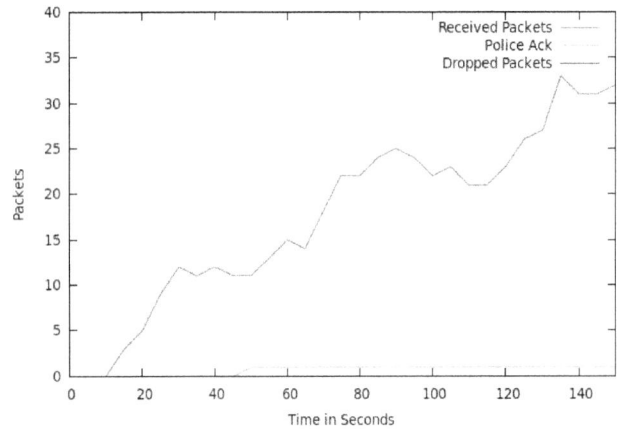

Figure 6. Scenario 2, the number of packets on the network.

6. CONCLUSION

As a conclusion, the ECDSA code was implemented successfully inside NS-3. Comparing between the two results (before, and after implementing the ECDSA code) for each scenario, we can see that there is no difference, which is somehow suspicious. In addition to that, the final results don't show much information, and this is due to a lack in the VANET simulation environment. At the same time, implementing the ECDSA code on messages didn't show major delay in time inside the environment. Instead, we can tell that it provides more security to the messages by creating a digital signature for each message on the network.

7. REFERENCES

[1] Arbabi, H.; Weigle, M.C. 2010. Highway mobility and vehicular ad-hoc networks in ns-3. *Simulation Conference (WSC), Proceedings of the 2010 Winter*, vol., no., pp.2991-3003, 5-8 Dec. 2010.

[2] Q. Chen, D. Jiang, V. Taliwal, and L. Delgrossi. 2006. IEEE 802.11 Based Vehicular Communication Simulation Design for NS-2. *In Proceedings of the International Workshop on Vehicular Ad Hoc Networks (VANET)*, Los Angeles, CA, USA, Sept. 2006.

[3] Biswas, S.; Mišić, J. 2010. Proxy signature-based RSU message broadcasting in VANETs. *Communications (QBSC), 2010 25th Biennial Symposium on*, vol., no., pp.5-9, 12-14 May 2010.

[4] Daihoon Kim; Jaeduck Choi; Souhwan Jung. 2010. Mutual Identification and Key Exchange Scheme in Secure VANETs Based on Group Signature. *Consumer Communications and Networking Conference (CCNC), 2010 7th IEEE*, vol., no., pp.1-2, 9-12 Jan. 2010.

[5] Aslam, B.; Zou, C.C. 2011. One-way-linkable blind signature security architecture for VANET. *Consumer Communications and Networking Conference (CCNC), 2011 IEEE*, vol., no., pp.745-750, 9-12 Jan. 2011.

[6] Giorgio Calandriello, Panos Papadimitratos, Jean-Pierre Hubaux, and Antonio Lioy. 2007. Efficient and robust pseudonymous authentication in VANET. *In VANET '07*, pages 19-28, New York, NY, USA, September 2007. ACM.

[7] C. I. Fan, R. H. Hsu, and C. H. Tseng. 2008. Pairing-based message authentication scheme with privacy protection in

vehicular ad hoc network. *In Proceedings of the International Conference on Mobile Technology, Applications and Systems*, September 2008.

[8] Studer, A.; Shi, E.; Fan Bai; Perrig, A. 2009. TACKing Together Efficient Authentication, Revocation, and Privacy in VANETs. *Sensor, Mesh and Ad Hoc Communications and Networks, 2009. SECON '09. 6th Annual IEEE Communications Society Conference on*, vol., no., pp.1-9, 22-26 June 2009.

[9] Manvi, S.S.; Kakkasageri, M.S.; Adiga, D.G. 2009. Message Authentication in Vehicular Ad Hoc Networks: ECDSA Based Approach. *Future Computer and Communication, 2009. ICFCC 2009. International Conference on*, vol., no., pp.16-20, 3-5 April 2009.

[10] Hsin-Te Wu; Wei-Shuo Li; Tung-Shih Su; Wen-Shyong Hsieh. 2010. A Novel RSU-Based Message Authentication Scheme for VANET. *Systems and Networks Communications (ICSNC), 2010 Fifth International Conference on*, vol., no., pp.111-116, 22-27 Aug. 2010.

[11] Vighnesh, N.V.; Kavita, N.; Urs, S.R.; Sampalli, S. 2011. A novel sender authentication scheme based on hash chain for Vehicular Ad-Hoc Networks. *Wireless Technology and Applications (ISWTA), 2011 IEEE Symposium on*, vol., no., pp.96-101, 25-28 Sept. 2011.

[12] Behera, S.; Mishra, B.; Nayak, P.; Jena, D. 2011. A secure and efficient message authentication protocol for vehicular Ad hoc Networks with privacy preservation (MAPWPP). *Internet Multimedia Systems Architecture and Application (IMSAA), 2011 IEEE 5th International Conference on* , vol., no., pp.1-6, 12-13 Dec. 2011.

[13] Biswas, S.; Misic, J.; Misic, V. 2011. ID-based Safety Message Authentication for Security and Trust in Vehicular Networks. *Distributed Computing Systems Workshops (ICDCSW), 2011 31st International Conference on* , vol., no., pp.323-331, 20-24 June 2011.

[14] Tat Wing Chim, Lucas Chi Kwong Hui, Siu-Ming Yiu, Victor O. K. Li. 2011. *MLAS*: multiple level authentication scheme for VANETs. *Published in: Proceeding ASIACCS '11 Proceedings of the 6th ACM Symposium on Information, Computer and Communications Security*. ASIACCS: pp.471-475, 2011.

[15] G. Yan, G. Choudhary, M. Weigle, and S. Olariu. 2007. Providing vanet security through active position detection (poster). *In Proceedings of ACM VANET 07*, Sept. 2007.

[16] Fonseca, E.; Festag, A.; Baldessari, R.; Aguiar, R.L. 2007. Support of Anonymity in VANETs - Putting Pseudonymity into Practice. *Wireless Communications and Networking Conference, 2007.WCNC 2007. IEEE*, vol., no., pp.3400-3405, 11-15 March 2007.

[17] Yi Qian; Moayeri, N. 2008. Design of Secure and Application-Oriented VANETs. *Vehicular Technology Conference, 2008. VTC Spring 2008. IEEE*, vol., no., pp.2794-2799, 11-14 May 2008.

[18] Ching-Hung Yeh, Yueh-Min Huang, Tzone-I Wang, Hsiao-Hwa Chen. 2009. DESCV - A Secure Wireless Communication Scheme for Vehicle ad hoc Networking. MONET. *Published in Journal Mobile Networks and Applications*, Volume 14, Issue 5, pp.611-624, October 2009.

[19] Gosman, C.; Dobre, C.; Cristea, V. 2010. A Security Protocol for Vehicular Distributed Systems. *Symbolic and Numeric Algorithms for Scientific Computing (SYNASC), 2010 12th International Symposium on*, vol., no., pp.321-327, 23-26 Sept. 2010.

[20] Samara, G.; Al-Salihy, W.A.H.; Sures, R. 2010. Efficient certificate management in VANET. *Future Computer and Communication (ICFCC), 2010 2nd International Conference on*, vol.3, no., pp.V3-750-V3-754, 21-24 May 2010.

[21] Wasef, A.; Rongxing Lu; Xiaodong Lin; Xuemin Shen. 2010. Complementing public key infrastructure to secure vehicular ad hoc networks [Security and Privacy in Emerging Wireless Networks]. *Wireless Communications, IEEE* , vol.17, no.5, pp.22-28, October 2010.

[22] Rabadi, N.M. 2010. Implicit certificates support in IEEE 1609 security services for Wireless Access in Vehicular Environment (WAVE). *Mobile Adhoc and Sensor Systems (MASS), 2010 IEEE 7th International Conference on*, vol., no., pp.531-537, 8-12 Nov. 2010.

[23] Sumra, I.A.; Hasbullah, H.; Ahmad, I.; bin Ab Manan, J.-L. 2011. Forming vehicular web of trust in VANET. *Electronics, Communications and Photonics Conference (SIECPC), 2011 Saudi International*, vol., no., pp.1-6, 24-26 April 2011.

[24] Mershad, K.; Artail, H. 2011. REACT: Secure and efficient data acquisition in VANETs. *Wireless and Mobile Computing, Networking and Communications (WiMob), 2011 IEEE 7th International Conference on*, vol., no., pp.149-156, 10-12 Oct. 2011.

[25] Rawat, D.B.; Bista, B.B.; Yan, G.; Weigle, M.C. 2011. Securing Vehicular Ad-hoc Networks Against Malicious Drivers: A Probabilistic Approach. *Complex, Intelligent and Software Intensive Systems (CISIS), 2011 International Conference on*, vol., no., pp.146-151, June 30 2011-July 2 2011.

[26] ANSI X9.62-2005, 2005. Public Key Cryptography for the Financial Services Industry: The Elliptic Curve Digital Signature Algorithm (ECDSA). American National Standards Institute, November 2005.

[27] FIPS 186-3, 2009. Digital Signature Standard (DSS). Federal Information Standards Processing Publication 186-3, National Institute of Standards and Technology, June 2009.

[28] SEC1 Standards for Efficient Cryptography Group, SEC 1: Elliptic Curve Cryptography, Version 2.0, 2009.

Author Index

www.ingramcontent.com/pod-product-compliance
Lightning Source LLC
Chambersburg PA
CBHW081551220326
41598CB00036B/6643